WILD THING

WILD THING

Finding hope and a home in the natural world

Randal Plunkett

First published in the UK in 2025 by Eriu
An imprint of Bonnier Books UK
5th Floor, HYLO, 105 Bunhill Row,
London, EC1Y 8LZ

Copyright © Dunsany Productions Limited, 2025

All rights reserved.
No part of this publication may be reproduced, stored or transmitted in any form or by any means, electronic, mechanical, photocopying or otherwise, without the prior written permission of the publisher.

The right of Randal Plunkett to be identified as Author of this work has been asserted by him in accordance with the Copyright, Designs and Patents Act, 1988.

A CIP catalogue record for this book is available from the British Library.

Hardback ISBN: 978-1-80418-955-9

Also available as an ebook

1 3 5 7 9 10 8 6 4 2

Typeset by IDSUK (Data Connection) Ltd
Printed and bound in Great Britain by Clays Ltd, Elcograf S.p.A.

Every reasonable effort has been made to trace copyright holders of material reproduced in this book, but if any have been inadvertently overlooked the publishers would be glad to hear from them.

This book is a work of Non-Fiction. Some names may have been changed to respect the privacy of those mentioned.

The authorised representative in the EEA is
Bonnier Books UK (Ireland) Limited.
Registered office address: Floor 3, Block 3, Miesian Plaza,
Dublin 2, D02 Y754, Ireland
compliance@bonnierbooks.ie
www.bonnierbooks.co.uk

To my wonderful parents, who built me to always go my own way and to never compromise, no matter how difficult things get and never to feel that I needed to fit the mold. You taught me the Dunsany way, a philosophy I follow every day and despite my past rebellion, I repeat the same words you made me utter for years with pride. I can never thank you enough for the lessons you taught me. I will do as you did and pass the same lessons to the next generation

To my beautiful family Laura, Catherine and Constance, you girls give me a reason to fight every day

*To my friends,
whose laughter kept me going when the words wouldn't come*

And to every reader who turns these pages – this book is for you

Contents

Prologue		1
Chapter One:	New York to London	7
Chapter Two:	The Disappointment	39
Chapter Three:	End of the Line	59
Chapter Four:	Zombie Estate	91
Chapter Five:	Going Full Vegan	105
Chapter Six:	Every Little Life	135
Chapter Seven:	Wilding the Gilded Cage	165
Chapter Eight:	Networking	201
Chapter Nine:	She was Proud and so was I	217
Chapter Ten:	Taking the Helm	235
Further Reading		267

Prologue

IT WAS LATE SPRING – THE EVENINGS WERE GETTING BRIGHT – AND I WAS DOING MY USUAL WALK AROUND THE LAND. 'Left to Wander' by Neurosis was blaring droney sounds through my headphones as I manoeuvred through the long grass. It had grown high enough to reach my shoulders and beyond; drying seeds brushed my lips as I walked through it. It was warm – well, warm for Ireland – and the air felt good against my skin.

Dunsany Estate, my home, looked so different now. The once-grazed farmland was almost unrecognisable. Tones of yellow and green glowed in the warm sun. The barbed-wire fences were engulfed by tall thistles and nettles. Soon they'd vanish completely under a green blanket. It had been three years since the last farm animal had been here. Nature was taking over, with grass growing tall, flowering and going to seed, wild flowers blossoming and the land asserting itself and gaining confidence.

I turned a corner, following a small dirt track from grassland into a wooded area with redwoods and Douglas firs, and within it a clearing. In the centre, a ghostly dead tree loomed, its component parts gradually crumbling and returning to the soil from which they'd come, the rotting wood already supporting an abundance of fungi, moss and lichens. Here, the sunlight dappled through the cover overhead and onto the shorter growth beneath the trees. The shafts of light, hitting the ground obliquely, seemed to move as insects swooped and swirled in the air. It was mesmerising.

I slipped the headphones off my head and onto my shoulders and the sound of the music receded. Only then did I realise how much natural noise there was all around me. I never walked without music blaring, so I'd never noticed before just how much *noise* the land made now. Millions of insects were buzzing, tornadoes of them spiralling in the yellow light of a summer's evening; hundreds of birds were chirruping, singing and batting their wings, the bushes and undergrowth were rustling as unseen creatures moved through them.

Just a few years before, the only birds we'd heard were crows, cawing and cackling as they wheeled through the sky above Dunsany Castle and its ruined church. I used to romanticise their sounds: they were trumpets of death, calling me, reminding me that I was fighting against the tide, fighting a pointless battle I'd never win. They were nature, mocking me and laughing at all the history I carried on my back. But today, instead of their doom-chimes, an orchestra of songbirds sang from the trees, the sky and the long grasses. The entire world seemed to be humming.

I'd walked around these lands hundreds – *thousands?* – of times before, but I didn't remember it ever having been as loud as this. With no castle, no house and no electricity pylons in sight, I might have voyaged back in time to an era before human activity changed everything. In that moment, I felt like the only person in the world.

Then, just a few metres away, the tall grass started to move. I turned to look and found myself face to face with a small group of native red deer: a young male without antlers – red deer shed theirs in the spring and grow new ones – and three does. They were just standing there, almost as still as statues, watching me.

I stopped. We all looked at each other for what felt like a long time. Their large, dark eyes contemplated me. My breath slowed, and so did theirs.

There are hundreds of deer in Dunsany, and there's certainly nothing unusual about meeting one on a walk. But this time, it was different. Usually they saw me and ran away. Usually I didn't pay them all that much attention. But this time, they seemed . . . unafraid. The young male looked at me with what appeared to be a keen interest. His eyes gazed straight into mine and he remained completely still, other than flicking his ears and tail when the insects bothered him. For the first time, I noticed that the deer themselves were covered with living creatures, insects that appeared to be hovering above them and jumping in and out of their fur: deer flies, horse flies and who knew what else.

There we stood as the sun started to set. Its yellow rays slanted onto the animals' brown coats, surrounding them with a nimbus of gold. They slanted onto me, too; I could feel the heat from the sun warming me through my black clothes.

Suddenly, I felt as though I was seeing the deer, and beyond them Dunsany estate – my home – and beyond that all of nature itself, for the very first time. As though I'd opened myself up and let the essential wildness of Ireland come in.

I rarely feel proud of myself. Why should I? I've never done anything special. I don't have any special talent or gifts. All I ever had was privilege, albeit accompanied by many caveats. I'd lived with a constant state of imposter syndrome because I was a regular underachiever. Despite all this, in that moment, I let a little pride manifest, mixed with wonder.

I've helped to do this, I thought. *I've created space for them. I've made a place where they're safe. I've stood up for victims with no voice: these animals, which have been persecuted by us for so long. I've even been there for nature herself.*

The spell broke and the deer started to move, turning and leaping through the tall grass and into the forested area behind them. Before they disappeared from view, the stag turned and looked back at me, still unafraid, as though he was saying goodbye, or so long, see you later.

And, just like that, just like the moment when you realised you've fallen in love with someone special, my purpose in life was revealed: I couldn't save all of nature, but I could do my best with the little bit with which I've been entrusted.

That was the day – in my thirties already, after a lifetime of feeling like a loser – I finally became a man, a grown adult, finally able to crawl out from the shadow of my parents' big personalities and my family's long, exalted past. It was confirmation of the essential goodness of what I was doing. It was evidence that could do – could *be* – more than I'd ever allowed myself to hope, or even imagine. It was, in an absolutely real sense, the beginning of the rest of my life. From then on, I knew that the rewilding of Dunsany wasn't just a pipe dream, but my life's work.

And as the land rewilded I started to change as a person, gradually shedding the hopelessness and inertia that had so often held me back, the darkness that had so often threatened to envelop the few hopes and dreams I'd allowed myself to have.

Chapter One

New York to London

I'M GOING TO START BY GETTING THE CRINGEWORTHY PART OVER FIRST: HELLO, I'M RANDAL. I'm often referred to as the twenty-first Lord Dunsany, but also as 'the Death Metal baron,' and sometimes as a rewilder or film-maker. I don't ride horses, I *hate* Pimm's and I don't own any tweed or polo-necks.

I'm going to talk about a lot of things in this book. Some may resonate with you; some will be off the wall. Some may even offend your sensibilities, and that's okay. You're welcome to disagree and even attack my theories and experiences if you feel inclined. Feel free, even, to throw a few insults my way. However, kindly refrain from calling me 'English bastard'. I'm an Irish man of Norman descent, not Cromwellian, so feel free to use 'French bastard' instead.

And with *that* out of the way . . .

Life started in New York. My earliest memory is standing in my crib, clutching the off-white bars and jumping up and down as I called for someone to come and get me. Eventually my nanny came. Her quilted dressing gown was soft against my face as she carried me to the small kitchen. She sat me on top of the counter and prepared scrambled eggs. I hated scrambled eggs later, but I remember those eggs being delicious. At some point both my parents appeared, so it must have been the weekend because I rarely saw them during the week, maybe just at bedtime or early in the morning. Then my older half-siblings, Daniel and Joana – Mum's children from her first marriage – emerged from their room, and we all sat around the small table, having breakfast. I was Dad's first child, and Mum's third. That little world of parents and half-siblings was all I knew.

That must have been about 1985, because I was born in 1983. It was an exciting time for my parents; New York was buzzing then, and they were just one of many talented young couples living and working in the city, taking advantage of all the opportunities it offered. Hearing them talk later on, it seemed that they knew everyone: all the old money but also the new elite composed of artists like Andy Warhol and Jean-Michel Basquiat.

Mum was from a once-wealthy Brazilian family, the Villelas, who traced their descent from Vasco da Gama. Her grandmother had allegedly owned an estate the size of Belgium. Mum herself was a well-known architect. She'd been married to someone else – a distant relative of Dad's – when they met, but apparently sparks flew and that was that. Mum left her husband, took the two children of her first marriage, and set up home with Dad. It was all very amicable, and I remember Mum's first husband as being rather like an uncle to me and my brother Oliver, the youngest.

Mum was as tough as nails. She had to be: she'd grown up in a macho culture in which girls, even the rich, well-connected ones, were supposed to do as they were told. Mum had dealt with these cultural expectations by becoming loud, assertive and fierce. Dad was gentler, quieter and more self-effacing. His childhood had been difficult: his mother – also Brazilian – had abandoned him to be raised by a cantankerous father, who was a damaged war hero, and a stepmother who, I'd learn later, wished him dead. By the time he and Mum met, he was a well-regarded artist who wore his family legacy quite lightly, but who was still drifting through life.

That legacy? He was going to be the twentieth in an extensive line of barons, dating back to the early days of the Norman settlement of Ireland. One day, he'd inherit Dunsany Castle and its extensive lands, and stride the halls where his ancestors had walked, looking over the battlements at the same view they'd woken to every day for hundreds of years. He'd do his best to leave an impressive legacy. As I was his eldest son, one day I'd be number twenty-one and expected to do all the same things, while keeping the whole lot safe for the next generation.

But I didn't really know or understand anything about that. Not yet. All I knew and cared about was my family, especially Margarita – or Dada, as I called her – an elderly former nun from Brazil whom Mum had hired to care for me and my younger brother Oliver. She didn't speak much English, so thanks to Dada, my first mother tongue was Portuguese, as it had been Dad's. Despite having left the convent, Dada was still very religious, and often prayed with enthusiasm in my parents' bedroom while we were playing. She may have hoped I'd pick up some of the fervour from her.

In fact, to some extent I did, as I regard myself as a cultural Catholic to this day.

Seen from outside, our life in New York probably looked very privileged, and it was: we had an apartment a stone's throw from Central Park, I had playdates with Ivanka Trump (a tall, funny kid in my memory, and my first crush), and my stepsiblings, Daniel and Joana, went to expensive private schools. In many ways, New York in the 1980s was a golden era for my parents, especially Mum. Capitalism was king, and anyone who was talented and hard-working could do well. It was an exciting, multi-cultural environment. Mum and Dad had many Jewish friends, and some of my fondest memories are parties at Passover; I even had a Jewish godfather, Alfred Taubman, a self-made businessman and philanthropist. Somehow, Mum had secured a dispensation from the Catholic archbishop. In the context of elite New York society, we were nothing special though. Donald Trump had a special nickname for Mum, 'No Project'. He used this both as a pet name and to let her know he wasn't going to hire her. In response, she'd call him 'Go to Hell'. Their back-and-forth startled their respective secretaries and employees, especially when Mum introduced herself as 'No Project' on the phone. She did work with Trump on a few occasions, on speculative enterprises.

Our apartment was on the thirteenth floor of a tall building, referred to as the fourteenth, because Americans take their superstitions seriously and don't have thirteen floors. It was in a swanky part of town, but it was small for a family of six. Mum and Dad had subdivided the larger rooms with chipboard walls to give us all some privacy. Oliver and I shared a room with Dada, while Daniel and Joana had small rooms of their own. One of my favourite occupations was leaning over the edge of the balcony and trying to spit onto the heads of people walking below, and I tried to teach Oliver to do the same, although he was too small to reach. Central Park was our local park, and when Oliver and I were very good, Dada bought us a hot dog each on our way home from the playground. To this day, when I smell hot dogs and that sweetish yellow American mustard I'm immediately transported to my early childhood.

Right down the road from the apartment there was a video rental. It was like Aladdin's Cave: small, dark and filled with delights. The owner was Middle Eastern – possibly Iranian – with a moustache and impeccable manners. He always seemed delighted to see us. Dad took Oliver and me there all the time. He rented us all the Disney movies, with the proviso that we had to watch one classic film for every cartoon. We saw films like *Bicycle Thieves* by Vittorio De Sica, Truffaut's *400 Blows,* Michael Curtiz's *The Adventures of Robin Hood* with Errol Flynn, Charlie Chaplin's *The Gold Rush* and *The Great Dictator.* Why Dad thought his tiny children should watch highbrow Italian and French New Wave films, I don't know. He had his quirks. I didn't always understand what I was watching, but I was invariably enthralled.

One day, when I was about five, Dad rented *Le Ballon Rouge*, by Albert Lamorisse. It is a short film from 1956 about a little French boy who finds a big red balloon. There was no dialogue, but somehow the director made it clear that the balloon quickly became his best – only? – friend. I cried when the bad boys got together to kill the balloon with their stones and catapults. After watching it once, I became obsessed with the movie and begged Dad to rent it every week.

I watched it over and over until I knew every scene by heart and could anticipate every single move. Mum and Dad worried because every time I got just as upset as the first, yet every weekend I demanded it. To this day, watching *Le Ballon Rouge*, or even just typing the title, brings me out in goosebumps.

Sometimes, when the movies were over, Dad told Oliver and me stories about our family castle in Ireland. 'It's beautiful,' he'd say. 'You'll see for yourselves one day.' He described the stuffed lions, the enormous paintings, all the wonderful objects our ancestors had left behind. 'And in front of the castle,' Dad would add, 'covered in trees, but still perfectly visible, is the ancient Norman motte and bailey that the very first owners of Dunsany built, a thousand years ago.'

'Eventually,' Dad told us, 'we'll have to go home to Dunsany Castle and build a life in Ireland. We'll pick apples from our own orchard. Won't that be grand?'

'But why, Dad?' we would say. 'We like it here!'

But we already knew that that's just the way it was. A shadow of dread began to loom over me. This happy existence would, one day, vanish like the end of summer and the start of autumn. The joy would fade like the glowing green leaves on the trees in Central Park.

'Dunsany is especially important for *you*, Randal,' Dad said. 'One day you'll be in charge there, and you'll need to figure out what to do with your life, and with the estate. Something very special.'

'But, Dad,' I said once. 'I'm only six.'

'Never too early to start figuring it out,' Dad said. He was smiling, and it was kind of a joke, but it also wasn't. No matter what path I took, it'd always come second to the many demands of our shared heritage.

In 1990, when I was seven, a notorious Dublin crime gang, led by a man known as The General, broke into Dunsany Castle and stole a number of valuable artworks, including three Van Dycks and a couple of more modern pieces by Jack B. Yeats. The loss of the art was very upsetting, and even more worrying was the fact that Granddad – the nineteenth Lord Dunsany, and named Randal, like me – was old and frail, and was very vulnerable in a large, unguarded castle a short drive from Dublin, which had a big problem with organised crime. Mum and Dad agreed that it was time to move closer to home. They compromised on London, where Mum hoped she'd have a good career as an architect, and which was close enough to Dublin that one could be in Dunsany in a matter of hours.

The day we left New York remains one of the saddest I've lived through. It meant saying goodbye to Dada. I remember that day very well. I stood in the open door of my bedroom, looking at the piles of boxes containing my whole life. The shrill sound of the tape gun was like my world being ripped apart piece by piece and my heart was breaking. Dada saw the tears in my eyes. Swiftly, she took me into my parents' bedroom.

'I don't want to leave you, Dada!' I said through my tears. 'Please don't let them take me away. I promise, I'll do anything, tidy my room, do my homework, I'll help more, just don't let them take me. I want to be with you!'

Dada broke down too. She knelt down to my height, pushed my curls behind my ears and whispered in my ear: 'My lovely boy, you're the closest thing to a son I will probably ever have. You'll have a new life in Europe, the life you were always supposed to have. You're important, Randal, God has a plan for you.'

Dada told me to be brave and to be good and said that whenever I looked up at the sky, she'd be looking at the same moon and sun as me. She dried my eyes, kissed me on the head and hugged me once more – hard. Then she returned me to Mum and Dad, who were distracted by the packing and didn't realise how upset I was.

The next day, everything in the apartment was packed away into trucks and a yellow taxi was parked out the front of the apartment building, waiting for us. Dad was carrying the last of our luggage. I stood beside Dada, clutching her leg. Mum motioned that it was time to go, and I squeezed Dada's leg even harder. She knelt down and hugged me goodbye, kissing me and holding me tight.

'Don't ever forget what I told you, Randal,' she said. 'Wherever you are, I'll always be with you.'

Then Dad took my hand, led me to the taxi and put me into the back seat. The door slammed shut and I pressed my face to the glass, fighting away tears with every inch of my being. The car took off and Dada slowly disappeared. I never saw her again. A part of my heart died that day. Even today, many years later, I still feel a piece of it missing.

Sometimes I wonder how my life would have worked out if we'd stayed and I'd grown up American. But that was never going to happen. Mum and Dad couldn't let it. There were obligations and duties I didn't yet fully understand.

The flight from New York to London seemed to last forever. It was raining when the plane landed, and London looked dark and dull as the taxi drove us to a family apartment in Burton Court. I remember desperately missing Dada, so much my body physically ached. I wanted her to tuck me into bed at night, to give me breakfast the next morning, to tell me

– as she always had – that I was her special little boy. But now she was far away, and Mum and Dad had made it clear that this was a new chapter for us all. I'd never really thought of Mum as my mother before – *Dada* was my mother – but I had to start now.

Obviously, Mum had always loved us, but she'd been so busy in New York we hadn't seen that much of her. In London she was less busy, and we spent much more time together. My chief memory of Mum from those early years is her stories. One was about a pet turtle she'd had as a child in Brazil and how she'd stood on his back to look over the garden wall, trying to appear taller to the neighbours. This sort of absurdity was very characteristic of her, and one of the things that made me feel close to her. I was fascinated by the idea of the turtle carrying its home on its back, of being both animal and home at the same time. Now that I was in a new and strange place, the thought was oddly comforting. I imagined myself likewise being able to bring my home wherever I went, and it made the transition to London a little easier.

Mum's first months in London were spent studying for architect's exams. She passed with flying colours and opened an office opposite Battersea Park. My parents bought a house. Gradually, Oliver and I got used to living in London. I began to find things I liked about it. One was the ageing punks with high, gaudily-coloured mohawks, leather jackets bristling with sharp metal studs bearing slogans such as 'anarchy' and 'UK subs' and well-chewed cigarettes dangling from their mouths. They haunted our local newsagent and were an exotic, fascinating sight, like tropical birds dropped in from some distant land. I stared at them enviously. I definitely wanted to be one when I grew up.

'Pfft, those people,' was Mum's comment on them. 'They have mental problems!'

I started out in a day school, where I was always bottom of the class. It wasn't clear at first why I was doing so badly. I seemed reasonably bright, but couldn't follow the lessons. Mum realised that I had dyslexia, as she had it too, and had struggled with it as a child, when there was very little understanding of the condition. Her father, a military man, believed in conquering problems with sheer will. He made her go up and down the stairs in their home repeating, 'I'm a winner, I'm a winner.' He wasn't one for indulging human emotion and promoted extreme behaviour as a way to defeat difficulties, in this case demanding repetition until the issue was conquered. Mum wanted me to use the same approach, as it had helped her. Unfortunately, it didn't work with me. Although she made me go up and down the stairs repeating these words, my grades didn't improve and I felt useless.

To make matters worse, the children at school ridiculed me. They made fun of my American accent. They teased me about my skinny frame and curly hair. I started wearing multiple layers to make myself seem bigger, covering myself with large coats and sweaters, even in the summer heat. When we had swimming in PE I'd feign sickness, as I dreaded being seen in a swimsuit. I became an expert at forcing fingers down my throat to vomit to get me out of sports.

When I look back at those early days in London, my overriding emotion is disappointment. It was probably difficult for my successful parents to have a kid who didn't seem able to learn or function. My older siblings Daniel and Joana, university students now, were very clever, and so was my younger brother Oliver. I wasn't. Nonetheless, I did find one friend, a kid called Emil.

Emil and his family lived in a cramped council tower block. His father was white, his mother black. They weren't 'together', or at least not officially. I remember Emil's dad as a kind man, skinny and dishevelled. Looking back, I suspect he may have been an addict. His mum worked tirelessly to make ends meet and put her kids through school. Emil and I played together every day. We ran through the tired corridors of his tower block, played in the broken lift, and spent hours in the basement, where some of the residents had started a small club for the local kids. One day, Emil produced a knife he'd taken from his big brother's room. I was impressed by how sharp it looked when he held it up to the light. Emil said that his mum and dad had had a big fight the night before, and that he'd been awake all night, listening through the wall to his mum's sobs. I put my arm around him and said that my parents sometimes fought too, embellishing a story to make him feel a little better. It didn't help at all.

Then Emil held the knife up where the elevator light shone off the blade.

'You're my best friend,' he said. 'You're kind of my brother.'

I nodded. 'Me too,' I said.

'Let's be blood brothers!' Emil said.

I'd no idea what he meant and was shocked when Emil used the knife to cut his thumb, which started dripping blood onto the elevator floor.

'Cut yours!' he said.

At first, I didn't want to. Emil got angry: 'If you're *really* my brother you need to prove it!'

Although I was terrified, I didn't want to disappoint Emil. I took the knife and, copying him, pressed it into my thumb. A shock of pain went up my body as I slit it open and a steady stream of blood flowed down my hand and onto the floor.

Bravely, I held my thumb up to Emil. He nodded: 'Now we'll be brothers forever,' he said.

We pushed our thumbs together and then pulled them apart. We both looked down at our bleeding thumbs.

'I think Mum has plasters in the drawer,' said Emil. 'Come on!'

That night, I lay in bed staring at the Donald Duck plaster wrapped around my thumb. I felt strangely warm. I'd found a home in London. Like a turtle, I'd brought home with me.

The summer holidays were nearly over when Dad announced at dinner that I was going to be leaving my day school and going to a boarding school, as was Oliver. The name of the school was Ludgrove, and Dad himself – like many generations of our family – had gone there.

'But I don't *want* to go, Dad!' I said.

Ludgrove was a posh school in a rural location many miles from the inner-city school where I'd met Emil. On my first day, I was shown how the names of the Plunketts who'd preceded me were literally carved into the dining-room walls on large wooden boards. The school had very restrictive rules. I could see Mum and Dad just once a month for a weekend. I could receive phone calls only once a week at a specific time and, like all the other kids, had to spend hours studying the classics, including Latin. As before, I was a target for the bullies. The children of the elite teased me because of my accent and my inability to understand British cultural norms. They all seemed to eat a lot of Marmite. I still associate its foul smell and taste with the English aristocracy, or 'toffs' as I preferred to call them.

Among the residents of the hellhole that was Ludgrove were Princes William and Harry, along with their bodyguards, though neither was in my year. I chiefly remember Harry because he was always in detention. Mum felt sorry for him and even befriended him, telling him how to escape detention by faking diarrhoea. She always had a soft spot for the underdog. I still recall the horror on his face as she explained how the ruse could work.

Mum and Dad were always busy, so they were always extremely late collecting me and Oliver on our monthly trips home. We usually sat at the door for several hours watching our peers leave with their families, staring down the driveway, hoping ours would soon arrive. I remember a worried Prince Charles rather sweetly fretting over me one day as I plaintively sat on my trunk, waiting for Mum. Say what you will about the man, but he was a gentleman. He made a point of thanking and paying respect to everyone, which is more than I can say for most Ludgrove parents.

I wasn't allowed to call home or to call my friend Emil. I couldn't stop thinking about Dada and wondering where she was and what she was doing. These feelings of loss continued to hover over me like a cloud until I wanted to die. I started to comfort myself by hiding alone under a fire escape near the school boiler-room. The boiler was down a flight of stone stairs with what seemed like a treacherous drop. I'd rush towards the balcony over the stairs, planning to jump to what I hoped would be my death. I'd stop short just in time. We'd been told the boiler was 'dangerous' and to keep away from it. I did the opposite. I spent every break staring at it, trying to suck in the carbon dioxide pumping from the pipes, thinking maybe that'd be easier than the jump. I thought less about dying than about simply no longer being. I liked thinking about it and returned to this topic repeatedly.

It was pleasurable, the way picking at a scab can be. I remembered Mum's attempts to motivate me for success by going up the stairs uttering those dreaded words, 'I'm a winner. I'm a winner.' I had my own mantra now: 'I can always kill myself. I can always kill myself'. That inner voice would stay with me for years. It was always such a comfort.

'By the way,' Mum said on one of my weekend visits. 'Your friend Emil rang.'

Excitedly, I asked what Emil had said. She said his dad had died and he wanted to talk to me.

'Here's Emil's number,' Mum said, handing me a piece of paper. 'You can ring him from school.'

Back at school that evening, I approached the headmaster's wife, who was known as the gate-keeper of the phone. I told her my friend's dad had died and that I needed to ring him.

'Don't be silly,' she said. 'Your little friend won't benefit at all from your coddling him; he and his family need to deal with their issues themselves.'

'But I *really* need to talk to him! I'm his only friend,' I said, on the verge of tears.

'Nonsense,' she said. 'Write him a letter. And don't cry. Crying is indulgent. Act accordingly.'

I wasn't allowed to ring Mum and Dad either, not until they called me next weekend. I wrote a letter – several, actually – and sent them home, asking my parents to forward them to Emil. Weeks later, I was finally allowed to ring him, but the phone rang out. I've never spoken to Emil since. Over thirty years later, that once-painful scar on the end of my thumb has shrunk to just a small mark, but the meaning behind it remains. Every so often, when I run my fingers along it, I think of Emil and wonder whatever happened to my first friend.

First year ended and we went to Dunsany for a long holiday to get to know our Irish granddad properly. In the Second World War, Granddad Randal had been a handsome, dashing hero, awarded medals for fighting at El-Alamein. A portrait of him in his full battle regalia hung in the dining room. The 1930s and 1940s had been his golden years, when he was young, handsome, a talented athlete and a brave soldier. Granddad's first wife, Vera de Sá Sottomaior – Dad's mother – was a beautiful Brazilian socialite who'd struggled with living in a rickety old castle in the middle of nowhere, and had left when Granddad was at war. After the war, Granddad returned a hero, but also had to rapidly adjust to his new reality as the less-gifted son of a literary giant – his father, Edward, had been a renowned writer. Publishing ninety or so books as Lord Dunsany, he was a pioneer in the genre of fantasy, often cited as having been a seminal influence on people like JRR Tolkien and HP Lovecraft, as a result of works like *The King of Elfland's Daughter*, which was published in 1924. He'd also been a great friend of some of the greats in Irish literature: William Butler Yeats, Lady Augusta Gregory, George Bernard Shaw.

But Edward's son, my grandfather, was a poor judge of character with no business sense. Randal and his father didn't get along, so my great-grandfather arranged his estate so that my grandfather could never sell it, just live off it until it could be passed to the next generation. By the 1950s – lonely, humiliated and still grappling with the psychological after-effects of the war – my grandfather had remarried, to Sheila Phillips, a woman who claimed to belong to a branch of an extremely well-to-do English family.

Despite appearances, Granddad had at least a superficial sense of loyalty to Dunsany, but I'm sure he also resented it.

Under his management, most of the gates had fallen off their hinges, squatters occupied parts of the land and houses alike, and many of the outhouses and ancillary buildings had started falling apart. Granddad had been very successful on the battlefield, but he didn't seem able to make the estate work. He was surrounded every day by the evidence of his many failures, and now that he was old and confined to home, the estate infrastructure was falling into even more serious disrepair, as was he. Granddad now had twenty-four-hour nursing care. The nurses came and went and we had very little to do with them.

Based in London, we continued to visit Dunsany for short holidays. I hated almost everything about these visits: the obligatory visits with Granddad in his stinking room, the strange coldness of my step-grandmother Sheila and the apparently endless vista of soggy fields that Oliver and I couldn't even play in, because they were rented to local farmers for grazing animals from which an apparently endless stream of steaming shit appeared to emanate. When we visited for Christmas, it was sometimes so cold in our rooms that ice formed on the inside of the huge old windows, and I remember my breath rising like a plume of smoke in the freezing air inside the castle while, outside, vast flocks of crows whirled against the endlessly grey skies.

Granddad still had a number of full-time staff, but most of them were elderly and had strong County Meath accents and we often didn't understand them. There were a few cleaners who'd been working for the family for years and a cook, who lived in the stable yard and mostly stayed in the kitchen, emerging only at mealtimes with plates of ham and bowls of cabbage. Some of the ground staff, who took care of the land, were from local families who'd been working on the estate for generations. Although I was just a kid and didn't warrant any special treatment, many of these people – who seemed impossibly old – appeared reluctant to look me in the eye and glanced to the side whenever they spoke to me, which made me feel even more uncomfortable around them. But, despite not being used to having children around, they did their best to be kind.

The one person who consistently made me feel uneasy was my step-grandmother, Sheila Dunsany. Behind those dark eyes of hers, not unlike the unblinking eyes of a crow, there seemed to be something actually evil. Sheila couldn't stop us visiting our own family home, although she tried. Despite our efforts to maintain a cordial relationship with Sheila, she didn't even try to hide her disdain for us. Always impeccably dressed in fashionable outfits and dripping with jewellery, she'd look down her long nose at Oliver and me in a way that made it very clear she found us lacking. Her accent was utterly extraordinary, like English fingernails being pulled down a blackboard, posh to the point of being almost incomprehensible. It was almost as though she didn't want those she considered her social inferiors to understand her. She reeked of tobacco and usually had a glass of something strong in one of her hands. Looking back now, I can see that she was half-cut most of the time.

In an effort to build bridges, Mum and Dad instructed Oliver and me to kiss Sheila. We had no choice; we'd be shoved towards her to stand on tiptoe and plant kisses on her ravaged cheeks. She smelled of face-powder and decay, accepting our kisses as her due, but never returning them. Then she'd flick her hands at us – those long pointed nails like talons – and tell us to run upstairs, as she'd things to do and didn't want little American boys getting under her feet. Obediently, off we'd go, often finding when we returned to our rooms that Sheila had turned the heating off again in the hope we'd be so uncomfortable we'd leave early. Mum and Dad started referring to Sheila as 'Cromwell the Second'. Cromwell is a hero in England and regarded as a saviour of parliamentary democracy, but in Ireland he's remembered as second in infamy to the devil himself, and in our family as having destroyed our church and forced us into exile in Holland for a period in the 1600s. During that time, the castle was emptied of its contents, which probably ultimately ended up in one of the Windsors' many palaces.

I do have some happy memories of visiting Dunsany, especially the exploring expeditions that Oliver and I enjoyed. We were used to living in an ordinary-sized apartment or house, and now we had a whole castle to explore, along with all its outhouses. We'd sometimes creep and sometimes run through the various small and large rooms of the castle, our footsteps making the floorboards creak. The glassy eyes of the animal trophies on the walls, and the painted gazes of our ancestors and other notables in their portraits, seemed to follow us. Outside we played in the formal garden, jumping over and through the square-cut box hedging and having water-fights with hoses. The farmworkers had a big, friendly labrador called Mac that we could sometimes persuade to join in the fun. There were some kids living in one of the estate houses and sometimes we played together. Their father, Granddad's cook's husband, taught me how to ride a bike. I've always been grateful for that.

As we got braver, we started to venture further away. We kids clambered up to the top of the motte in front of the castle and sat on its flat top, surveying the landscape. From up there, we could see across acres and acres of land, over the fields to where Dunsany ended and someone else's land began. There were some scruffy bushes growing on the top of the mound, and trees had climbed up and rooted on the far side, but the growth was relatively sparse, and there was little to obstruct our view. Granddad's gardener said there was gold buried somewhere up there, dating to Cromwell's days, when the family had needed to hide their valuables somewhere fast. We never found any, though. Perhaps it's still there.

At the weekends, we were allowed to rent our beloved videos from the local Xtra-vision video rental. Oliver and I loved action movies, particularly *First Blood* and *Rambo II*.

With me in charge of our mutual safety, we went to a forested area about half a kilometre from the castle, through which the Skane River flows. The Skane is a small tributary of the River Boyne, and it wasn't very deep where it flowed through the estate. Oliver and I could get right in and wade through the water, pretending we were involved in guerrilla warfare. I remember the water being dark and murky as we crashed through it, kicking up mud that was an odd, greyish colour. Occasionally a bubble rose to the surface and burst malodorously. We'd shout: 'We got us some Charlie!' I don't recall ever seeing any of Ireland's common waterbirds standing along the edges of the Skane, as they do on the verge of any river or canal that harbours life, and we certainly never saw any fish. It never occurred to us to wonder why the water smelled so bad.

Oliver and I rarely ventured into the fields as they were generally filled with cattle. As city kids, we couldn't tell the difference between cows and bulls. 'Walk with a stick!' one of the farmworkers advised us. 'Everyone in Ireland walks with a stick.' He explained that if we had a good stick each, and waved them at the cattle as we went by, they'd be scared and would run away. But we looked at our own small, scrawny bodies, and then the big, hefty bodies of the cattle, and were unconvinced. Sometimes we saw rabbits, but they often looked strange and unwell, rather than like cute Disney rabbits. They were sick, Dad said, with myxomatosis. The disease had been introduced to Ireland in the 1950s, and Irish rabbits were increasingly resistant to it, but every so often a new wave came in and destroyed most of a generation.

Dad loved the countryside and nature and tried to teach Oliver and me how to tell the difference between oak and an ash, and which wild plants were edible and which were not. A few times we made a little bonfire so that we could have a barbecue. We kids enjoyed the sausages but weren't even remotely interested in Dad's attempts to teach us about the glories of the great outdoors.

Having spent just a year as a boarder at Ludgrove, finishing off primary school, now I was supposed to attend a secondary school. I was to move on to board at the prestigious Eton, travelling back to see my family only for the holidays. Many generations of Plunketts had also gone to Eton, and had used their great education to achieve wonderful things.

'You're going to love it,' Dad said encouragingly. 'It'll be so much fun. You'll be with other boys your age. There'll be midnight feasts in the dormitories. And we're not far away; you'll be able to come home often.'

Dad was a terrible liar, and I could tell that he was lying then. He'd have been an awful poker player, because when he told an untruth, he'd look away. Because I knew he wanted me to believe him, I pretended I did.

I attended the interview for Eton. The principal asked what I wanted to do with my life. I said I wanted to write stories like my great-granddad Edward, the famous writer. We were all very proud of him. Perhaps with all this in mind, Dad had always encouraged my love of storytelling. He said he was a patron of the arts and gave me extra pocket-money for every story I wrote. But the headmaster was unimpressed with ten-year-old me. I was the first Plunkett to be rejected by Eton, the news delivered on the phone one afternoon when Oliver and I were on a visit home from Ludgrove. Mum was livid, vibrating with rage and hurling insults at the stuffy British professors.

'Don't worry,' Mum said. 'The last will be the first and school doesn't matter. I myself left school at thirteen and ended up being more successful than any of my classmates!'

Mum said the same thing every time I got a report card with straight Fs and Es.

This setback, and the fact that Granddad was getting older and needed more help, prompted Dad to decide that it was time for us to move to Ireland permanently, despite Sheila's protests. So we moved into Dunsany Castle, our family home. Dad may also have been prompted by the fact that Cromwell the Second was – according to the few domestic staff left – steadily emptying the house of valuables and doing much more damage than even Ireland's top mobster had managed to wreak. It appeared that Sheila was packing up the family silver and either distributing it among her relatives or selling it all over town, while she told the great and glorious that *she* was the one with the money, who was keeping the estate afloat. At one point, the housekeeper had intercepted a family member of Sheila's leaving the castle weighed down by a heavy suitcase. Before she reached her car, the suitcase broke open and thousands of pounds' worth of silverware fell onto the gravel. Sheila was more than capable of presenting her old, drunk, befuddled husband with papers to hand his belongings over to her, and he was more than capable of signing them.

Looking back, I can see why Dad felt so strongly about moving. His father was now bed-ridden, old and frail and drunk all day long. Without some oversight, Sheila might end up dispensing with the entire estate, trust or not. Later I found out why we'd moved to London first instead of Ireland. Dad had wanted us to move into a property on the estate known as the Dowager House. Traditionally, this was reserved for the widows of the family when they retired from the castle, allowing the next generation to move into their new role as stewards of the estate. Sheila immediately sold the large, beautiful Georgian house for much less than it was worth, as it wasn't protected by the trust that held most of the estate for the next generation. Dad was livid and offered three times the purchase price to the new owner, but they wanted more than he could afford. We'd have to move into the apartment on the castle's second floor, where we'd stayed on our holidays from England.

For weeks, Mum and Dad fought about the whole idea of moving to Ireland. They kept the worst of the arguing for when Oliver and I were in bed, but I'd creep out of bed and perch at the top of the stairs to hear what they were saying.

'I hate Dunsany with every ounce of my being!' Dad shouted. 'It holds only bad memories for me, but I'll dedicate my life to fixing it so Randal never has to suffer as I did!'

'We're *Irish*,' Dad told Oliver and me. 'We need to put down roots in Ireland, like we should've done a long time ago. We're not English, so being educated in England doesn't even make sense. We're going to leave London and go back to live full-time in Ireland instead. The place of our people. You boys will go to Irish schools. It's going to be great.'

Dad explained – as he had so often – that we were descended from Normans who'd settled in Ireland in the early Middle Ages, choosing the exact right spot to build, open fields and lay down roots. They were the *good* settlers, who loved Ireland, shared a common faith with its people and took care of everyone, unlike the later settlers, who were English, and just ruined everything. Our castle had been our family home for almost nine hundred years. He didn't want to be the one to break that chain.

'First me and then you, Randal,' Dad said 'Dunsany is our special place. It should be our home, too.'

Living full-time in a castle probably sounds quite grand – and I suppose it was, what with all the old masters and *objets d'art*, the hunting trophies leering at us from the walls and the sweeping views across the estate's spreading parkland – but it was freezing cold too. Our apartment had majestic views over the grounds, but it also had a chipped, grubby, dark Formica kitchen that had been installed in the 1960s and never updated. Dublin, the capital city, with its theatres, cinemas and bookshops, looked close on the map, but there was no motorway then, just a warren of winding little roads unmarked by signposts. Oliver and I had to rely on one another a lot for company. Perhaps mostly to get us out of the house. Mum and Dad acquired a dog, Xulé, from the household of Oliver's godfather, Lord Congreve from Waterford. We'd always wanted to have pets, but hadn't been able to in New York or London. I'd wanted an Alsatian like our Uncle Congreve's – he had several, and they reminded me of wolves – but Xulé, who came to us as a puppy, was a bundle of joy and quickly stole all our hearts. 'Chulé', which is pronounced the same way, is a Portuguese word that refers to the stench of smelly feet, and the puppy's name was Mum's little joke. He came everywhere with Oliver and me. Mum and Dad loved him too. We eventually acquired another, Pitouka.

'A Jack Russell is the right dog for a Plunkett,' Dad said happily. 'Look at the tombs in the church.'

I went to look and there they were: ancestors carved in stone back in the Middle Ages, their feet resting on what looked like little Jack Russells accompanying them into a Norman afterlife.

On a wall in one of the castle's many halls hangs a small portrait of a portly alleged Cromwellian loyalist who'd inhabited our home during those unhappy years of the mid-seventeenth century. The painting hangs in the back stairwell, far away from the family portraits. The story relates that he'd suffered the consequences of having slept with the wrong woman and, as punishment, was left to live in what remained of Dunsany after Cromwell had half-destroyed it. He'd arrived as a young man and spent most of his adult life here. Having loved food, wine and women, he was now deprived of all three. When Charles II returned to power, he reinstated former supporters of his father to their lands and properties, and the Plunketts came home. This Cromwellian is said to have been waiting at the door, bags packed. He presented them with his portrait and said it was a small token as he'd been looking after this pile of rocks for years. He added, apparently, that he was returning to England as quickly as possible, as Irish women were ugly and our food was lousy. This story has always made me laugh, because he was from Sussex, which – *checks notes* – is not known as a culinary jewel. The old story maintains that he died in old age in the arms of a young woman, so things worked out for him in the end. I once asked Dad why we still had this portrait of the fat old Cromwellian in our back stairwell. Dad said that, although he was our enemy, he's still part of the shared history of Dunsany, and that you have to take the bad with the good. He would not be joining the rest of the family in the dining room, but would remain on the back stairs, which is also known as the dead corridor, as it's filled with paintings and heads of dead animals. That made sense to me. I've always smiled at the idea that Dunsany is more than a building or a family, but part of a bigger story.

Cromwell the Second was known among elite circles in Dublin as a patroness of the arts who spent a lot on high fashion and works of art. She was on charitable committees and lent her name and help to all sorts of fundraising endeavours. In this persona she'd plenty of admirers in Ireland. They could never have imagined how she described them. Sheila loathed the Irish and often complained about them – how uncouth they were, she said, how uncultured. She made fun of their accents and complained when Granddad invited Irish people, particularly locals, to the castle. They'd held a noteworthy argument over lunch one day a few years before, when they'd both been younger and stronger, while the staff listened through the door.

'You've done it again!' she'd screeched. 'You've invited more of these filthy, dirty people into my house! You know I can't stand these bloody Irish!'

'Well,' Granddad had roared back, 'what the fuck do you think *I* am, if not an Irishman?'

The employees heard a crash. Granddad had picked up his bowl of soup, flung it across the room and thundered out. Years later, the housekeeper at the time, who had overheard all this, said she'd been afraid that Granddad would kill Sheila. You can say what you like about the Plunketts – and, believe me, many say a lot – but one thing that we've always been sure about is that we're Irish. Irish and proud.

The worse things got between my grandparents and parents, the more Mum filled my head with stories about how terrible Dad's childhood had been. Mum said that Sheila had wanted Dad dead, because without him her own family would inherit the castle. When he first arrived from Brazil, where his mother had stayed, Dad didn't speak English well and had a strong accent. Sheila punished him for his poor English by denying him food. When he made a mistake, there went his dinner. Apparently, Dad became so thin that one of the young housekeepers, Joan Flynn, a sparky local woman, fed him on the sly, risking her job in the process. Joan would make him hide under the table in the kitchen and sneak him food, with the butler keeping an eye out. After some months of this, my Dad's grandparents, who lived between here and England, returned from a long trip overseas. They were horrified when, on meeting Dad for the first time, he was served a plate of dinner and he quickly ducked under the table to eat it.

My great-grandfather questioned the staff, and Joan told him everything. After that, Dad's grandparents took over his care. This, Mum explained, was one of the main reasons why my great-grandfather had placed Dunsany in a trust; he'd lost all faith in Granddad and Sheila.

When Dad got older and went away to boarding school, and from there to college, Sheila burned all the pictures of him: the few we have were saved by Joan, who managed to grab them from the fire. When Mum told me these stories, I found them hard to believe. But Joan herself, now elderly, confirmed it all. She'd come back to work for us in her later years, and it was touching to see how much she and Dad loved each other. She was still very protective of him, and he regarded her as a sort of guardian angel. Mum told Oliver and me never to discuss Dad's childhood with him, because he didn't want us to see him as a victim, and Mum didn't want him to have to revisit old pain or to feel embarrassed. Dad never spoke ill of anybody; he always wanted to see the best in people. Even then I could see that, despite his many talents, his social agility and his profound sense of duty, beneath it all there was a sort of fragility. I still feel angry and upset that someone could have treated an innocent child so viciously that part of him would never recover. I also feel angry and upset with my mother for sharing these stories with Oliver and me before we were old enough to hear them.

Despite all the tension our presence was causing, Mum immersed herself in trying to normalise the immensely strained family relations. Surely, she thought, her father-in-law would have some love for his own grandchildren. Periodically, Oliver and I were sent downstairs to talk to our drunken, bedridden granddad and sometimes – horrifyingly – to give him a kiss.

'He's still your grandfather,' Mum would say in encouraging tones. 'And deep down I know he's fond of you. Just give a little kiss to show that you care. It won't kill you.'

Granddad spent almost all his time in bed now and sometimes suffered from waking nightmares. He could be awful: during one robust exchange of views with Mum, he yelled at her, 'Go away, you boring woman! I think we've had quite enough of colonials for one day!' It was the poshest, most absurd insult I've ever heard, but Mum didn't see the funny side.

Granddad put back a litre of Black Bush whiskey every day. A crate was delivered directly to the castle every week, together with a little box containing some small tins of snuff, from the last shop in Dublin to stock the revolting stuff. He started his mornings with a glass of Black Bush and milk. All he ate was white bread and canned oxtail soup, washed down with more whiskey. In the evening he had a cup of Complan with a whiskey chaser. All day long he snorted snuff, which dribbled down his chin, stained his pyjamas and made him smell utterly revolting. Mostly he seemed indifferent to Oliver and me, but very occasionally he'd hoist himself up on his elbows and tell us about when he'd been our age, and his favourite activity had been dragging his bicycle to the top of the old Norman motte and then freewheeling down: 'I'd get up to such *speed*,' he always said, 'that I'd reach the road at the end of the avenue without so much as touching a pedal.' I suppose this was Granddad's effort to reach out to us, but we paid his stories of boyhood very little attention.

Just once in a while, something would happen that'd make me feel sorry for Granddad, and even a little warm towards him. Like when he'd start ranting about my little dog – 'Get that fucking dog out of here!' – and then relent because for some reason Xulé was fond of him and would lick his hoary old toes with enthusiasm and affection. 'Oh, all right then,' Granddad would mumble. 'The dog can stay. He likes me.'

Mostly, though, I waited for Granddad to die. He seemed the living embodiment of all our problems as a family. The symbol of the rot that had set in at Dunsany. Sometimes I fantasised about picking up a pillow and smothering him. Putting us all out of our misery.

'I'm only small,' I'd think. 'Nobody'd ever suspect *me*. And there's no way he could ever fight me off. He's weak and frail.'

Looking back now, I can see that at least some of my grandfather's dreadful behaviour probably related to the terrible things he'd seen – and perhaps done – during the war. Even all those years later, he suffered from appalling nightmares and would start screaming in the middle of the night, waking everyone in the castle.

Dad had found us a school locally, Headfort. We'd be joining in for the 1994 school year. Headfort, with its old-school aesthetic, was very different from Ludgrove. The kids were normal and didn't look down at me because of my accent or heritage. I have happy memories of building forts, starting to make friends and actually enjoying life – I was allowed home at the weekends! – although I did very poorly academically. For the first time since moving from America I wasn't shunned and disliked by the other kids. We rode horses and I was quite good at show-jumping and started winning medals. I started to feel that maybe I'd be happy in Ireland after all. Mum and Dad bought me a horse – Boner – and I focused on getting in with the horsey crowd.

Apart from the family dogs, Boner was the first animal I ever really got to know. He'd been rejected by a local riding school because he was difficult and threw the young riding students onto the ground. But somehow he and I just clicked, and I was able to ride him.

Around this time I wanted to start listening to music, and when Daniel was home from college for the holidays, I asked him to lend me some tapes. He pulled out an old tape: *Powerslave* by Iron Maiden.

'It's heavy metal,' Daniel said.

The very words excited my curiosity. That sounded cool.

'Can I listen?'

'There you go,' he said, tossing it over. 'Maybe you'll like it.'

I took the tape back to my room, slid it into the tape-deck I'd been given for Christmas and hit play. Over the next few minutes I learned something very fundamental about myself: I love heavy metal. Really, *truly* love it. The raw energy, the distorted guitars, those pelting drums . . . I listened to that tape until it broke, and then begged Dad to take me to Dublin to buy more and to pick up copies of *Kerrang!*, a magazine dedicated to the genre. We went to the Sound Cellar, a basement shop that had all the music I loved. At first the owner thought we were lost, because most of his customers weren't middle-aged dads accompanied by their young kids. But after the first few visits I knew him as Tommy and we were friends. I still buy records there today. At the time, I was still so short I couldn't see the shelves properly, and all the hardcore stuff was behind the counter, so Dad had to pick me up to see. Soon I was spending two hours there at a time, poring over the music, until eventually Dad started going off to do his own chores while I stayed there, in my element. This was one of Dad's most loving acts as a father, because he liked classical music and a little light jazz, and found my tastes absolutely baffling.

Shortly after finding the Sound Cellar, I discovered 2FM's *Metal Show* hosted by John Kenny. RTÉ 2FM is popular Irish radio and back then on a Sunday evening, they took it dark. I tuned in religiously to hear all the classics and the new acts: Marilyn Manson, Morbid Angel, Type O Negative. I was the only kid in school who loved heavy metal. I spent the weekends growling at the mirror in my bedroom, trying to emulate my idols. I started skipping lunch and saving my lunch money to buy more music. The other kids thought I was a weirdo, but I didn't care. I was in love. Back home, when the shouting started, I'd just put on my headphones and turn the volume up until heavy metal filled my ears.

When I was twelve, primary school ended, and while most of the other kids went to St Columba's, a boarding secondary school on the outskirts of Dublin, I was sent to King's Hospital, a private school for the middle classes not too far from Dunsany. The brief moment of belonging I'd experienced ended. My mid-Atlantic accent and unorthodox upbringing and family marked me out as a target. The other kids picked on me for my long hair, for being skinny, and basically anything they could poke fun at. 'A freak', they'd call me, 'rocker man' and 'satanist'. Oh, and my personal favourite, 'English cunt'. They felt free to make their feelings known because my family was 'posh'. I shouldn't be here, they told me, saying that my home was land stolen from the true Irish. I was miserable, and failing every class and in every way. My nascent interest in horse riding went south too, because I got home so late, and had so much homework, there was no time to ride. Boner was sold to another family.

Despite having previously planned to build a career as an architect in London, now that we'd decided to embrace our collective future as the custodians of Dunsany, Mum had thrown herself wholeheartedly into this project. She'd briefly attempted to kickstart an architectural career in Ireland, but the night she was awarded her licence, the chair of the Royal Irish Institute of Architects leaned into her and whispered, 'I hope you're not coming here to ruin our architecture.' This had enraged her so much she grabbed the microphone and announced to the room, 'What architecture? All you have here are bad copies of English architecture.' Then she threw the microphone on the ground and walked out.

Soon Mum's new life's purpose was preserving and improving every aspect of Dunsany. Perhaps because she was also descended from an old family with a lot of history, Mum could understand why the castle and the estate mattered so much to Dad. So – much as she deplored the lack of decent coffee in the local SuperValu – Mum was now all in. She started talking about what we might be able to do with Dunsany when Granddad was gone. There were various beautiful properties from different periods in history, most of them now in states of decay. Mum's rich imagination and her years of architectural experience helped her to see them not as they were but as they could be, and she began to draw up elaborate plans to renovate them into bijou residences that could be rented out to supply the estate with a ready supply of funds.

Perhaps it was all going to work out.

Chapter Two

The Disappointment

DAD WAS GETTING STUCK INTO HIS ROLE – RISING AT SIX TO PAINT, AND SPENDING THE REST OF THE DAY DOING ADMIN AND MANAGING THE ESTATE. One day that'd be me, having to let my passions take second place to the great Dunsany project.

'It's not always easy', Dad said, 'to inherit a family tradition like this, but it's a privilege and a responsibility that the firstborn son just has to accept.'

Daniel and Joana were starting out on their adult lives. Oliver was nerdy and seemed to breeze through life; he loved reading large fantasy books and playing video games, both of which I struggled with. They all seemed so much more accomplished than me.

Dad had started to prepare me for the future in our traditional family style, telling and retelling the stories of our ancestors and all the amazing things they'd done. He repeated them and made me do the same until they became a reflex.

He walked me around every room in the castle, into every nook and cranny, intoning our family mythology. He told me I had a sacred duty to continue the tradition, to keep Dunsany Castle and its lands safe for the generations to come. One of the ancestors – Oliver, like my brother – was a *bona fide* saint from the seventeenth century, finally canonised in 1975 after centuries of being just a Blessed. His severed head is on display as a relic in St Peter's Church in Drogheda, but his crozier is in our dining room at Dunsany Castle. How was I supposed to compete with someone like *that*?

I enjoyed hearing stories about my great-grandfather Edward, the writer who published as Lord Dunsany and who'd raised Dad. Dad described him as a larger-than-life personality with a creative mind. I also liked hearing about Horace Plunkett, my great-grandfather's uncle. Horace had helped form the best bits of modern Ireland by fostering the cooperative movement among smaller farmers, and lending his support to organisations like the Irish Countrywomen's Association and An Túr Gloine, which trained and encouraged stained glass artists. I admired him because he was noble in spirit; someone who stood up for ordinary people and supported those with few resources. But I felt sorry for him too. Despite everything, he was never completely accepted by those he helped, because he was a member of the aristocracy. The Irish elite didn't like him either, regarding him as a socialist. Horace had spent his life working for Ireland, and it angered me that he'd been undervalued and underappreciated.

Alongside the stories of our ancestors, Dad repeated the rules of Dunsany: 'You cannot sell what you didn't bring. You must add to the castle modern things of your time, which will eventually become history. You won't celebrate other people's histories; you'll make your own.' Every time visitors came, these rules were explained to them too, along with those old stories about our ancestors. When Mum and Dad had guests over, Oliver and I'd have to stand back and smile while Dad showed them around the castle and told them about our ancestors, the wonderful things they'd done and the rules they'd followed. I was always forced to listen and nod as if it were the first time I'd heard it all. My parents made me repeat the rules to their guests, like some sort of party trick. It was awful.

Although I hated this performance, I understood that Mum and Dad were doing it all partly for me, to help me to grow into the role I'd have to fill later on. There was no other choice because, much as I didn't want this for myself and wished I'd been born second, I loved Dad and didn't want to upset him. Still, I grew angrier, more frustrated and despairing with every single retelling. The stories were supposed to make me feel closer to Dunsany but instead they made me resent what I was and – even more – what I was expected to be. I didn't give a *shit* about most of our ancestors because they were all dead and no longer mattered. I wanted to live for the right reasons, not to placate people who were no longer even alive.

Sometimes it was hard to reconcile the competing stories of the Dunsany dynasty. Were we a noble, wonderful family full of visionaries and high achievers, or a dysfunctional lot, turning on one another and failing to support the smallest, weakest members? Maybe we were both. I started to hate the old stories, which I'd heard so often that every single word was indelibly engraved in my memory. When Dad launched into one of his many narratives, not only did I know which words he'd use, but when he'd pause for a wry laugh, when he'd throw in a witty aside. Being a Plunkett, a custodian of Dunsany, seemed most of all a performance, even when there wasn't an audience looking on, but especially when there was.

Mum also instructed Oliver and me to put on smart clothes and serve the table like two little waiters. 'If you know how to serve, you'll know how to manage,' Mum said. 'It's the first step towards success. You'll thank me when you're running the estate.' I learned silver service and a good patter for guests, but success continued to elude me. I noted that while Mum loved meeting and entertaining new people, her relationships with them were often quite transactional. She wanted her friends to be people of influence who could help her to meet other people of influence and hopefully put Dunsany Castle and Dad's art career on the map. His talent and skills weren't in question, but as most of his career to date had been outside Ireland, he didn't have the right connections. By befriending and painting portraits of Ireland's leaders in politics and industry, Mum hoped Dad's profile would rise and that he'd take his rightful place among the finest artists in the country.

Despite being privately owned, the castle was considered a national monument. For tax reasons, Dad opened it for a certain amount of time every year. That meant that there were sometimes guests whom nobody even knew traipsing through our rooms and ogling everything, including us. Sometimes Oliver and I'd be trying to watch *X-Men* or *WrestleMania* only to have to greet a small crowd of tourists whom Dad was showing around. Wherever the visitors came from, they'd ooh and ahh and tell us what lucky boys we were, to be growing up with such a marvellous heritage. Used to this, we'd nod and smile politely, our hands clenched into fists behind our backs, waiting for them to go.

I was increasingly aware that many locals regarded us as big nobs and resented the land we owned and the fact we didn't welcome the local hunts – the Ward Union and the Meath Hunt. Historically, many of the big houses and castles of Ireland do have links to the hunt, and the hunters seemed aggrieved that we didn't want to. My family had been resisting the intrusions of the hunt for a long time. Ironically, most of the people involved in the local hunt were from well-heeled backgrounds and had little reason to be resentful, because they very much ruled the roost in their communities. Hunt members seemed to dominate the local knacker yards, and refused to accept carcasses from anyone who got too aggressive with the hunt. For generations, they'd been tormenting not only Dunsany and other bigger landowners, but also farmers with smallholdings who were fearful of being penalised.

The hunt was easy to spot, with their horses, baying hounds, silly archaic costumes, and noisy retinue of cars, companions and assistants. They made a godawful racket as they ploughed across the fields of Dunsany and our neighbours' properties, frightening farm animals, damaging crops and hedges and leaving an astonishing mess. Dad tried to deal with them in his characteristically gentlemanly fashion, writing carefully worded, diplomatic letters to the leaders. It didn't help. When they encountered fences or locks, the hunters broke through them to allow passage to their horses, dogs and accompanying vehicles. Their horses' hooves mashed the ground into mud and their hounds – up to thirty or forty – bayed after inoffensive foxes or deer. The drivers accompanying the hunt tore around small country roads in their beat-up trucks and vans. The farmers renting our land complained when their precious crops were damaged. But none could speak out for fear of reprisal: denial of the use of their local knackery, intimidation, or even violence. Then Dad started going out to try reasoning with the hunters. Often our family mealtimes were interrupted when we heard the hunt on the land, and Dad jumped up and left to remonstrate with them. Many Christmas holidays were ruined by the hunt.

One December when I was about eleven, shortly after Dad had been assertive in not allowing the hunt to wreak havoc on the land, we all went to the local hotel for lunch. The hunt members were there too, nursing their pints at the bar, shifting in their seats and glowering at us. As the pints went down, the glowers escalated to angry comments and yells, which the hotel staff tried to ignore – they were nearly as intimidated as we were. I remember feeling angry Dad didn't resort to violence like my heroes Jean-Claude Van Damme and Steven Seagal. He preferred making his detractors look simple and primitive to breaking some teeth.

One Christmas Eve, just after Dad declined permission to the hunt to ride across our land, one of the gate lodges, thankfully uninhabited, was set on fire. By the time the guards came, there was no evidence of who had set the fire, but we had little doubt. We were relatively lucky to have lost only a building to the ire of the hunt because various local people were beaten by thugs demanding access to their land for this destructive pastime.

We also had many problems with poachers. Sometimes the phone rang in the middle of the night – a helpful neighbour saying that someone was shooting somewhere on the estate.

Up Dad would get, dragging on his clothes over his pyjamas, pulling on rubber boots and his winter coat and getting into a car in the hope of intercepting them before too much destruction had been done.

Mum had always worried about people setting fire to the castle, or descending on it with pitchforks, ready to attack us. A neighbouring family castle, Killeen, had been burned down in 1981 by nationalist extremists responding to the Troubles in Northern Ireland, who may have mistaken unoccupied Killeen for Dunsany. This episode of arson, so close to home, lent weight to her fears that the locals all hated us, and that we weren't safe. We knew we could expect limited sympathy when terrible things happened. Although our family had historically been Catholics, we were regarded as Anglo-Irish and all those awful stories about dreadful landlords and the Protestant ascendancy were told as if they applied to our ancestors, although they didn't.

After our gate lodge was burned down, we ensured that there was always at least one person in the castle, in case the arsonists wanted to take on a bigger target. The people who disliked us and prized the hunt were probably only a small minority of the locals overall, but they seemed to be everywhere. We'd go to the SuperValu in the village and hear half-muttered curses as we encountered a member of the hunt in the frozen goods section, or leave to see our car blocked in or find that someone had run a key down the side of the vehicle, leaving vicious scratches in the paint.

I noticed Mum's concerns and fretted over them. The fear that angry locals might come and kill us all grew and grew until I worried about it constantly. One night I woke to hear a terrifying noise. It sounded like the incoherent yells and shouts of an angry, drunken mob. Judging by the sounds of hard, heavy objects crashing against each other, I was sure they were all carrying cudgels. Screaming, I rushed into my parents' room, where Dad explained that it was the deer's rutting season and the frightening sounds were just the male deer fighting. Eventually he persuaded me that this was true, but still I crept into his bed and spent the night, cowering, in the crook of his elbow.

Music, and particularly the heavy metal that I loved, calmed me and brought me joy. Walking angrily around the large farm or the local town, trudging across the grass and through the forests in my black boots and trench coat, growing out my hair and obsessively listening to Sepultura, Morbid Angel, Obituary, Deicide, and Marilyn Manson, made me feel like part of a community. I imagined meeting the other fans of my favourite singers and bands, and what it would feel like making friends. I dreamt of finding a young goth girl who'd link her arm with mine as we shared our hatred for the world and lay under a tree debating which Darkthrone album was the best. I begged Dad to let me go to concerts in Dublin, and he patiently brought me, leaving me at the door. As they were usually over-eighteens only, and I'd no way to call home, I generally ended up listening to the band from the street outside.

At home and at school, I obsessively drew dark pictures of figures being mangled and cut up, and devils poking at writhing, screaming mortals. My classmates made fun of me, probably because I was freaking them out; that was the era of the Columbine High School massacre in the States. The killers had dressed like me, shared my taste in music and also struggled to make friends. Honestly, I can understand why people might have been concerned.

Having always struggled with my lessons, I remained at the bottom of every class and utterly miserable. Because I'd no friends, Mum arranged for some boys from my class to come to the castle to celebrate my birthday. Doing her best to make me happy, and desperately out of touch with Irish teenagers and their habits, she made an elaborate meal and, despite my protests, served it in the formal dining room, beneath the gaze of various Plunkett ancestors. This made all the guests snigger, and when I went into school on Monday I knew everyone had been laughing at the pretension on display. I felt bad for Mum, because she'd only been trying to be nice and didn't want to hide who we were.

After many tests, I was diagnosed with severe dyslexia and slight dyspraxia. An excuse, I suppose, for my manifold failures; but I've never liked excuses – I didn't even then – so I've always done my best to reject those labels. In my family, weaknesses are to be conquered. My parents spent a fortune on extra tutoring over the summer, and Mum continued to insist that I chant 'I'm a winner' every time I went up or down the castle stairs. I did – but under my breath I'd also chant, 'and I can always kill myself,' a much more comforting thought. My escape button.

My parents didn't know how dreadful things were, but they were worried about me spending all my time in my room with no friends. They encouraged me to walk around the estate. They said the fresh air would do me good, and perhaps Dad hoped that getting to know the land better would give me a sense of belonging. But our patch of glorious green Ireland did nothing for me. It was just window dressing for a place that I experienced as a prison. I found it very difficult to separate the land from other aspects of my heritage.

When I thought about the dreaded day when Dad died and I'd be trapped here forever, I felt an awful sense of impending doom, which spilled over into a dull sort of hatred for not just the castle and the weight of expectations, but even the very ground it was on, and the fields all around it.

Granddad died when I was sixteen. He'd reached the grand old age of ninety-three. Sheila was eighty-six and living in a nursing home in England. We'd all been waiting for this moment, and certainly Granddad's death was no tragedy, as his quality of life had been terrible for years. It was truly astonishing he'd reached that age on a diet of whiskey, canned oxtail soup and Complan.

As is the family tradition, Granddad was buried on the estate where he'd spent most of his life. Most of our ancestors are buried in the family graveyard around the ruins of Dunsany Church, but Granddad had left instructions to bury him at the summit of the old Norman motte just beside it, where the most remote Plunkett ancestors would have had their first seat, and from where, as a little boy – before life and the war embittered him – he'd launched his bicycle. Up the side of the motte we all traipsed, even the ageing friends and relatives who found the walk a hard slog. I remember feeling nothing much as we watched Granddad's coffin being carefully lowered into the dark, cold Dunsany soil. For better or worse, Dad was Lord Dunsany now. Number twenty in a line that dated back, unbroken, to about AD 1180.

Daniel turned to Dad and said to him quietly, 'I suppose you're happy now he's dead.'

'Not really,' Dad said sadly. 'After all, he was my father.'

If it had been me, I'd have pissed on his grave, but Dad was a better man than I've ever been. Granddad's grave was marked with a simple wooden cross, and within weeks nettles, brambles and docks had started to colonise the site until you could hardly see it at all. Sheila died shortly afterwards, in England. We didn't attend the funeral. Gradually, all the paraphernalia relating to Granddad's illness was removed. Someone took away his clothes and other personal items. His tatty old mattress and nicotine-stained sheets were consigned to the dump. The stench of snuff and oxtail soup receded. Now Mum and Dad were in charge of the castle and determined to make their mark on it.

To find a vision of what Dunsany could be and work towards that becoming a reality, Mum and Dad started digging deep in their pockets for money to invest in the estate. The farm had been badly run for years. Buildings had begun to fall down, shed doors hung rotting on their hinges, gates were broken and in disarray. Dad arranged for new gates and new fencing. A promising start. They also made some eccentric choices towards realising their vision. They spent a fortune on renovating the decrepit properties on the estate. Mum hired builders to tear up floors, take out kitchen units that she considered passé and break up functional, if unfashionable, bathroom sets. Frames were removed from windows and roofs dismantled ahead of replacement. But before any of these projects were finished, they'd run out of money, or steam, or both, or the renovations would not be up to Mum's standards and she'd have the builders pull them apart again. Mum and Dad had design expertise, but neither seemed able to manage a project or stick to a budget.

One of the main sources of income for the estate had always been farming, and now it was mostly from renting the land to local farmers. While the Irish Land Commission had acquired portions of the estate back in the 1920s, the castle still came with more than a thousand acres of land and roughly five hundred acres of woods. In his younger years, Granddad had made a lot of money from his thousands of cattle. He'd sold most of them to Goodman, a progenitor of the current Larry Goodman, whose family has dominated the Irish beef-processing business for generations. Celebrating his business successes with whiskey, he often spent days admiring the cheques he received. Unfortunately, in his drunkenness, he frequently misplaced them. Now Mum and Dad found uncashed cheques all over the house. I've often wondered what would happen if I tried to cash them now.

Back in the early Middle Ages, when our Cusack ancestors lived in Dunsany, the owner had two daughters. Having no heirs, he arranged for them both to marry noble Plunketts. He had only one castle and was determined that both girls would have equally fine homes. So he came up with the perfect solution: each girl would position herself at the furthest part of the estate. When the signal was given, the two would run towards each other. Where they converged would be the border of their future estates. As it happens, our girl was a little more big-boned, so her older, more formidable sister became the owner of Killeen, and our younger, less agile ancestor became Lady of Dunsany. Through the ages that followed, both sets of ancestors had cut down trees, drained fields and made farmland where once there'd been forests, bogs, streams and natural grasslands. In the process, the wildlife that had roamed free receded to the margins, and the cattle reigned supreme. Dad once described the diminished populations of animals and birds as the 'cost of our success'. He was right. Since antiquity, everything we'd done to make the estate fruitful for us had reduced its viability as a habitat. The wild birds and animals were still paying the price.

Mum and Dad were worried about my failure to thrive at school and concerned that my growing fascination with death and my explosive, nihilistic personality were leading me astray. Rejecting the idea of another local school, they made the unexpected decision to pack Oliver and me off to a swanky school in Geneva, Institut Le Rosey, where the annual fees cost as much as many people would spend on a family home. They took out loans and even a mortgage to pay them. Mum said it was an investment in our future and would open up doors, transforming us into a more international family.

'We're not paying for the education,' she said. 'We're paying for the *contacts*. In this life, it's all about the networking.' Oliver and I would be meeting the children of some of the most powerful people in the world, and making incredible connections that would help us to get on in life. 'It's not too early to watch out for a nice girl who comes from money,' Mum advised. If I married into money, she explained, we'd be able to replace the roof on the castle, complete the renovation of the estate buildings and restore the fortunes of Dunsany.

The day we drove away from the castle towards Dublin Airport, Mum and Dad were in the front and Oliver and I were in the back seat. The castle disappeared as we drove around a bend in the avenue and past our ancestral church and graveyards. As if they were saying goodbye, the crows that roosted in the ruins of the church swirled overhead against the bullet-grey sky. I didn't know how I felt about going to Switzerland, but I did feel some vague relief at leaving Dunsany, with its sodden fields and depressed cattle.

At Institut Le Rosey, I was one of the poorest kids, which will give you an idea of the typical student intake. My classmates at Le Rosey and the other upmarket schools in Geneva with whom we went out drinking were the children of international bankers, oil tycoons, Mexican drug lords, Russian oligarchs, African presidents and warlords and the descendants of assorted dictators, including great-grandchildren of Spain's Francisco Franco. Many were given monthly allowances bigger than the annual salaries earned by their long-suffering teachers, with separate funds for clothes and toiletries. A lot of the kids had bodyguards. They all wore Gucci and I felt like I was slumming it. Mum had bought us new clothes from Gap, which I'd considered quite fancy, but suddenly I was surrounded by thirteen-year-olds swinging handbags worth more than our Ford Sierra. They had Rolex watches and I'd a glow-in-the-dark Swatch. The only other kid who dressed in simpler clothes, like mine and Oliver's, was Guillaume, whom we later discovered was the Hereditary Grand Duke of Luxembourg. Guillaume and I occasionally smoked together behind the sports facilities.

Being Irish was a bonus at school, because several of the employees were Irish too, and they were particularly nice to us. Even the English thought we were cool. For the first time since leaving London, I made a few friends, although Mum's advice to always consider the importance of networking meant that these relationships sometimes felt quite business-like; the other kids had probably been given much the same advice. There were a few kids who liked rock music and we formed a band and played Biohazard covers. For me, this was a way of doing something with my roiling anger. I still spent a lot of time listening to Morbid Angel and Slayer, much to the distaste of my Turkish roommate, who preferred Turkish pop music. He was a nice guy, but by the end of the school year he thanked God we'd never be sharing a room again because he'd had more than enough of my 'shit music'.

Along with the rest of the kids, I endured regular drug testing, but also enjoyed visiting bars in Geneva where we were allowed to smoke and drink, and where some of the new-rich kids flashed the cash, spending as much on champagne in a single night as the average industrial wage in most wealthy countries. Thanks to those rich kids, we all drank a lot – sometimes with the teachers, too – and often returned to the boarding school more than a little tipsy.

I remained very insecure about my appearance. I'd already started lifting weights and now I was becoming obsessive about transforming my body. I'd always been quite small and thin. I needed to control something in my life, and my body was going to be it. I rose ever-earlier to work out in the school gym while my classmates slept. I force-fed myself so much I often had to go to the toilet to vomit. I started to accept the vomiting as a daily reality. I took protein powders, drank special shakes and begged the kitchen staff for extra meat. I did all this every day. I got stronger, but never felt big enough. Mum had always told me that my head looked too big for the rest of my body, and had alternated between saying that I was too thin or too fat. Now she said that with my newly earned muscles I'd started to look grotesque, like a clown. 'You'd better not get your hair cut too short,' she advised me when I came home on holiday. 'With those big shoulders, you'll look like a pinhead.' Despite my mother not understanding the pain these jabs caused me, I muscled on.

I failed my first year at Le Rosey and had to repeat it. Academically, there was a hierarchy in the school, with the Korean and other Asian kids at the top, the Russians and other eastern Europeans next, then the Americans and west Europeans, and right at the bottom the Turkish students and me. I put in another year, failed my exams the second time around, was deemed unsuited to the International Baccalaureate, and was invited to leave. I was nearly eighteen then, and it was becoming increasingly urgent for me to get at least some basic qualifications. In a final push, Mum and Dad sent me to a crammer in England, Cherwell College in Oxford, which specialised in one-to-one tuition for dissolute teenagers from affluent backgrounds who needed extra help to get into university.

'Don't worry,' Dad said. 'The new school will help you get some A-levels.'

I knew I wanted to study film, and my parents were happy about that – they were both very comfortable in the world of artists and creatives – but without support I wasn't going to get onto any university course. At Cherwell, I took classics, English literature and film studies.

The English teacher, James Evans, with his arty glasses and flowing black trench coat, was a bit of a New Romantic. When he realised I'd a taste for the macabre, he produced novels and poetry about death, ghosts, monsters and the supernatural. 'I think you'll like these,' he said. 'Give them a try.' Initially sceptical, I started reading, and discovered it could be fun. When he encouraged me to analyse classic fairy tales from the Brothers Grimm and others, I was in my element.

The film studies teacher, Louise Longson, and I bonded over the French *nouvelle vague* and Italian neo-realism.

She was a driving force in me taking film studies. My classics teacher, Rachael Pallas-Brown, gave me a taste for Greek tragedy.

None of these teachers seemed to find me stupid, and I've always been immensely grateful for that. I still struggled with writing and crafting an essay, but I started to enjoy academic learning and a path started to open through the dense forest of my many inadequacies. The fairy tales in particular gave me the language I needed to express myself. I found it easier to deal with symbols and metaphors than to face reality head on.

Also for the first time, I met other young people who shared my interests. Within a week or two of arriving in Oxford, I'd smoked my first joint, and now I started getting into drugs and having fun. I adopted a uniform of baggy pants and long hair. I had cornrows, went to squat parties, and pretended to be a normal kid, a run-of-the-mill disillusioned youth. I got my first job as a barman at the Zodiac Club and, not long after, I started making more money as a rock DJ. I never did or said anything to make my friends suspect what awaited me at home.

Perhaps I wasn't the sharpest knife in the drawer, but I tried hard at school and worked at making friends. While I did do plenty of drugs and cut loose at the weekends, I never got carried away. I held down a steady job, my teachers seemed to like me and I was making the grades. I was working on my image too. My hair was getting longer and longer as I continued my project of obsessively building muscles and I was much bigger than ever before. This earned me some attention from the girls I met – and from some of the guys too, which weirded me out a little.

I was also deeply depressed. I'd developed violent tendencies that I mostly directed inwards. The suicidal thoughts that had been a feature of my childhood since we left New York regularly played on my mind and I embraced every little pain as a release. With each month that passed, the downswings into depression were worse. Some days I'd take the bus – any bus – and sit on it for hours until the driver stopped and made me get off. Every so often, a certain evil word would creep into my mind and send me spiralling into waves of despair. That word was 'Dunsany'. The waves of depression could hit me at any moment and a spell could last for weeks.

Then something extraordinary happened. One weekend I took a bunch of magic mushrooms and had my first taste of MDMA. Unfamiliar with it, I took the whole baggie rather than just one dose. I was off my head for days, but when I came down I'd stopped experiencing the waves of deep depression that had been part of my life since early childhood.

Although I engaged in quite a lot of risky behaviour in those years, I never even came close to becoming addicted to alcohol or drugs, despite enjoying plenty of both. Like everything else, ultimately they were sacrificed on the altar of my quest to be stronger and bigger with each day that passed. The only thing I've ever really been addicted to is exercise.

Holidays meant I had to return home. Reluctantly, I did. The castle was, as it has always been, stern and beautiful. The view from the front included centuries-old trees planted by my ancestors, and inside, the walls were lined with those ancestors' portraits. They all seemed to be looking down at me in judgement, as though they knew my every thought and that I'd be the one to bring the place crashing down.

I was sure that, if there was a heaven, they were watching me herald in the Apocalypse.

The castle remained fucking freezing, and while the grand rooms spoke of when there'd been over fifty domestic staff, around every second corner there was an outbreak of mould or dry rot that had to be arrested, because while the castle seemed to be determined to give in to entropy, nothing was more important than keeping it safe for future generations of Plunketts. I glumly sat and watched DVD after DVD, my back resolutely turned to the big diamond-paned windows with their view of the fields. I couldn't wait to get back to England.

'You're next, son,' Dad said. 'It'll be all yours when I'm gone.'

I stopped protecting Dad from the views I held about our ancestors and heritage and started becoming more aggressive in rejecting the very idea that there was anything special about Dunsany at all. I made it very clear I'd no intention of becoming the sort of person who was happy to be Lord Dunsany, leader of a castle and estate that, I felt, was nothing but a millstone around our necks. Then I felt bad for complaining about the prospect of having something – a castle! – that most people could only ever dream of.

Somehow, during this brief, frenzied period, I got some A-levels – not great grades but better than anyone had anticipated – didn't need to check into rehab (unlike many of my classmates) and was accepted at Kingston University in London to study film. Kingston wasn't the Oxford or Cambridge education that 'should' have been my lot, but it was still better than anyone had been expecting for me. Perhaps things were looking up.

Chapter Three

End of the Line

I WOKE IN MY NEW APARTMENT IN KINGSTON, A LONDON SUBURB. I glanced up from my pillow at my newly decorated room, plastered to the ceiling with band posters and heavy metal banners. The cream walls had been transformed into darkness with gory logos and men in corpse paint holding bloodied skulls.

Yes, what a dork.

It was September 2003. I was nineteen and it was the opening day for freshers. From now on, there was going to be no non-essential learning. I was going to learn how to be a film director and live every day like my last because, wonderful as this newfound freedom was, I was on borrowed time.

The whole idea of university excited me. All those American teen movies – *frat parties*! – came to mind. I was sure I'd be spending every night in deep conversation with film connoisseurs and arts people who'd leave these halls and become creators.

On my first day, I arrived in a huge auditorium and sat down in the third row. As I looked across the faces of about two hundred young people, they all seemed pretty sensible and regular. Run of the mill, even. Overhearing the students around me talking, my excitement faded. I'd hoped for a year full of quirky filmmakers, but they felt more like the future staff of an accountancy firm.

Where are the lunatics? I wondered. *Where are the disruptors? Who's going to help me make films?*

'I like your T-shirt,' someone said.

I turned around to see a man covered in tattoos accompanied by two guys who also looked out of place among the normies. Perhaps all wasn't lost yet!

The best thing about being a student in London was having my own place as I bonded with the other oddballs in my year over horror films, our shared disdain for Usher and R&B and our appreciation of pizzas. Together, we watched cult films and travelled everywhere in search of engaging events. My house became our frat house. There we watched banned videos and chatted about sci-fi, books, girls and music. As there was no club scene that we appreciated in the area, we created our own: four fully grown men bouncing to XTC in a cramped living room in the wee hours of the morning.

In a more middle-class suburb our loud, obnoxious, dissonant music would probably have aggravated the neighbours, but thankfully the only neighbour who took any interest in us was Nikki.

Nikki was a slim, attractive young mother about a year older than me. Once in a while she turned up on my doorstep in her dressing gown, clutching a spliff. She must've been lonely, because she seemed to invent reasons to drop around – looking to borrow a lighter, asking me to fix her laptop, wondering if I could give her some milk. She said the council had given her a place on the block and that she and her kid had been in a shelter before.

'My boy's daddy beat me up and ended up in prison,' Nikki explained.

'For beating you up, seriously?'

'Nah, not just that, he also stole some laptops and got done.'

I didn't know what to say.

'We've all been there, I suppose,' I attempted.

She laughed hysterically: 'You're sweet.'

Sweet?! I thought. *Not had that one yet.*

I could never tell whether or not Nikki was trying to flirt with me. Did she have a crush on me or was she like this with everyone? Often, minutes after I got home, I heard her using the flap of my letterbox to knock on the door.

'What you up to, darlin'?' she'd ask. 'Any plans this weekend?'

'The usual,' I'd say. 'Got lots of coursework to do.'

This was all lies. I invariably left all my coursework to the last moment. But while I liked Nikki, all my instincts were telling me that she was the kind of trouble I could do without, a spinning bright red flag with bells on it.

My first year came and went. Mum and Dad wanted me to visit often – 'You're so close! You could be back every second weekend!' – but I broke out every excuse not to. I said I was studying every waking hour and couldn't possibly fit in visits, even short ones. When I thought about home, I always envisioned the freezing cold castle, under a heavy panoply of menacing dark clouds, its corridors so damp and dark even the electric light couldn't penetrate their shadows. Less of a welcoming home than a trap, its strange and melancholy beauty like an anglerfish's dangling light. The fields always wet and churned to mud by a thousand heavy hooves.

The neon, noise, chaos and endless fun of London made Dunsany seem a million miles away, and I didn't want anything to do with it.

I remained obsessed with my appearance, still sure I was small and weak-looking. Trying to control my life and kill the blackness that periodically engulfed me, I toiled at the gym so hard that sometimes I had to stay in bed for a week, unable to move with the pain.

'You're doing too much!' the trainers would say. 'You have to be careful.'

I ignored them all. I wanted to destroy myself and build something I could tolerate. I wanted to be admired for anything, anything other than having a castle or a set of impressive ancestors. I wanted something that was *me*, and I was willing to suffer for it.

Mum and Dad were still desperately trying to make the estate financially viable, while dealing with ongoing challenges in their own financial lives and with hostility from some elements in the local community. They struggled to negotiate with squatters and the frequent ingress of the hunt, which still felt like an invasion of barbarians and caused horrendous damage. But in the early 2000s, the public mood in Ireland had turned decisively against hunting, and now every time there was a big hunt, there were usually protests there too: Green Party types with wellies and home-made placards, shouting at the hunters or regarding them with silent sorrow. My parents told me all about the protests when we spoke on the phone, or during my rare visits home: 'Maybe the tide is turning,' said Dad. 'Perhaps this will help to keep the hunters off the land.'

The rise in public protests was good news because now we weren't the only ones standing against the might of the hunters, and their ire wasn't focused exclusively on Dunsany, but on everyone in their way. It had become much more difficult for them to spin a narrative about Irish traditions being quashed by the castle people, which was nonsense, of course, but a convenient fiction that made it easier for them to excuse their own behaviour.

In March 2004, in the thick of the hunting season, the local hunt barged once again onto Dunsany and started galloping across the land, the horses' hooves sending heavy clods of wet, dark soil flying while every living creature fled for cover. Mum was at the end of her rope. She grabbed an antique rifle from the display in the hall and rushed outside, joining a small group of hunt saboteurs. Leaping into our Jeep, they all made their way to the hunt. Turning the tables on the hunters, Mum loudly accused them all of 'pretending to be Irish'. She did her best to wave the ancient weapon – which was almost too heavy for her to pick up – in a menacing fashion and told everyone that if she saw them again, she wouldn't be afraid to use her blunderbuss.

Unsurprisingly, this colourful incident made the local newspapers, and for a brief moment Mum was a hero. She made the radio and the papers and came out of it looking much better than the hunters. It was glorious and I admired her for fearlessly confronting a cartel of savages in silly uniforms.

I'd finished my term and had returned home for the summer of 2005. Dad was excited to see me and hugged me tight, kissing my head.

The prodigal son returns, I thought.

Dad was excited and bursting with energy. Both my parents were. I realised I'd missed their enthusiasm. On the phone, we only ever talked about problems.

Right now, Mum and Dad were both focusing on him. They'd been working hard to relaunch his art career. Mum felt responsible that he'd set aside his paintbrush for so long to help her. She'd pushed him to do a grand exhibition in Rome, where he'd once had a good reputation and a burgeoning career, before his future at Dunsany scuppered it. Now that Dad was in his sixties, and this was his last chance to build his artistic reputation, Mum had rented a beautiful apartment just off Piazza Navona. Dad was going to launch a big exhibition in the Brazilian Embassy there, and Mum was going to make sure that the Who's Who of the Celtic Tiger elite attended, as well as all their most successful friends. Together, everyone would toast Dad's success. Ahead of this grand event, Dad had been working non-stop, getting better all the time. Mum said we'd spend the summer in Italy to support him and that we all had a duty to give him this happiness as – finally – he embraced his talent. She was on a high, entirely confident she could deliver this spectacle in Dad's honour. We all believed her and promised to do whatever we could to help. How could we not? Neither of them had been this happy for years.

Dad was making the final changes to his paintings ahead of the exhibition as we arrived at the apartment in Rome, which Mum had decorated just for him. It was a scorching summer, and my parents were on fire too. The exhibition was truly spectacular. The guest list was filled with ambassadors, people of influence and all kinds of cultivated types.

Within the first hour Dad sold his first painting for a pretty sum and the champagne bottles came and went.

A formal dinner followed the show. Watching Dad from afar, I noted that he seemed tipsy. Unlike Granddad, who'd been able to clean out a bar, Dad had never been able to handle a drink. As I watched him stumble, I saw him move to sit on a bench next to a colleague. Suddenly, he tumbled badly, completely missing it. Mum came rushing over and so did the waiting staff. She made excuses: 'He can't drink, he has no head for it.'

I got Dad some water and gave it to him, asking if he was all right. He smiled and nodded, but I could sense that something was wrong. Over the coming days, we all noticed that Dad was beginning to walk funny. He bumped into people, knocked over plates and used the wall for support. By the end of our stay in Italy, he was beginning to see double.

Terrified, we took Dad to his dear friend, Dr Sandberg, who'd come to Rome for his exhibition. Dr Sandberg made him an appointment at his clinic and they started to run tests. The relief that it wasn't a brain tumour was quickly dispelled by his worsening symptoms, the initial success of his exhibition overshadowed by our grave concerns about his health.

Eventually, Dad was diagnosed as having a rare neurological condition known as progressive supranuclear palsy, or PSP. It's a bit like Parkinson's disease and multiple sclerosis. There's no cure, and all that's certain is a slow, arduous death. Dad already had mobility issues, the inevitable vision problems had begun and ultimately he'd be all but paralysed.

Dr Sandberg delivered the devastating diagnosis along with the information that Dad would probably be wheelchair-bound and unable to talk before too long. He could say nothing to soften the blow. There were some experimental drug combinations that had shown positive results in slowing the progression of the disease, but it certainly wasn't going to be all that long before Dad joined the rest of the ancestors in the family plot overlooking our home.

Despite the awful prognosis, Mum was determined we'd find a cure and that we had to keep positive and keep Dad healthy. He'd need a rigid routine of exercise to help slow down the effects of his illness, and would take every medication available. I knew that as soon as I graduated I'd need to come home to look after Dad.

Hours before my flight to London to finish college, I stood in the dining room, glaring at Granddad's portrait. 'It should've been you,' I whispered. It wasn't fair: Granddad had been awful but had lived a long and – in his strange way – fulfilling life. Dad, who'd just found happiness and fulfilment as an artist, and who was a wonderful and kind man, was having it all snatched away.

It was raining as the plane landed. I sat in silence on the bus to Kingston, knowing the worst was yet to come. My grades slipped in the final year and I struggled to sleep, worrying endlessly about Dad. Whenever I could, I resorted to escapism: movies, drugs, whatever gave me a moment's piece from thinking about Dad and his rapidly approaching death.

One day I got home from college and found a tall guy leaning against my door and chatting on his phone.

'Sorry, bruv,' he said amiably, moving aside to let me pass. I smiled and went inside. Shortly afterwards, I heard the letterbox flap banging: my neighbour Nikki's signature move. Looking through the peephole, I saw her standing at the door.

Here we go, I thought. I opened the door and found her standing beside the guy I'd seen earlier. He was Trev, she said. He was her baby's father, and would be staying with them for a while. As Nikki spoke, I remembered her confiding that Trev had beaten her so badly that she and the baby had fled to a women's shelter, and that the council had had to find them a home. Now she was moving him in?

'D'you need anything from the shop?' Nikki asked.

I politely declined and started to make excuses, closing the door.

'Hold up, bruv,' Trev called out. 'You got any blue Rizla?'

Aficionados of marijuana often like to use long rolling paper, and the blue-packeted paper tends to be softer on the throat.

'Sure,' I said.

I went into the living room, grabbed a half-finished packet, and handed it to Trev.

'Cheers, bruv,' Trev said. 'Much appreciated, my man.'

'He's alright, ain't he?' Trev remarked as an aside to Nikki.

'Yeah, he's a dote,' she said, smiling.

Jesus Christ, I thought, *don't get me involved with your upcoming drama and for God's sake don't steal my laptop.*

I watched them from my kitchen window as they walked into the street. A storm was brewing; I could feel it.

I saw Trev quite often over the next few weeks. He was always smoking outside my place when I arrived. One evening I got home, trying to choose between going to a party being thrown by a nursing student with a crush on me or spending the evening alone, worrying about Dad. I was putting the kettle on when I heard a loud thump at my door. It was Trev, asking to borrow my phone charger. Reluctantly, I lent it to him.

'Oy, Randal,' Trev said as I went to close the door. 'You like Charlie?'

It was the first time he had ever called me by name.

'Which Charlie?'

'Ha ha, joker, I mean white, man.'

He was talking about cocaine. I said I liked it well enough.

'Good,' Trev continued, ''cause I got some bangin' stuff. You want a line?'

Tentatively, I followed Trev into Nikki's house, realising I'd never been in it before, though she'd been in mine countless times. Neither she nor the baby seemed to be in as Trev chopped up a line on the coffee table.

'Go on,' he invited me. 'Hit that shit.'

The coke fired through my nostrils and they tightened and then slowly numbed as I got the metallic aftertaste. He was right; it was *strong*.

'What you got on later?'

'Not much, got invited to a house party,' I replied. 'You?'

'Just chillin' bruv, just chillin', you want some gear to take with you?'

'No, my friend, I'm good.'

'Go on, man, I got you.'

I stared at him a moment before the numbness in my face prompted repeat business.

'Sure, why not? Fuck the world, right?'

'Fuck the world, mate!'

I bought a baggy from Trev and phoned my friends. Shortly afterwards, with the promise of a high, they arrived. I'd already come up with a plan: get completely smashed and then turn up to the party. I was determined not to think of home.

The nursing student hosting the party was texting me now and again to see if I was on my way. But we were already late, and I was a good few lines down. I was going hard and already had a head start. As we waited for our cab, we listened to the latest Red Chord album, *Fused Together in Revolving Doors*. I could feel the accumulated effect of the lines of cocaine as my phone beeped with frequent messages. Suddenly light-headed, I went to the bathroom and stood in front of the mirror over the sink. A wild, wide-eyed figure stared back at me. I was a mess. I threw water in my face to try and improve the situation, but I remained on a knife edge. My pupils looked like large black holes in my skull and a cold sweat was forming over my skin.

As I climbed into the taxi minutes later, my heart was beating a hundred miles an hour, my ears were hearing underwater sounds and I could feel every hair on my body standing on end. I lay my head back and looked up at the street lights, moving past in slow motion. I was cold and my heart was racing. *Is this it?* I wondered. *Did I overdose? Is this the end?* The car radio was playing 'Meat is Murder' by The Smiths. I'd never heard it before, and it felt so poignant, a sad ballad lulling me away.

Thankfully, the cocaine was beginning to wear off by the time we arrived at the party. I fell out of the cab and was greeted by the nursing student, who was excited to see me, but surprised by the state I was in. I said I'd had some cider and that it didn't agree with me. The party came and went. I never told anyone how close I'd come to hitting the iceberg.

Weeks later, Trev was still living with Nikki. I heard them partying all night long. Then the fighting started. I'd walk out the door as she screamed at him and he stormed off, calling her a slut. Once I found her crying on the steps. I wondered why she'd shacked up with a guy as violent as him.

With the strains of Eminem emanating through the party wall one weekend, I could hear Trev and Nikki fighting, and then screams and beating fists at my door. In tears, Nikki burst into my house, her face swollen and bruising fast. As she launched herself inside and closed the door, I could see Trev just behind her.

'He beat me up again!'

'Oy!' Trev yelled, banging on the door. 'Get your fucking ass out here now; you've no business getting him involved in your mad shit.'

'Go fuck yourself, Trev!' Nikki roared back. 'I'm sick of this!'

Trev was big and clearly off his head and I was a posh kid with a pizza in the oven. Things were about to turn nasty and I knew I had to do something.

'Trev, listen,' I said through the door. 'I think you should calm down. Nikki doesn't feel safe and if you continue, I'll be forced to call the cops.'

'Mind your business, mate! Send that fucking little bitch out here now or I'm gonna fucking kick this fucking door down!'

I moved to the phone and began to dial when I suddenly heard the sound of a power tool. In my fright, I thought it was a chainsaw, although it was probably some sort of drill.

'Fucking open the door or you're all fucking dead!' Trev shouted.

The power tool revved, then suddenly stopped. Nikki and I panicked. I was sure we were both about to be murdered, as I'd seen in countless horror flicks. But then we heard feet scuttling down the stairs. Through the window, we saw Trev get in his car and drive away. Just as the police started to answer, Nikki moved towards me, pressing her finger down on the phone, ending the call.

'What the hell are you doing?' I asked. She didn't answer. She just hugged me for an uncomfortable moment.

'Thank you,' she said as she unlocked her door. Suddenly, I could hear her son crying from next door.

'The police will trace the call and come here,' I said. 'We hung up on them'.

She gazed at me, her face swelling fast and her eyes focused on the distance. 'I'll call them,' she said, closing the door. I never saw Nikki again. Not long afterwards, all her possessions were gone from her windowsill, and shortly after that, I saw several bags of rubbish outside. Another family moved in, and not long after that I moved house too.

I've never forgotten the look Nikki gave me that night. After she'd gone, I'd sat on my couch feeling utterly useless. Despite all my muscles and tough talk, I wouldn't have been able to help if things had escalated. I felt like a complete loser and a fraud. Worst of all, I was scared and knew that I was weak. I was reminded yet again of my glorious ancestors and their accomplishments. How ashamed they'd have been of me, unable to protect a vulnerable young woman at her time of need.

The film course lasted three years, but it took me four as I needed to pick one last module to complete. I wrote a thesis on video nasties. At Dunsany, Mum was struggling trying to look after Dad, whose health was declining fast. They needed me back.

I returned home on a grey summer's day. Mum rushed to the front door to meet me, with Dad wobbling behind her, leaning heavily on his stick. I could see they were happy to have me home. I looked up at the mass of crows flying between the castle's towers. They seemed to be looking down at me. I knew that they – or their antecedents – had seen many generations pass through. I'd be the latest, if not the last, and certainly the worst.

Over dinner, Mum talked to me enthusiastically about all the wonderful things she was doing and how I'd be helping to run Dunsany now. I knew better than to argue. Mum was in charge and everyone else was a sounding board for her ideas. I was fine with that. What did *I* know about running an estate? Dad had barely touched his dinner. He was struggling to get the food into his mouth with his fork. It kept dropping before he could reach it. Later, I helped him to change into his pyjamas and put him in bed. His legs didn't move properly. His reactions seemed delayed, and he was increasingly unable to shift his weight correctly, so I found myself bearing his weight to help him move around.

Dad was beginning to struggle with painting, too. I'd watch him close an eye to help mitigate his double vision. He'd always done a lot with clean architectural lines. It had been amazing watching him work freehand, drawing shapes and forms that most would have struggled to create with even the best tools. Now his work was changing, becoming softer and fussier, more primitive and, dare I say, splodgy. He was struggling to stay motivated. Next, Dad was increasingly dependent on a wheelchair and finding it more difficult to eat. Every time he choked, we watched as if this was the end. We lived from one cough to the next.

This situation was awful for everyone but truly terrible for Mum. She'd been here before. Her father had died slowly from lung cancer, and she'd spent much of her young life caring for him instead of going to school. She'd probably never imagined going through such torture again. Mum had told me that, as her father's condition worsened, he'd often asked her to distract him from his pain by singing to him. Now, she was sometimes reminded of a piece of music she'd once sung for her father. An explosion of emotions would follow, and a meltdown she couldn't control. Soon Oliver and I were struggling to care for both our parents as Dad's health declined and Mum's emotional episodes escalated.

People who can express themselves are much more likely to be happy, even when things are very tough. I've seen this in others and experienced it in myself. Mum never could. She found happiness through setting goals – for herself and for others – and achieving them. She'd spent most of her adult life being praised for her wonderful projects. Now she could only express her creativity in her surroundings. Since Dad's diagnosis, and as his health declined, she'd slipped into a life of seclusion and her home had become her canvas. She laboured to design bedrooms and living spaces in the house so beautiful that we, her children, would want to spend time with her and at home.

Mum had started her biggest feat in the house yet: the gallery. Or, as it was once called, the west wing. It was in a dire state and its rebirth was going to be her expression of love for a man who would be dead soon. She was going to build a temple, a museum, where Dad's work could be properly appreciated. Having committed to furthering his career while there was time, she was determined to give him a taste of artistic success before it was too late. She'd do it even if it killed her. So she arranged for the creation of stained oak and beech floors made from trees from the estate, some of them replicating in wood the images Dad had created in paint. The sink in the bathroom was a take on one of Dad's designs for a perfume company. The doors were custom-made, eight feet high. She was bringing all her skills, and all Dad's designs, to create something truly extraordinary: an edgy art gallery that belonged in New York, not County Meath.

'My love,' Mum would say as she wheeled Dad around the construction site, 'this isn't just going to be a place to show your work. You'll continue painting here.'

I've never witnessed such devotion and love in anyone. I remember realising she truly believed that one day Dad would be painting in these rooms. The grim reality was that his condition was steadily worsening. He was less and less able to paint and his food choices were increasingly limited as he was choking ever more. The gallery was still far from complete, but even if it had been, he was no longer able to use it.

Mum and Dad had started to fret a lot more about money, even more than usual. How would we manage the vast expense of keeping the castle intact and running the estate? How would *I* manage when they were no longer there to help? Keeping the estate running had always been a struggle, but this was different. A place like Dunsany consumes vast amounts of money. Straight out of college, with a film degree that probably wouldn't have got me a job in a café, and a distinct lack of killer business instincts, it didn't seem like I was going to be in a position to earn much anytime soon.

Panicking that I'd be unable to manage once Dad had passed, Mum became increasingly desperate to protect my future. She started inviting wealthy guests for dinner, along with their marriageable daughters. She was in the market for a rich girl who'd marry me and provide an injection of cash. She hoped to find someone savvy, smart, well-mannered, and from an old-school family, who'd dedicate her life to me and to Dunsany. She'd have to be willing to sacrifice comfort and freedom to be a caretaker of this cold castle, to accept the rules of Dunsany unquestioningly. Mum didn't want me to see the roof collapse, along with all my hopes and dreams, one leak at a time. This was her desperate way to buy me a chance at an easier life. Writing this now, my first impulse is to laugh at the madness of it, but looking back as a much older man, I also feel desperately sad for my mother. There was more chance of me finding gold in the back garden or winning the lottery than finding a twenty-first-century woman who'd fulfil those requirements.

'If we'd stayed in New York,' Mum would say, 'you'd probably have married that nice Ivanka Trump girl.' She was joking, but she also wasn't. She'd tell me to dress up well to make a good impression. I felt like a prize bull on display at the local mart, and I knew the various marriageable daughters were as mortified as I was.

Mum and I needed more help to manage Dad's rapidly escalating needs. Oliver, who lived nearby, was helping as much as he could, but it wasn't enough. Dad was choking with ever-greater frequency, so Mum began blending his food. We were struggling financially. We'd assumed Dad's many years of paying health insurance would assist us with his care; he'd used a British insurance company as we'd lived in England many years before. Despite his Irish address and the Irish bank account that had been making payments every month for years, once he was ill they wouldn't cover any of his healthcare in Ireland. And as he had a pre-existing condition, no other insurer would take him on. Dad was eligible for help only from the Irish state, which provided a special chair that helped him up and down and a steady supply of the nappies he needed now.

Despite being in a deep financial hole, we continued to spend on the best doctors, additional therapies, anything we thought might help. Mum almost never left Dad's side. Even when she did the books, or the little administration she could handle between cleaning him, preparing softer and softer food and trying to make him walk, she sat right beside him.

Even as his condition progressed, with his slurred speech and reduced ability to speak coherently, Dad continued to talk to me about Dunsany, about how I had to find a way to care for it and make it mine.

'Dunsany's special. It's more than a building.' He'd say these words laboriously, slowly, his mouth struggling to form each one. 'The place is *alive*. So many of our ancestors struggled and died to protect it. I'm telling you; it'll give you what you give it.'

His words haunted me. I knew he wasn't crazy and I wanted him to feel at least a little relief. I could see him struggling to find a reason to stay alive when Mum and I argued over how to run Dunsany. At my angriest, I threatened to sell it and move to Vegas. Poor Dad would raise one finger, trying to interject.

How painful to see your world collapsing like a house of cards. To see your whole family unhappy, knowing that much of that is because you're ill. To be locked in a blurry darkness in which only the sound of fighting reminds you that are still alive.

I took Dad's hand and said: 'Don't worry, Dad. I won't let the place fall apart. You and Mum trained me well.' His eyes twinkled when I said those words. He squeezed my hand, warmed by my lies.

Dunsany is far from anywhere you might find work in the film industry, and in 2008, Ireland's economy was on its knees. What little film industry there was was heavily focused on Dublin. Ireland is small and cliquish and it appeared that the only way into an already struggling film industry was through personal connections. I didn't have any, and I'd no time to build any as I was caring full-time for Dad.

One of my few outlets was working out with the basic weight-lifting equipment I'd bought to keep in shape. I thought maybe I should forget film-making, retrain as a personal trainer and open a gym – right here! – because if there was one thing I *did* know it was how to build muscle. I contemplated renovating one of the outhouses and turning it into a gym for private clients. A useful side benefit would be that I'd remain in great shape. I still feared becoming 'too small'. Living in the castle, where almost everything was outsized, made me feel even punier than I had in London. Being a personal trainer might give me an opportunity to make some friends in the area, too. But my parents didn't like the idea of a future owner of the estate working in sweatpants and doing something as narcissistic as body-building and helping strangers to make themselves as grotesque as, according to Mum, I was slowly becoming.

'Come on!' Mum said, impatiently. 'You can be a filmmaker right here and run the estate at the same time. You can't do either if you're sweating in front of a mirror.'

My parents had agreed that Oliver and I shouldn't settle for less because of Dad's condition. 'They both need careers,' Dad had said. 'If they don't have the tools they need, they'll have to get them'.

So before Dad's illness progressed even further, Mum sold some of her assets so that Oliver and I could each spend a year on getting some more education. I enrolled on a short course in digital film-making, and Oliver started studying video game design. The only course in Europe that I could access was the SAE Institute in Amsterdam, and Mum and Dad both quite liked the idea of my spending some time in the Netherlands, where our family had found a refuge in Cromwellian times, and where one branch of Mum's family originally came from.

I can see now that part of Mum's reason for encouraging me to go to Amsterdam, aside from the networking opportunities and her hope I'd acquire film-making skills, was to offer me a sort of *rumspringa*, an opportunity to be young and have fun before getting down to the serious business of learning how to manage Dunsany while also caring for my dying father.

In Amsterdam, I met a man called Karim Traïdia, a guest lecturer who taught the essence of directing actors – the *real* stuff. I think I was the only student who knew who he was before he walked in the room. Karim had made several acclaimed films, including *The Polish Bride* – a wonderful movie that won multiple awards, including the Grand Golden Rail in Cannes. Karim's approach to directing didn't disappoint: I learned more in an afternoon with him than I had in all the years of hitting the books. His kindness, warmth, intellect and artistic vision attracted me from the start.

I was in awe of his ability to tear at the fabric of what makes a character act, and of his unparalleled insight into the human spirit. We became friends.

Karim taught me that, no matter what a film is about, the director needs to have a personal relationship with it: something he loves, something he fears, something he wants. Really good directors don't just know how to manage all the technical inputs; they know how to infuse a film with their own feelings and emotions – something of *them*, an expression of their spirit – in a way that makes the story bigger and more important. Never before had I met someone so comfortable discussing the landscape of emotions, and how they can be visually portrayed.

Karim also talked about the challenges and benefits of being an outsider. He was an Algerian, born when Algeria was still a French colony, and he'd lived in France, and now in the Netherlands. It can be hard getting into any industry when others perceive you as different, he said, but there are also hidden benefits. It's easier to be objective, easier to look beyond the immediate emotions involved in any experience and to see the story.

I'd always been embarrassed about my own background and culture, knowing that many Irish people would never really see me as one of their own. I'd always felt more like an observer of Irish life than a participant in it. Never one of the gang. Karim taught me to accept my heritage as something I couldn't change, acknowledge this discomfort, and to confront these feelings through art. These conversations reshaped my entire outlook and they still resonate today. I consider Karim a mentor in the best sense of the word.

Before the course ended, Dad's health had deteriorated further, and I knew he needed me. The sabbatical was over and I returned home. Thanks to Karim, I wasn't quite the same man as I had been when I left.

Now Dad relied on Mum for all his physical needs and had become her purpose for living. Keeping him alive for as long as possible was the only reason for her to get up in the morning. His gallery was nearly complete, but he could no longer paint. He tried to talk, but could only manage a gurgle or a mangled single word. We spoon-fed him concoctions of blended vegetables, which he regularly choked on. Teaspoon by teaspoon, these meals could take hours. We used a special wet wheelchair to wash him, and we dressed and groomed him. I don't know for sure whether or not Dad's mind was still clear. His only responses now were a delayed thumbs-up or a raised finger. His eyes no longer moved and his body was beginning to bend from wasted muscle. He'd been handsome once, but now he was a hostage in what remained of his body. We played the TV for him, trying to find films or shows he might enjoy. Too often it seemed to track back to depressing news of bombs landing and people dying. I don't know if he even noticed, but we needed to believe we were helping him. In the darkest of moments, I wondered why we were all working so hard to keep him motivated to stay alive. For what? To suffer? To buy us more time? He was a prisoner alone on an island. We all were.

Looking back now, my biggest regret from that time is that there was so much tension at home. Individually, we were all doing our best to help Dad and make his illness easier to bear. Together, we were all rubbing each other the wrong way, often bickering loudly even as we bathed or fed him and willed him to stay with us for as long as possible, and then a little more. I know that Mum and Oliver were doing all they could, and

I was too, but I wish Dad hadn't had to listen to so much arguing as the life faded from his eyes. All I can say in mitigation is that we were doing our best.

I'd been fantasising about killing myself, or at least ceasing to exist, since childhood. I was still doing it now. I sat upstairs in one of the castle's large windows looking out at the parkland in front of the castle. The majestic trees that my forebears had planted. The sprawling fields in pasture for animals or tilled for crops. The river where Oliver and I had played so happily as children, which had provided us with hours of pure joy. I imagined going onto the roof and jumping off the battlements, falling past each storey of the castle as the view of the fields flashed by my eyes, and landing with a heavy thud on the gravel outside the front door, the muscles I'd spent years building reduced to a bloody pulp that would seep out of my body and into the ground of Dunsany. Knowing that suicide was an option was a relief. There was always a way out. My favourite little whisper remained 'you can always kill yourself.' When the going gets too tough, there's your exit.

In the winter of 2010, I'd started making short movies, using the skills I had gained from college, inviting friends from Amsterdam and London to participate, and reaching out to like-minded Irish creatives by placing ads on Film Ireland, a website for professionals in the Irish film industry, and other online sites. I started to save and to do odd jobs to get some cash together to make films. At first, we had no equipment other than a handycam I'd bought in London. It was hardly top of the line but, in the right hands, it was a cinema camera. We'd no lights or materials, so we made them. We bought construction lights from the hardware store and used various household items as flags and reflectors.

All around me there were decaying buildings and other quirky agricultural relics. There were fields and forests. To some, this was decadence and decline, an estate well past its prime, but to me it was all a film set. We were going to use it to tell stories. They wouldn't be pretty or refined but I was going to make films. It was a start. Whether I liked it or not, I was here now and I was trying to make my new reality work. My parents had made so many sacrifices to give me a skillset to pursue this career. The rest was up to me.

The first productions were, inevitably, not all I wanted them to be. They looked cheap, the inferior quality of our equipment clearly showed, our technical skills were amateur and the writing was clunky. The films suffered from a lack of identity and there was no unifying theme, but rather a general focus on all things dark and macabre, linking to my childhood in an old, shadowy castle, to the fairy tales that had fascinated me since discovering them as an A-level student, and always to the dark music that had seen me through so many tough times. The themes ranged from necrophilia to zombies; basically, the full gamut of human experience.

Although these early efforts were far from perfect, I started to feel that I had some potential. I'd left college with the idea of being a director but, after finding no one who could write well, I was forced to start writing. Once we shot the films, I couldn't find anyone to edit them, so with some YouTube and lots of evenings spent on various forums, I began to learn. For years I'd considered myself not to be technically minded, but as I laboured to learn all these new skills I started to get good at them. Every time I hit a wall, I said to myself, 'Fuck it, gotta learn that too, I guess.' Having always struggled with learning in formal education, now I was finding myself able to do it on my own.

When I was a child, my parents had always taught me that if you want to be a good manager or a boss, you should have at least a basic knowledge of all the jobs and be prepared to do any of them. By the end of my first few shorts, I'd been the sound guy, the camera guy, the light guy and the editor. I sucked at most of these jobs, but I was learning fast. By the time I'd started my second short, I was also beginning to learn how to critique my own work. I'd not yet, however, applied the rule Karim Traïdia had taught me about directing: the best ideas and stories have an element of truth from the storyteller, and if they don't, you're doing the filmic equivalent of cover songs.

Then I directed a short film called *Walt*. It told the story of a young boy living in rural Ireland. He was approaching puberty, dealing with bullying at school, the recent death of his mother, and a challenging time at home with his father, with whom he longed for a closer relationship. There were tender scenes when he met a kind older man who needed help and offered companionship. The landscape of Dunsany also played a starring role, its fields, forests, water all the subject of lingering shots. The actors in *Walt* walked the same paths my ancestors trod every day for generations; the camera made love to a tamed, domesticated, grazed and fenced landscape. We'd moved the farm animals to other parts of the estate to provide an illusion of wildness, although the clearly visible cropped grass spoke loudly of them, even in their absence.

Maybe you'll see *Walt* one day, so I won't tell you the ending, but I will reveal that the plot twist is when a sweet friendship turns into . . . well, cannibalism. Even then, in the throes of making the movie and caring for Dad, it didn't take a genius to see how I was using the film to work out my own issues. The actor I cast to play the older man known as Walt was John E. Regan, who looked a bit like Dad, and the little boy, played by Cian Lavelle-Walsh, was dealing with the same problems that had blighted my younger life and were still following me around. Karim Traïdia's words echoed in my mind as I worked: insert your own fears and pain and make them part of the characters and the story. Like a bird struggling to fly for so long, I'd flapped and suddenly began to hover, creatively. I was beginning to find a way.

At the same time, almost despite myself, I was developing some interest in the land. I was open to the idea of continuing something my father had dreamed of: creating an organic farm so we could cease being landlords and work the land ourselves, maybe even create a gourmet brand of our own. It was a nice dream and a good plan, but most important it was a way of showing Dad that his dreams and desires weren't fading as his disease took hold.

Organic farming was already quite big in Ireland. The Irish Organic Association was founded in back in 1982, when farming without the help of chemicals and other modern innovations was still seen as eccentric. Dad had always taken a great interest in it, as he was instinctively averse to the use of chemicals on the land. In his day, his grandfather had also been very vocal about these kind of practices and their dangers. By the 2010s, the number of farmers interested in taking an organic approach was growing quickly. We took back some of the land and found a farm partner, Rob, to do things under our instruction, with a view to taking back the rest as I learned more about farming. I thought I might even take the official exam I'd need to qualify for farm subsidies. I was becoming reconciled to dividing my life between art and estate management as my great-grandfather, and then my father, had done before me.

Dad went into his final illness in 2011. He was now so unwell he was moved to his own little room at the local hospital in Navan. We were told the end was near. He'd been a giant to me all my life, but he looked very small against the white hospital linen, with tubes entering and leaving his body. We took turns to stay with him, never leaving his side, as he could go at any moment.

I'd pulled the night duty. I watched the sun set from the window near his bed. We sat in silence for what seemed an eternity. And then, uncontrollably, I began to speak. I couldn't tell whether Dad could hear me or not but I talked on. I told Dad I'd never sell Dunsany. I said I knew that, deep down, he probably wished Oliver had been his first-born son. I told him not to worry, because all his dedication to preparing me hadn't been in vain. I'd look after the memory of all my ancestors, who'd lived and died before us. I'd be a monk to this place, a good apostle. I'd carry the torch with no further question, and dedicate my life to protecting the estate he'd suffered for. He could rest now, it was safe with me, this giant stone baby that would never grow up, these soggy fields on which the cattle splattered fresh excrement every day. I didn't know what to do with it all, but I'd figure something out. I'd learn to love it. I'd become the man he wanted me to be.

Dad, of course, said nothing. He just kept breathing slowly, the slight movements of his eyes barely visible beneath the paper-thin lids. I stayed with him for hours, watching the barely-there rise and fall of his chest. It was the last thing I ever said to him. There are so many other things I wish I'd said too, but didn't. I suppose everyone feels that way.

In the morning, I went home to wash and rest, planning to return for lunch. I was getting ready to leave when Daniel burst into the room. He put a hand on each side of my face and told me Dad was gone. From another room, I heard the unnerving sounds of my mother wailing. I'd heard something like that before, when farmers separated the young sheep from their mothers and days of suffering followed. I didn't budge. I patted Daniel on the shoulder and thanked him. I was determined not to cry. Crying was for the weak, I thought. It was *indulgent*. That's what I'd been told, all those years before, when my best friend Emil's father had died. Now I felt I'd been weak for too long and would never again show the world a single tear.

Dad was waked in the gallery he never got to paint in, his paintbrushes on a cart in the corner of the room, where they remain today. I remember feeling numb as I looked down at him in the light beechwood coffin we'd selected at the undertakers. It was the same colour as the gallery's Escher-esque parquet flooring. The undertaker had dressed him in a smart navy blue suit that was too big for him, with a crisp white shirt and one of the golden-coloured ties he'd liked. Dad had always been a snappy dresser.

Mum's sobs filled the room as people filed solemnly past the coffin, paying their respects. Although Dad's life had become utterly miserable, she'd worked tirelessly to keep him alive for as long as possible and now she was utterly bereft. Dad had been seventy-one; old enough for his death not to be a tragedy, but still young enough for his loved ones to feel he'd been stolen too soon. And we were all utterly exhausted from years of caring for him, years of doing everything we could to delay this moment for as long as possible.

After the funeral, we buried Dad in the small family graveyard around the ruined chapel opposite the castle. He'd always wanted to be laid to rest among his ancestors, for his mortal remains to become a part of Dunsany soil. I was glad Granddad was some distance away at the summit of the old Norman motte. A crowd attended: friends, relatives and some locals. We all stood under a leaden sky punctuated with swirling crows as the sombre, beautiful words of the funeral service were intoned. After they lowered Dad into his final resting place, people started filing past, shaking our hands and muttering condolences.

'I'm sorry for your loss, Lord Dunsany,' someone said.

'Thank you,' I replied on auto-pilot. Moments later I realised – *holy shit* – he'd been talking to me. I'd dreaded this day my whole life and now it was here.

Within days of Dad's death, everything was falling apart. Mum and I were fighting about what was going to happen next. I yelled that I could sell the estate now if I wanted to, and there was nothing she could do. As soon as the words left my mouth, I felt guilty; my last promise to Dad had been that I'd take care of Dunsany. We were arguing in Dad's room, where he'd spent most of his decline, and where he'd been confined to bed just days before. It seemed as though his spirit might still be there, hovering somewhere above our heads, watching with dismay as two of the people he loved most turned on one another.

We calmed down, of course, and took back the harsh words we'd been throwing at one another, but the aftermath of

Dad's death continued to be tough, though in some ways we'd been waiting for this for years. First Mum's life, and then mine and Oliver's, had revolved entirely around Dad's escalating needs. For years, every time he coughed, Mum had spiralled into panic, and we'd all wondered if this was the end. We'd lived in a state of constant fear that we weren't doing enough to keep him alive. Now the weight of anxiety had finally been lifted, but it had been replaced by a new set of problems.

Financially speaking, the estate was a mess. Dad had been sick for so long, the estate had been poorly managed for years, and Granddad had nearly run it into the ground for decades before that. There'd been an economic crash, and we were still living through a global recession, which had hit Ireland's open economy particularly hard. Incomes from farming were down, rents were falling, and expenses were rising precipitously.

I felt guilty for complaining about having inherited a beautiful castle at a time when so many people were losing their homes, or couldn't get enough money together to save for a deposit or pay their rent. I knew that I really couldn't complain openly at such a difficult time, but I also resented the situation I was in. It was impossible to keep on top of things like opening all the windows every day, and prohibitively expensive to heat every room, so the castle started to suffer: black mould, moths and condensation were wreaking havoc in the less-used rooms and serving as an eloquent visual metaphor for the lengthy and inevitable decline of the Irish aristocracy.

Xulé, the little dog who'd been with us since my childhood, was old and grey now. I woke one morning to hear Mum wailing again. Poor Xulé had died in the night. Mum was devastated.

'I don't want to bury him!' Mum said. She suggested that we get Xulé stuffed so that he'd stay with her always. The idea was grotesque, but it was obvious that she was transferring her grief at Dad's death onto this smaller loss. Eventually we agreed to bury Xulé at Dad's feet, in the style of the Plunkett ancestors. The thought of him being united with Dad seemed to make her feel a little better.

Having always seemed much younger than her years until now, Mum seemed utterly lost and older than her age. It was hard to remember that once she'd built New York skyscrapers so tall they'd touched the clouds. Before Dad's illness, Mum had been bold – fearless, even. Now, she became ever more anxious at the thought of leaving the castle. For fear of what might happen if she left Dad alone, even for a few hours, she hadn't left Dunsany for years. She seemed to have decided to continue living in a reduced world, to feel as though her leaving the castle would hurt it, or somehow invite evil-doers in. Blessed with an abundance of talent and ability, she continued to sink it all into the estate. Desperate to care for someone, for something, she bought whole chickens and bags of potatoes and vegetables, and prepared elaborate roast dinners for the dogs – roast meat, gravy, roast and mashed potatoes, buttered vegetables – until they became grotesquely overweight and the family vet begged her to stop, saying that she was literally killing them with kindness.

At that time, Daniel was in London – he had married and had children of his own – Joana had moved to Brazil, and Oliver still lived in a family property a short distance from the castle, where he was working on starting his own video-game business. When my elder siblings came to visit, Mum went all out, preparing their rooms with the nicest linen – 'You'll sleep well on that; it's from the eighteenth century!' – and extravagant flower arrangements, trying to show with these things how very much she loved us all. Her dream was for all of her children to be so impressed by her adoration of them they'd live in the castle too. Inevitably, she was disappointed if the visit wasn't 'perfect' or people didn't connect with one another as she'd hoped. After these visits, Mum would return to the kitchen to cook for the dogs. My siblings, understandably, would return to their own lives. A look of relief always seemed to cross their faces as they said their goodbyes and drove up the avenue and away from Dunsany.

Chapter Four

Zombie Estate

WITH THE COST OF SUPPORTING DAD'S CARE NO LONGER WEIGHING US DOWN, WE BEGAN WORKING HARD TO INCREASE OUR INCOME AS WE PICKED UP THE PIECES AND STARTED REBUILDING OUR LIVES. Oliver was slowly creating his first phone game. Mum continued to try and restore the broken property engulfing us.

With more time on my hands than before Dad's death, I was finally able to finish editing my short, *Walt*, which I'd filmed during the final stages of his illness. I'd been quite aware of its autobiographical qualities when I made it, but the fact that I'd poured my fears into it was even more obvious now. Watching *Walt* today, it's a clear parable about me; about my fears that Dunsany and its constant demands would eat me up and spit me out.

I regret that Dad never saw any of my serious attempts at film. I wish he'd been given the chance to watch this one, to see I wasn't without potential. All sons crave their fathers' approval; I know I always did. Having struggled at every turn through school and through life, I still often contemplate what it'd be like to show Dad – who loved me regardless of how difficult I could be – any kind of personal achievement.

Walt was the first of my films to have any meaningful level of success. It won several awards and did the festival circuit. I received some positive feedback, which was encouraging, particularly as it had been made on a very low budget, with most of the equipment cobbled together from whatever I'd managed to find in IKEA.

A little more confident, I started making connections with other creatives in the Irish film industry. At least some of them were prepared to accept me at face value. We began to work together. *Walt* having been my first serious film, I was determined not to let the momentum fade, so I quickly started a new project and became more ambitious. My next film, *Out There,* would deal with how I was feeling at the time: the desire to run away, to disappear from my new duties. Making *Walt* had been good for me: expressing myself through it had lifted a massive weight from my shoulders. Now I had to address the even bigger ball of black emotion festering in the pit of my stomach, and once again, the only way I could deal with my emotions was through film. I regard *Out There* as my first proper grown-up effort at directing a film. We even shot it with a real cinema camera, and it's much more technically accomplished than *Walt*.

Zombies were just beginning to get big in popular culture at the time and I thought that we could do a great movie at Dunsany using this appealing trope. Although *Out There* was very personal, it also had lots of gentle nods to films I admired in the genre. A man wakes up in a forest, apparently utterly alone. Once again, the landscape at Dunsany wasn't just the set; it was also a protagonist as the action flickered between terror on the land and another, happier existence before the protagonist's arrival. Scenes shot in dense forest made nature look aloof, even hostile.

In a way, the estate was just another one of the zombies. The intensive farming to which it had been subjected for generations had reduced it to a sort of half-life. It was beautiful on the surface but deadly – even horrifying – when you looked more closely. The short film captured the claustrophobia and sense of being lost that I felt at home, as well as the terror of the protagonist, among the beautiful colours and elegant shapes of Dunsany. Scenes shot in and around the estate outhouses – state of the art in the nineteenth century, crumbling now after decades of inattention – captured an imagined dystopia. The story resonated with me. It was like admiring the bars of your own gilded cage. *Out There* is a zombie flick, but it's also about someone who fled his obligations and was ultimately destroyed. The betrayer and betrayed were both, of course, me.

Using Dunsany to tell stories that explored the human condition and also exposed my personal fears and anxieties made me start to loathe the land a little less. At least now I was using it to do something I loved. And by putting all my own fears, resentments and angers into my films and showing them to the world – by confronting them through the medium of art – I started to feel better about myself: less of a loser, less *small*, more hopeful for the future.

As soon as *Out There* was released in 2012 I decided to promote it relentlessly. I spent countless hours contacting every single blog, website and film festival I could find, sending them a link to *Out There* and asking them to review it. I treated this quest like a job, putting in two hours a day, every day, for six months. If I wanted to succeed, I'd have to do so not through talent or connections but on pure grit. I told myself I'd treat it like a war.

When I wasn't dedicating myself to promoting the film, or if I felt lazy, I imagined my opportunities as a finite quantity of liquid being poured down the sink, only to be consumed by my enemies. This vile image kept me more focused than ever before. When my neck ached from too many hours at the computer, or I was rejected and wanted to give up, I whispered something new to myself. Not 'I am a winner, I am a winner' as Mum had made me repeat as a child or 'I can always kill myself' as I'd repeated during my weakest moments, but a new mantra: 'I've only just begun to fight.'

Out There featured in over forty film festivals, won several awards and was nominated for many more, including Best Industry Short at the Lit Film Festival in Limerick. Most excitingly, it was selected to play at the Cannes Film Festival.

Visiting Cannes for a few days was thrilling, even if *Out There* was in one of the less flashy categories. Finally, I felt, Dunsany Productions and I were going places, even if we weren't getting much attention on our own turf; one major Irish festival rejected *Out There* even after its outing at Cannes. The programmer was overheard in the cinema lobby commenting that I 'had enough already' and 'the Irish film industry didn't need his sort stealing the opportunities of those who aren't blessed with everything' when questioned about this strange little film and why it wasn't featured.

Mum, whose agoraphobia had steadily deteriorated, didn't attend any of the screenings. She had many excuses, from 'Who'd look after the dogs?' to 'The house can't be left alone.' I didn't push. I felt bad for her. Once she'd been the heart and soul of the party and now she was staying alone with the dogs because of her entirely rational fears of being burgled, and also for fear of the unknown. I also wanted her to share in my small taste of success simply because I didn't really have anyone else who could. I went to my premier at Dublin's Irish Film Institute by myself.

By the end of summer 2013 Oliver had relocated to Texas, where he was doing well. I remained at Dunsany with Mum. We spent so much time together I could predict her every move. With Dad gone, she focused exclusively on me and the castle, and lived in constant fear. She kept all the shutters closed, even on the fourth floor, always frightened that burglars would scale the walls and break in or that a storm would launch trees through the windows. We moved from one room to another in the dark: modern ghosts haunting our own ancestors. Mum grew pale from lack of sunlight and so did I. We were still trying to offset the financial strain following Dad's death, so we rarely turned on any heaters, and the castle suffered from cold and damp.

A once fashionably dressed architect frequenting the parties of New York's elite, Mum now wore faded tracksuits, big bomber jackets and a scarf. She was a sad sight and, dressed much the same, so was I. It sometimes felt as though the castle, with its endless demands, was sucking the life out of her, transforming her gradually into a shell of her former self, a Brazilian Miss Havisham to my Estella, each trapped by a place we were supposed to love. Mum was living in the past, her love for me impossible to extricate from her efforts to keep me under her control, even as I moved into and beyond my mid-twenties. She showed no anger or bitterness as, superficially, she tried to make my life easier by doing everything for me.

The castle was affected by Mum's behaviour too. It deteriorated as the darkness and humidity grew. One day I noticed a painting of Dad's – one of his Cubist-inspired works, from the 1980s or early 1990s – hanging crookedly. Damp had warped the frame, deforming it. It had twisted so violently it stood right out from the wall, like a hand grasping for help; the castle reminding us of our downward spiral. Increasingly, I felt like that warped frame. My psychological armature was being eroded and twisted from inside and there seemed to be nothing I could do.

Since Dad's death, every day was the same. We lived in constant panic, dreading every time it rained or the wind blew that the castle would collapse. We learned to fear the postman, who any day might bring a bill we couldn't cover; we seemed always to be just one step from financial ruin. Our nights gave us no peace: we slept on alert for any sound of intruders or of the castle falling apart. Many nights Mum woke me, saying she'd heard a noise and thought it might be water flowing. I'd get up and we'd walk around the house, inspecting every room for any sign of water or a leak. We rarely found anything, but these night checks accompanied every storm or rough weather (I still often carry out these checks. I can't explain why, but if I don't, I struggle to sleep). As always, I turned to exercise for relief, transforming my stress and angst into kinetic energy, trying to get bigger and stronger at all costs. This was the closest I had to a form of escape, although each bout of exercise was short.

It would be easy to say we'd become paranoid, but there were justifications for our panic, because disasters occurred regularly and often without warning. But I knew that my mother and I had fallen into a strange, dysfunctional relationship. In a way, I'd fallen into Dad's place, and found myself almost acting the role of a husband. I was trying to write scripts and kickstart a career in the film industry, but when I was working Mum came to see me at least once an hour. Why? I don't know. Making sure I was still there? Telling me what she was doing, lest some disaster befall one of us? Engaging in pointless conversation because if she didn't talk to me she wouldn't talk to anybody? I was her sounding board; she had no one else. She needed to express herself and, unable to, had become desperate for the slightest attention, which she needed like a drunk needs booze. On the rare occasions when I left, she rang me constantly. She'd left me food, she'd say, would leave the back door unlocked, could I let her know what time I'd be home? One Christmas I planned to visit my then-girlfriend's house for the afternoon, and Mum followed me outside and flung herself on the car bonnet, saying that I wasn't allowed to leave at Christmas and that she'd rather die than let me go.

You might assume she didn't want to be alone at Christmas, but we'd given up on Christmas a long time before then. I hated Christmas with a passion. During Dad's illness I'd spent many holiday periods in the emergency room with him as he was treated for conditions like pneumonia, which could have been the kiss of death. When I wasn't in a waiting room or hearing the eternal beeping of a hospital monitor, I was waiting for the phone to ring. It was invariably a concerned neighbour saying that the local fox and deer hunts were on the move, invading us again like a cancer we were powerless to stop.

For all these reasons, I'd learned to loathe Christmas and all the festivities. Every year it reminded me of my fear that my whole life would be dictated by the constant need to be at Dunsany, always being pulled away from family meals or dropping what I was doing to face external threats, as Dad had done before me. It was an annual reminder of my responsibilities.

Why bother fighting back against the hunt? you might wonder. Why not just let it be? The reality is that if you start throwing your hands up and saying 'Fuck it', it'll end badly. If you ignore illegal hunts, thieves will follow and inevitably this situation can escalate out of control, as it had before Dad came home.

I was working upstairs when my phone rang: it was Mum, from downstairs, letting me know we had visitors who were requesting a meeting. I came down to find her in the hall with two very well-dressed men.

'How do you do?' the older of the two said. 'We hope you don't mind us dropping around like this.' He introduced himself and his son. We all shook hands. They were very polite. Charming, even.

'How can I help you?' I asked. I felt wary, as I always do when strangers arrive unannounced. We've had so many run-ins with burglars. These guys were wearing expensive flashy Swiss watches and tailored shirts. They were also wearing hand-made Italian shoes, which is unusual in Ireland, even among the very wealthy. What did *that* mean? Through the hall window, I saw a gold Range Rover. Something felt off.

The older man quickly got to the point. He explained that they were hoteliers. They were designing new hotels with an African theme, he said, which they hoped to launch as a new trend. In particular, they were working with a new hotel in the west of Ireland that was going to be remodelled in this style. They were visiting stately homes to look for hunting trophies that could be used to make moulds for casting resin replicas.

'We've found plenty of zebras,' he explained, 'but we're looking for other types of animals too, elephants and so forth. Your neighbour mentioned you might be able to help . . . said he thinks you've a rhino.'

'You must come in for tea!' Mum said. She rushed them into the dining room, and ran off to make tea. We made small talk beneath the gaze of my various ancestors. I noticed that our visitors paid no attention to the silverware, although Mum had brought out the good stuff. Their eyes slid over the artwork on the walls with no sign of interest. Perhaps that was reassuring. If they wanted to burgle us, surely they'd be casing the joint?

Against my best instincts, after the tea I showed the two men the hunting trophies, many of which were stuffed into the old decommissioned kitchen where once an army of servants worked hard to make lavish meals. They kept their cool, but were speechless when they saw the rhino head. It was enormous, the horn alone as long as a man's thigh-bone; rhinos use these horns for various purposes, including fighting, asserting their territorial authority and foraging for roots. One of the men casually sauntered towards it and put his hand around the horn to measure its width.

'Oh,' he said, 'this is fantastic! So beautiful. I've waited a long time to see one like this.'

They looked around the room, found a stuffed warthog and asked if they could take moulds of both the rhino and the warthog. They'd be just perfect, he said, for the hotel: 'They just scream "Africa"!'

They offered us €5,000 in cash to borrow both the rhino head and the warthog so that their specialist in Dublin could make a mould. The money was tempting, but I was dubious. I suggested they put together a detailed proposal in writing and email it so we could think about it. 'Ten thousand,' was his immediate counter-offer. 'And we can go to the bank right now.' Now I knew for sure that something fishy was going on. I reiterated that I needed to see a written proposal first.

'Maybe we should've taken their money,' Mum said as they drove away. 'There's a new leak in the roof.'

Something didn't seem right. I called the Gardaí, explained what had happened and asked what they thought.

The Gardaí arrived within moments – they'd never done that on the many occasions we'd reported hunting and poaching – and took a detailed report. They were aware, they said, of Irish crime gangs searching for rhino horns, which were worth a fortune on the illegal market. These had already been implicated in several burglaries, in Ireland and elsewhere. The horns were sold to Chinese crime cartels, who peddled them to practitioners of Chinese medicine. Ours might be worth as much as a quarter of a million euros.

A week later, we received a phone call from our visitors and another offer of a bag of cash. They'd upped the price to twenty grand. Mum told them the head was gone. We called an acquaintance in the auction business and disposed of the rhino head in exchange for future favours. We assumed the story was over.

A few weeks later, Mum left the castle on one of her very rare forays off the estate. She needed to see a doctor and the only one she trusted was my father's doctor, Dr Sandberg in London. That day, I had a visitor who drove a Jeep similar to mine. Shortly after he left, after nightfall, I was sitting in my office. The castle was creaking and groaning, but then it always does when there's a strong wind. The dogs started scratching and whining to go out, so I brought them to the front door and opened it. They rushed into the darkness, barking. I peered out to see what all the fuss was about. Through the gloom, I saw two men exiting a small car and a few more standing at the window that led into the room where the rhino head had previously been stored. They looked up and our eyes met. I saw them collectively realise I hadn't been the driver in the Jeep that had just left. I slammed the door shut, grabbed one of the double-barrelled shotguns my ancestors had used to kill game from the corner of the hall and dialled 999 on my mobile phone. The Gardaí said they'd come as quickly as possible, but the castle is quite remote, and even if they weren't as slow as usual, I was alone with a bunch of criminals.

I started creeping from one side of the dark castle to the other with the admittedly stupid idea of surprising the intruders and scaring them away with my gun. It was to my advantage not to turn on the lights, as I knew the building like the back of my hand, and they were working blind. There were more of them than me, but like any creature, I was capable of being dangerous when threatened in my own habitat. Thankfully, by the time I got to the old kitchen where the trophies were kept, I could hear the thieves' car skidding away. They'd managed to get into the castle; the door to the old kitchen was ajar. As the rhino head was no longer there, they'd left disappointed. The police arrived an hour and a half later and a very friendly guard started to brush for prints. I told him I'd grabbed one of my ancestors' guns to frighten the intruders.

'Hah!' he said jovially, indicating towards the taxidermised heads. 'Probably the same gun they used to shoot one of these lads back in the day. Good job you didn't shoot; it could easily have backfired.'

'The one time I leave the house,' Mum said when she got back from London, 'burglars try to break in. I'm never going anywhere again.'

And she didn't. Mum stayed where she was, and the hunting trophies remained where they were, their glass eyes as emotionless as they'd been before this intrusion.

Our visitors called one last time and once again Mum told them the rhino head was gone. A week later, we heard someone walking on the roof over the old kitchen, and Mum saw someone looking in the window, but by the time the guards arrived they'd departed, leaving no trace. We never heard from them again, but a few years later some gangsters managed to grab a rhino head from the Irish Natural History Museum, which is right next door to the Dáil, the houses of parliament.

Those days weren't all awful. There were good times. In many ways, Mum was a great companion. We were never short of banter. As a Brazilian with Latin sensibilities, she was always up for some entertainment and we often enjoyed heated debates about politics or film. We had fun together as long as I never questioned her decisions or queried how she was running Dunsany. If I did, within minutes conversation escalated to a series of vicious exchanges. The slightest pushback caused her such anxiety and explosive anger I worried she might have a heart attack, or even literally explode with rage. Once, angry over my dissent, she lit a sheet of newspaper on fire and threw it at a painting. 'We might as well burn the castle down now!' she shouted.

Mum was stubborn; she'd never have admitted there was a problem, let alone accepted help, and nobody who loved her dared defy her. She believed, as she'd always seemed to, that I was incapable of making even the smallest decisions without her help and input. She said I was in charge now – which on paper I was – but regularly overruled me and dismissed my views as childish and uninformed. This often happened in front of guests and staff. She'd point out that she'd sunk plenty of her money into the estate and knew much more about business than me. That was true, but she was also getting older and out of touch, and what had once been confidence often now manifested as hubris.

I didn't have great entrepreneurial instincts but I could see we were making mistakes. We were the *Titanic*, soon to crash into the iceberg. Whenever I protested, war broke out. I threatened to leave, numerous times, but eventually became resigned to my powerlessness. What was I going to do; kill my mother? Leave her alone, here? I couldn't, and for every fight we had, she also offered lots of encouragement and love. She lived for me. Had I needed anything, she'd have sold all she had to give it to me. How could I hurt someone like that? She was still dealing with her grief. She was my best friend. I'd never given up on Dad, even at the worst, and I wasn't going to give up on Mum either. My job now was to look after Mum and try to mitigate some of her less-good decisions until my time came.

Mum had always wanted me to marry money. Now her pursuit of a suitable bride intensified. She upped the ante from inviting around friends with marriageable daughters to actively trying to match-make. Embarrassing scenes ensued as she sought wealthy heiresses and tried to push us together. At one point, a good female friend of mine from a 'suitable' background came to visit, and Mum told her behind my back that I was romantically interested, but too shy to say anything. Having no idea that this conversation had occurred, I continued to treat my friend as always. Confused and disturbed, she understandably distanced herself. I'll always regret that this friendship, which had been important to me, didn't survive Mum's completely unhinged behaviour. She was in no way dissuaded. No wealthy heiress within fifteen years of my age was safe from her increasingly transparent attempts to see me married to one of them. As a grown man in my thirties now, it was mortifying. I lost count of how often I sat through yet another matchmaking effort, or listened to Mum talking about how I needed to find the 'right' sort of bride – one who'd bring lots of money to the table and be prepared to hand it over, while also not wanting to get personally involved with Dunsany at all. Not much of a deal.

While such schemes may have played out in Jane Austen's day, when heirs and heiresses could be auctioned off to the highest bidder, this was the twenty-first century. Mum had always tended to read what she wanted into situations, to narrate stories about life that had more to do with her wishes than with reality. Now she seemed to want reality to bend to her will.

Chapter Five

Going Full Vegan

SEVERAL YEARS EARLIER, SHORTLY AFTER DAD'S DEATH IN 2011, OUR FARM TENANT HAD GOT INTO A SQUABBLE WITH US OVER SUBLEASING THE ROUGHER LAND. At one point he'd leased it some unsavoury characters who'd abandoned ponies and horses on the land, as happened so often in those recessionary years. Ultimately, the animals had to be seized by the authorities, and we all agreed that subleasing was no longer an option. As subleasing the land for grazing had risks – the animals regularly broke out and damaged his crops – he agreed to leave the land idle.

This was good timing, as the subsidies system was making changes in nature's favour. The Irish government sponsored a scheme encouraging farmers to allow the margins around their fields to grow wild; the Rural Environmental Protection Scheme, known as REPS. Introduced in 1994, this was the first nationwide scheme to encourage farmers to protect the country's natural and cultural heritage. Its keynote policy was that small strips of land should be 'set aside' in areas considered environmentally sensitive. Now the policy was shifting towards a certain amount of rewilding becoming a prerequisite for receiving the subsidies that most farmers rely on. They were being forced to allow 5 per cent of their land mass go to a category called 'Greening'. For our farm tenant, this meant he could use the marginal land in his leasehold as a portion of his greening contribution.

Without the animals, the once-compressed, messy scrubland steadily filled with thistles, brambles and other wild plants. To a limited extent, wildlife started to rebound here and small areas of tangled grass and wild flowers began to form. I remember finding it quite interesting, in an abstract sort of way, that such tangible change could occur quite quickly. Although the areas were being left to rewild were restricted in size, a variety of plants took root and it was soon evident that there was much more insect activity in these areas than in others. Occasionally we saw rabbits, and sometimes a pheasant. I didn't know what I was looking at yet, but these were the very first seeds of rewilding at Dunsany.

To raise money, we'd bought a herd of cattle, which would be fattened at Dunsany and sold on. We planned to grow a herd and develop an organic farm in partnership with Rob, a neighbour and a friend. We'd share the grazing land with Rob in exchange for his help and guidance through the trials and tribulations of developing a business we didn't understand very well yet.

Our first bullocks arrived covered in blood from being dehorned late, and Rob and I tended to their wounds, a revolting and distressing task. In the process, I'd looked into the animals' eyes and seen their distress. *Are we so civilised?* I'd asked myself. *How can we really be so oblivious to our savagery and then wish for something better for ourselves?* I felt so sorry for the dehorned cattle. You may have heard there's no sensation in cows' horns, and that removing them doesn't bother the animals. That's simply untrue; a convenient lie to make us feel better about the terrible things we do in pursuit of a cheap hamburger. Amputated stumps actually itch terribly as they heal. The bloody stubs attract flies, which make the itching even worse. The cattle pushed their big heads against tree trunks, fence posts and the ground, and made agonised sounds as they tried to relieve the dreadful sensations. Eventually, as their wounds healed, they started to feel better, and I relaxed a little as I watched them from the castle windows.

The longer the animals stayed, the more apparent it became that each had a unique personality. And yet, we – Rob and I and society in general – saw them as commodities, soon to be slaughtered, cut into convenient portions and packaged for the supermarket refrigerator shelves.

I pushed meat around on my plate one evening, watching the streaks of blood and grease it left behind. Since starting to work out in my teens, I'd been obsessed with eating enough protein. I'd been sure I needed to eat lots of meat to build the muscles I wanted. But right now, for the first time, that steak looked revolting.

Deep down I knew that, despite all the fancy talk, bodybuilding and a meat-heavy diet were unhealthy. After all, it was well known that too much red meat causes heart disease. *Will I spend my whole life working out in the hope of a long, healthy life only to die of a heart attack like so many of the bodybuilders I've followed for so long?* I wondered. Having spent time with my cattle, I'd been losing interest in eating steak for a while. I'd always known that cattle had to be killed, but having close contact with them had left me feeling morally confused.

Could I be a vegetarian? I guessed that was possible. I looked into it further and to my surprise there was in fact a lot of data on it. After watching several documentaries and reading a lot of science papers online, I became curious. I decided to try being a vegetarian for month. At worst, it'd be a detox. I'd also learn whether I really needed meat for my health. I'd read and believed that meat was the food we were meant to eat and that to deny it would destroy our health. Was that really true?

I'm a methodical person and I don't jump into things lightly. I'd always been told that vegetarianism is unhealthy. The vegetarians I'd met at my various schools had always seemed frail. All the health magazines I read agreed that if you didn't consume enough iron or protein you could wither away in a matter of weeks. I began to research the counterargument. It appeared that the research showed that veganism was even better than vegetarianism. I read about vegan athletes and influencers who seemed to be healthy despite eating no animal products. I also found a lot of data showing that veganism can reverse heart disease and diabetes, that it could reduce the incidence of cancer and – to my surprise – is good for the environment.

So scratch being vegetarian, I'll go full vegan for a month instead, I decided. At worst, I'd be able to debunk the next vegan who threw their spiel at me as I'd be able to say I'd tried it. At best, if veganism was the real deal, it would stand to the test. So I stopped eating animal products of any kind.

Within a week of removing meat from my diet, I felt great. The stubborn stores of fat at my waist grew smaller, and I gained strength almost immediately. Normally, I increased the weights I lifted gradually, but now I found myself putting more weight on the bars without the slightest issue. I was sleeping better and feeling more alert. I was now eating less than half the protein I had before, with all of it coming from plants. Within the first weeks the results were so dramatic that even I had a tough time believing it wasn't just a placebo effect.

A month or so after starting my diet, I had to go to a wedding. As there were no vegan options available at the meal, I made do. Almost immediately after reverting to consuming animal products, I felt and looked like hell. My body, which had adjusted quickly and seamlessly to the plant-based diet, was now utterly rejecting animal products. My skin broke out and I felt drained and needed several coffees to function in the morning. After that, I had no doubt. Being vegan isn't just good for the planet; it's also good for me. Not one single scrap of animal-derived food has crossed my lips ever since. Mum became vegan too.

Now I was furious with myself for having been so closed-minded to all the vegans I'd met. I'd even teased them, assuming they were weak and weird. I found myself questioning everything I'd believed in and wondering what else I was wrong about. Everything in my world was beginning to change, from what was outside my window to what was on my plate.

I began to study physiology in more depth and to listen to the claims of those advocating plant-based diets. Some of their arguments were extremely compelling. Our bodies demonstrate that humans evolved to eat plant-dominated or plant-only diets. Why do we see colour? So we can better judge ripe fruit or vegetables. Why do we have jaws that grind from side to side, like any herbivore's? To process grains and plant matter. Why do we have long digestive tracts and alkaline saliva? To absorb nutrients from plants and kickstart the digestive process. We have all this in common with herbivorous mammals like deer and goats, and while humans *can* eat a meat-heavy diet, our bodies – unlike those of obligate carnivores, such as wolves, cats and lions – are not really supposed to, and we typically don't achieve optimum health on a flesh-based diet.

Merely surviving is different from living in an optimal way for health and longevity. If one examines the longest-living populations, their diets are usually based on a larger ratio of fruits and vegetables, with less processed food, less protein and plenty of carbohydrates. They also have active lifestyles and tend to eat less than most western populations. As I absorbed all this new information, I wondered why it had taken me so long to understand what now seemed so obvious.

In the Bible, Jesus is alleged to have said: 'Do unto to others as you would have them do unto you.' I knew many churchgoing people, all of whom seemed to have convinced themselves that cruelty to animals is acceptable because people are all that matters. But no animal is evil; evil has been created by humans. Animals kill to eat and to protect their young, but only humans kill for malice.

In the aftermath of releasing *Out There* and the flurry of interest that followed, I had lots of meetings, which concluded with absolutely nothing gained. Nothing had changed. The success I thought I'd achieved turned out to have wings made of lead. I realised that if I wanted to make film work for me,

I'd have to do it alone. I might have pushed its door open a centimetre or two, but I'd failed to exit my gilded cage. Still, the success of the short had made me more confident and ambitious and I'd started to dream of bigger things.

I've always developed stories slowly. I fixate on various themes and do lots of reading and research. Some of the themes I'd touched on in *Out There* were evolving. With my new interest in veganism and growing awareness of how we were slowly killing nature, I began to develop an idea for a new film.

Origami was a story about loneliness and isolation, a world in which most of humanity has disappeared, swallowed by a new nocturnal predator. The script followed a Japanese protagonist, a stranger in a strange land, like me. I'd been told I wasn't truly Irish for so long, and the character in the script wasn't Irish at all. He'd be culturally lost in a version of rural Ireland that wanted to attack and kill him. I could relate to a character who came from very far away and found himself lost in a hostile environment, alone and surrounded by nature, that wanted humanity to disappear so it could flourish.

I've always felt very drawn to Japanese culture: because of the samurai movies I watched with Dad as a child and partly, I suppose, because of all the Asian art in the castle, collected years ago by my great-grandfather. I imagined my Japanese character feeling even more lost and at sea in Dunsany than me. He obsessively made little origami animals – cranes, turtles, llamas – in homage to his lost culture. Perhaps he was the last man clinging to these cultural artifacts. If he perished, so would his ancestors and his way of life. In a way he was carrying the flag for his ancestors, just like me.

In 2014, during the early stages of *Origami*, fate provided my mother and me with exactly who we needed at that time in our lives. Through Tony Kiernan, a film and sound engineer at Moynihan Russell Studios in Dublin, I met a film editor, Stephen Lourdes. I'd been friends with Tony for several years, and I quickly became friendly with Stephen, too. We agreed to work together, and I invited him to Dunsany.

Almost straight away, Stephen and Mum hit it off. They became friends. When Mum found out that Stephen might be interested in working on some documentary ideas about the eighteenth Lord Dunsany, she invited him to live with us. That way, he'd be able to commit fully to the project. Before long, Stephen and I were working together on other projects. Mum soon seemed relaxed with him living with us, more so than she ever had with me. They would share a bottle of wine in the evenings. Working with her was still tricky and demanding, and she still desperately missed Dad, but the arrival of Stephen, and his absorption into the family, gave her an essential social outlet other than me and gave me some breathing space to focus on the estate, on my career in film and even a little on building my own social network.

I bought myself a book on origami, spent hours watching YouTube tutorials and started doing the same thing. I sat at my desk and folded and folded, little paper animals falling from my fingers onto the floor, filling the small, dark room I used as an office. In the gloom, my only view a brick wall, I'd hung old film posters: the Polish version of *Solaris*, an array of Toshiro Mifune masterpieces. Among the cinema art, old Japanese theatre masks, collected by my great-grandfather and hung on the walls ever since, watched over my obsessive, lonely work. The soundtrack was walls of sound by Jesu,

Swans, Neurosis, Isis, Cult of Luna. Their lyrics spoke of doom and dystopia and suited both the script of *Origami* and my mood. 'The race to render your vision', Neurosis sang,

> A fracture in the world can devour
> Return to the light of the bearer
> The radiant breaks down into life
> We are left to wander . . .

I folded every day. Obsessive as I'd been in promoting *Out There*, my new objective was to feel my protagonist's truth. I needed to know what it was like to sit alone in the dark folding origami, worried that if I stopped I'd forget how. Repetition was second nature. For years, Dad had made me recite the stories, the history of this place, like a mantra. For this character, clutching a fading connection to his home was all he had left. I folded until my floor was heaped with paper animals made from old newspapers, magazines, any paper I could find, in an array of colours and shapes. When the weather was stormy, the draught blew them across the carpet. Anyone spying on me would have thought I'd lost my mind. Mum didn't. She understood that obsession is powerful and a route to success.

Among the origami I folded, the hardest challenge, and also the most rewarding, was the turtle. I'd been fascinated by turtles since hearing Mum's stories about her pet turtle in Brazil, and I also identified with them. Like a turtle, I seemed to be indivisible from my home, which both sheltered me and weighed me down. Also like a turtle, I seemed to have no choice but to move painfully slowly towards my goal, although it wasn't yet clear what that actually was.

Whereas previously I'd worked out my own issues through the medium of film in a not entirely conscious way, in writing the script for *Origami* it was much clearer what I was doing. I'd poured myself into the script completely, as never before. In the story, the hostile landscape was Dunsany. The lost man was me, and the origami animals were my ancestors and the stories passed down by my father. The feeling of freedom this realisation gave me was like ecstasy.

As my hours continued to pass in that dark office, I started thinking about the nature beyond the castle walls in a different way. I became aware of how very *silent* Dunsany was. There was a certain amount of birdsong early in the morning, but not nearly as much as you'd expect. The silence that otherwise prevailed was punctuated only by the cattle bellowing as they waded around muddy fields, eating every blade of grass down to the ground and shitting most of it back out. Where were all the animals and birds? Why did so few animals populate the land? It felt like there should have been many more. The only creatures that seemed to be thriving were the cacophonous crows circling above the roofless family church.

Before he got ill, Dad had forbidden the farmers to shoot any animals. Of course, they'd protested, saying the crows were destructive creatures that damaged crops and whose numbers should be kept down. Now Dad's description of the animals of Dunsany as the victims of our success echoed in my mind. I'd often heard people talking about nature and animals in terms of the circle of life, which suggested a simple cycle that just kept happening over and over again. But as I continued to work towards creating *Origami* that concept seemed to capture only some of what I saw. I started thinking of the behaviour of the animals and plants until I saw the cycle of life as less like a two-dimensional circle and more like a spiral. A spiral that had started to spin off its axis, throwing all life off-kilter.

Trying to make sense of all this, and desperate to get away from Mum and her endless problems, I started going for long daily walks. I'd pull on my rubber boots and waterproof jacket and grimly tread the landscape, my feet growing heavy with mud, earbuds in place and metal music blaring a sound track. These solitary walks, listening to my favourite music, reminded me of how alone I was, how I was walking the land largely to get away from the realities of my home and from my mother, whose vast emotional needs and endless demands seemed to have eclipsed every other social relationship. I should've been in a mosh pit at the weekends, not holed up in the middle of nowhere.

Listening to the music that had provided a soundtrack to my endless construction of little paper animals, the sounds that had comforted me since discovering heavy metal as a child, I fell into a rhythm as I pounded out a route in the long grass, making a clear path that I followed every single day. I started to know every twist in the path, every tree, every bump and curve in the landscape, as intimately as I knew my own face in the mirror. On one level, these walks reminded me of everything I was missing, the experiences my peers were enjoying. While they were out in the world building their lives, I was here, surrounded by beauty but weathering emotional turmoil at every turn.

Studying film had taught me to be an observer, to look for patterns or see the consequences of actions. I had learned to question why things work as they do. Now I felt like a detective, with a puzzle in front of me. I started to experience things I'd never seen before, and to view with fresh eyes sights I'd seen a thousand times. It was almost as though the land was whispering to me, saying we'd taken enough and now it was time to give something back. The concept of debt played on my mind: we'd taken and taken for so very long, never properly considering the cost of this behaviour. I began to watch the farm animals from afar. I was vegan but profiteering from meat production, which I increasingly understood to be destroying the future. Things were unravelling, everything I saw on the farm was wrong and I didn't know how to change it.

I'd been using Dunsany as a set for several years, but my relationship with the land had always remained functional and perfunctory. While sometimes my head was turned by a particularly lovely flower, or the scent of a flowering honeysuckle in the fragile heat of the Irish summer, or my imagination was captured by the light filtering through the trees in a particular way, mostly I'd only cared for it inasmuch as I could use it to tell a story or pay my bills. I cared for it because it gave me something tangible. Now, as well as trying to get inside the head of my protagonist, I considered my antagonist. Who would that be, in the story the film told? The nocturnal monsters that nature sent to kill the humans, were they once victims of our animal farming? Mutated, perhaps, from all our genetic modification? No, because they were the consequence of an action. *Who's the real antagonist here?* Was it me and people like me? *When you know something's wrong, how can you knowingly not stop it?* I wondered. *Who's the wronged who will exact revenge?* Then it hit me: it was nature itself, of course. The real antagonist is nature itself. It's been wronged so long it's sent devils to destroy us. I was excited at this realisation, which was like the sound of a puzzle piece clicking into place. I'd been considering the story from my limited perspective and had missed an integral part: how we got here.

Just as I wanted to understand the protagonist's burning need to preserve his culture, I needed to experience the other elements of the story. I needed to know what it felt like to *be* part of the landscape, rather than just a witness to it. I needed to see what a truly wild landscape looked like, rather than just imagining one and then improvising. I needed the landscape to express itself. I needed to be *involved* with that expression. That's what was missing.

We were nearing the end of the agricultural year when Rob, our farming partner, called us for a meeting. The sale of the animals had yielded less money than expected, although we'd invested heavily and increased the herd. Rob said that if the grass was richer, we'd make more money.

'We need to boost the nitrogen,' Rob said.

'What does that mean?' I asked.

'Chemical additives will make the grass richer,' he explained, 'and put more weight on the animals next year.'

Mum turned to me and shook her head. We wanted our farm to be organic, not driven by chemicals.

'Organic's a pipe dream,' Rob insisted. 'There's no profit in it.'

'There isn't much profit in this either,' I replied.

Rob turned back to my mother: 'We can do better with chemicals,' he insisted.

The meeting ended shortly after. Mum and I looked at one another. Damned if we do, damned if we don't. A crazy notion popped into my head.

'I need the land for my next film,' I said, 'but I need it to look natural, not like a farm. The money I'll save on location costs will be more than we'll make this year. If we leave the land alone, it'll have time to recover. It might have more nutrients after a break from grazing and I'll have a set for my film.' She wasn't convinced, so I edged closer and used my best manipulation and guilt tactics.

'Do you want me to do well in my work?'

'Of course, my love,' she said. 'More than anything.'

'Then let's take a year off from animal farming. Two at most. We're vegan now, anyway. I'll shoot my film, the land will recover and we can think about another approach to the organic when it's done.'

I had her. Mum would have died to make me happy and for me to stay with her. I also knew she feared chemical farming. She suspected Dad's condition had been caused by chemicals. She was in. We'd lose some money but the animals weren't making us that much in any case. The rest of the land was still leased and would still provide an income.

A few days later, I told Rob we were beginning a new day at Dunsany and would be removing animal agriculture from the land for the foreseeable future. He looked at me like I'd lost my mind.

'Well, what are you going do with the land?'

'We're going to leave it to nature.'

'You what?'

'Leave it to nature,' I repeated.

Rob studied me for a moment before edging in close and whispering, 'Is this some sort of tax dodge?'

'Nope, not a tax dodge. We're going to let the land recover naturally.'

'But you can't! The land will be destroyed. The weeds will be bigger than the castle! You won't be able to walk the fields.'

Rob was literally in shock as I calmly informed him we'd made up our minds.

'But the ragwort will take over!'

I wasn't listening.

Before long, the last of the animals were gone. I stood looking out across the bare fields, free of domestic animals for the first time in a long time, maybe a hundred years. I wandered through them, greeted only by the sounds of the crows flying above. I felt like I was walking on the moon.

The fields that had previously been left fallow for some time were already beginning to change as the plants reclaimed them. There was no more bellowing, no more churning of the ground to mud by the cattle's hooves. No more anguished screams from sheep and cattle as the little ones were separated from their mothers and they were all left to cry out their pain until they realised that there was no way back and just gave up.

To these we added all the forested areas and the rest of the land known as 'the park' – the fields surrounding the castle. The forested areas had previously been heavily managed, with every fallen tree removed, every slight change monitored and interfered with. Now we just left them to their own devices. My employees thought we'd lost our minds, but were also happy to have less work, particularly as our workforce had dwindled since Dad's death.

Where Mum had tried to put her own stamp on Dunsany by renovating parts of the castle and the outlying properties, now I was going to put my own stamp on it by allowing the land to do its own thing. In the immediate term, there'd be a painful drop in the estate's income. In the long term, who knew? There was no obvious way to monetise over six hundred acres being left alone. This was a gamble, but it felt right. I couldn't really be vegan and profit from the slaughter of animals. I couldn't make a movie about nature and not listen to it.

The moment spring came, change started happening quickly. It was as if all this time nature had been waiting in the wings for an invitation to the party. The first year, I walked the land every day, watching the grass grow. I wanted to understand what was happening because I hoped to use this knowledge in making *Origami*.

I became curious about the plants I saw. Before, most of them had been scruffy, anonymous weeds to me. I'd never given them even a moment's thought. Now I used my camera phone to photograph them, and I learned their names and how they fitted into the complexities of the natural environment. Every picture I took led to a journey of discovery that never once disappointed me and almost always led me down dozens of delightful tangents. How could I not have realised before that every plant – no matter how small, no matter how apparently humble – had its own story and played its own important part in the bigger picture of nature? Why had nobody ever told me that each plant is much more than just one singular entity, but actually a little world, with its own inhabitants, its own natural cycle throughout the seasons?

Like everyone else, I'd long been used to thinking of plants as being divided into 'weeds' and 'useful plants'. Weeds were to be pulled out, cut down, rooted out, destroyed. They strangled the plants we wanted to see live – the *good* plants – while themselves contributing nothing. Now, undisturbed, the plants I'd been used to thinking of as weeds grew taller, thicker, stronger. They pushed out leaves and flowers and on them caterpillars, wool carder bees, earwigs and countless others grew and thrived.

The insects – oh boy, I'd never seen so many! The fields that had once had just horseflies were now filled with all kinds of winged species I couldn't even identify. I'd never thought very much about any of these tiny creatures before, but now I realised that when you take the time to look, each is utterly extraordinary in its own unique way.

I began to query why we even use the word 'weeds'. Referring to a plant as a 'weed' is a value judgement. It says the plant in question is a pest, with no purpose or place in the world. Something to eliminate. 'Weeds' were often referred to as invasive. Yet as I read, I realised these plants weren't alien to the land. They were native. Native but 'invasive'? How is that possible? 'Native' means they should exist in our ecosystem as part of a delicate balance.

The more I read, the more I realised that every single plant – no matter how scruffy, no matter how apparently unimportant – plays a significant role in the environment. Each interacts with the others around it. Each is also a tiny ecosystem, supporting insects that will, in turn, support bird and bat populations. Remove just one species, and the entire system goes out of balance.

The summer of that first year came and began to settle in. The grass grew long. It flowered and seeded. Butterflies – more than I'd ever seen before – started to fly above it. As I walked, observing the changes happening right outside the castle, gradually I started to notice something else. Birdsong! It suddenly seemed so *loud*. On summer evenings I'd walk and watch the tiny birds shoot over the wild grass as they grabbed insects in the air. These were swallows. We'd had a few before, but not like this. They flew in waves, circling and then dropping. Where had they all come from? I heard the pheasants too. They seemed to love the newly long grass. As I crossed the meadow, they'd leap up and fly away. It was fabulous.

A consequence of leaving the grass that year was that, as it grew taller and taller, the castle seemed to get smaller. Less intimidating, too. For as long as I could remember there'd been a knot of resentment in my belly because I felt trapped in a life I hadn't chosen and that didn't seem to fit me. That knot had started to loosen now. I began to feel something new. Optimism? Hope? It had been so long since I'd been happy. Had I *ever* been truly happy? I struggled to find the words for what I was feeling.

Summer ended and the wet months followed. The once-tall grass began to fall on itself, making the grasslands look like a green sea. That wet autumn ushered in a chilly winter; the grass began to break down into the ground, forming a lush green carpet with big, lumpy clumps. Now came the deer to feast on all the uneaten grass. I continued to walk daily, observing all these subtle and non-subtle changes. I felt like a young baby whose first experiences are touching and observing the new world around them. That's exactly what I was doing too.

By the second year, *Origami* hadn't advanced enough, so I told my mother: 'One more year.' So one more year it was. She liked not seeing strange vehicles or men walking the fields, as she had when we were farming, as she was understandably anxious about strangers who might be examining the castle with a view to breaking in. And as the view from the castle changed, she admitted she found it lovely. She was more comfortable and relaxed. I was too.

By now, anyone could see there'd been a massive increase in the number of birds. I started observing buzzards fly overhead in considerable numbers. Before, I'd only ever seen one, on its own. Now there were several flying together and getting into fights with the crows.

Ragwort, thistles, ground elder, yarrow, dandelion, vetch, clover and more grew higher than I'd ever seen them before, reaching up proudly towards the pale Irish sun as though they knew I'd declared a truce. I continued to walk the land. It was a daily pilgrimage to my family's past and to my present and my as-yet-unwritten future. It was a way to escape Mum, whose huge emotional needs in the wake of Dad's death filled me with guilt and made me resent her. It was a scroll that unfurled endlessly, showing me the cast of millions of living beings, each one working so hard every day to stay alive and to create the next generation, living in and on the estate.

I walked early in the morning when the birds were waking and starting the dawn chorus. At that time of day, a strong but not unpleasant smell seemed to hang suspended over the grass. It was the scent of badgers, which have a number of scent glands that they use to communicate within and between badger communities, all-important messages about territory, identity and finding a mate.

I walked in the middle of the day when the land lay exposed under sun, cloudy skies or falling rain. I might see far above me the trails left by airplanes, while below, the long grass rustled with animals. I often disturbed rabbits going about their business. Sometimes they paused to watch me with their big brown eyes, their whiskers twitching worriedly as they tried to ascertain whether or not I meant them harm.

I walked in the evening as the sun started to slip down to the horizon, when the night insects rose, the birds grumbled and chirruped as they settled to sleep and the flittering, dark shapes of bats could be seen against the deep blue or grey of the darkening sky while they hunted for insects.

Often I walked for hours, around and around the same routes, as I realised that every time in the day, every shift or change in the climate, every time one season slid into another, I was experiencing different things. I was being told a new part of the story. My walks became longer and longer as my love for Dunsany deepened and grew and I saw nature changing all around me.

Ragwort has a tall green stalk that supports frilled leaves and bustles with bright-yellow flowers, the colour of the sun. As the spring turned into summer, those stalks would fill with moving creatures. The most striking were the orange and black caterpillars that swarmed over the plants like a tiny, tiger-striped army, devouring the leaves with single-minded purpose. Earnestly, the cinnabar caterpillars inched their way along the ragwort stalks, munching and growing until they were ready to move into the next stage of their development. These were the juvenile cinnabar moths, which would spend the winter as pupae and emerge the next year to spread their red and dark grey wings and lay their eggs on a new generation of ragwort.

Everyone in Ireland with a connection to the land is taught to hate and fear ragwort. A native plant, it's identified as a pest and treated as if it were invasive. This is because the plant is toxic if consumed by some animal species, notably cattle, which are a staple of the Irish agricultural industry, as well as horses, goats and various others. Some of these animals seem to instinctively realise this, and tend to avoid it, but horses – to which it's extremely toxic – find it appealing. The plant is particularly dangerous when dried, so if it gets into hay intended as feed, farmers have a problem.

Two very powerful lobbies, the beef and the horse-racing industries, have campaigned against ragwort for years. Under Irish law, it's illegal to allow ragwort to spread, so landowners are required to eliminate it. Every summer there are angry letters in the Irish newspapers about how this law is unenforced, even on state land, because ragwort – again, *a native plant that's naturally endemic to Ireland* – will grow almost anywhere. It flourishes alongside motorways and national roads, its bold clusters of yellow flowers making an ass of the law.

Ragwort, like every other plant that naturally occurs in a given landscape, isn't 'bad'. It's an integral part of an area's biodiversity, and home to a variety of species for which it's not toxic, but essential to life. So long as it's left in its natural condition, most of the animals to which it represents a threat recognise it as hostile and leave it alone: the real risk comes when we interfere with it as an element of animal husbandry.

When I first started letting the ragwort do its thing undisturbed, plenty of people said I'd regret it, because after a few years there'd be nothing *but* ragwort. Our agricultural workers and all the farmers I knew had warned that it would 'take over', would 'ruin the land'. I was warned to watch out because the council might fine me and the penalties could be large. In that second year, I worried I'd made a grievous error. The ragwort *was* dominating quickly. The green grass was bursting with it. I couldn't afford a fine, especially as the rewilding was already costing us income. If we were fined, there was no way we could continue.

People said the only way to avoid a fine and absolute chaos was to kill the ragwort with a chemical spray. Everyone said the land needed to be proactively managed and that if it wasn't I'd eventually have to spend a fortune to fix it. They often pointed out that Ireland, like most places, had been intensively farmed for generations, and what might look like a wild landscape is actually anything but. The implication was that nature had already been interfered with in so many ways, it no longer knew how to cope on its own.

In response to all this fear-mongering, particularly from neighbouring farmers, Mum was very concerned. We'd started to argue about whether I'd made a mistake. I needed to do something. I was mindful that all the farmers advising us had years of farming experience, and I didn't. I knew that one might argue I'd no business getting involved in something that, with my sheltered existence, I'd no experience of. That perhaps I should just stay in my lane. But I'm naturally stubborn and increasingly felt that nature was a force far superior to any mere human and didn't need to be coddled by us, her children.

The naysayers were often older farmers who referred to crows and foxes as 'vermin' and shot them on sight. They used chemicals without wearing protective masks. But they were right in saying that if I didn't do something about the ragwort there was a very good chance the council would fine me.

Pondering this dilemma, I went for a walk in the walled garden, built in Victorian times. This was where Denis Toomey, our oldest employee, worked. Denis was at least the third or fourth generation of his family to have worked at Dunsany.

He'd lived his whole life in one of the estate cottages, without even electricity or running water until Dad returned. When Dad sought to rectify the situation, Denis hadn't been impressed.

'I don't need it,' Denis had said.

'You don't need running water?' Dad had protested, 'Where do you get a glass of water?'

'The ditch,' he'd responded.

Dad had supplied Denis's place with water and electricity, but I can't be sure he ever stopped drinking from the ditch. He was old-school like that. He was in his mid-eighties now. Although he'd officially retired, he never stopped coming. Dad had held him in very high regard.

Denis – an elderly, thin man now – was dressed in an old farmer-style blazer, the sort of thing you'd see in period films, and he was caked from head to toe in earth and grime. I called out and he turned in surprise. After exchanging some pleasantries, I got him to sit down and take five minutes from the watering to chat. Nervously, he did. He'd grown up when employees wouldn't make eye contact with the head of the household. I explained my predicament regarding the ragwort, hoping to gain some insight. As an old-timer, I thought he'd have some tricks up his sleeve.

I often struggled to understand Denis. He spoke very quietly, with the thickest accent I've ever heard. An old-fashioned accent from the nineteenth century. Denis explained that ragwort had always been a problem in Dunsany.

'What would you do about it before chemicals became a thing?' I asked.

He smiled. 'We'd pull it.'

I paused a moment, hoping he'd elaborate.

'Come again?' I asked.

He looked at me as if I'd two heads: 'We'd *pull* it!'

I felt like a man on a quest who'd visited an oracle for guidance and had it now. To beat this beautiful yellow flower menace, I had to pull it.

I moved into the castle. If I was going to war, I'd need tools and weapons – in this case, my trusty headphones and some workman's gloves. The first was easily found but the second was more troublesome. After much digging in our toolshed, I found one lonely glove with a hole in it. I smelled it; it reeked. I tossed it away in disgust. I couldn't pull over a thousand ragwort with bare hands; I needed something. I wasn't going to bring a knife to a gun fight.

In search of my car keys I went into the kitchen, thinking I'd have to drive to town to buy workman's gloves. Clearly, as the Plunketts had only a singular workman's glove, we weren't used to manual labour. Then I spotted a glow of pink. I moved to the sink and retrieved a pair of pink washing-up gloves. The Plunkett family may not be great with manual labour, but we do know how to wash dishes to a reasonable standard. Pink, though? Really?

I arrived at the entrance to the front field, glancing across the two hundred acres of meadow. The yellow ragwort bounced in the wind as the butterflies hovered over them, as if they were dancing. Like a soldier about to charge at his enemy, I braced myself, pulling on the pink washing-up gloves that contrasted attractively with my black Behemoth band shirt.

I peered again at the vast landscape, flicked my headphones over my ears and moved in. I attacked, pulling ragwort aggressively. My arms flooded with blood and heat as I yanked and yanked. From a distance, I must have looked like a bent-over rice farmer as I toiled. Hours passed and finally I stood and peered across the planes of grass. I'd barely made a dent.

Walking home, I considered the situation. I decided I could win this battle. I'd just have to make it part of my day, every day. It'd be my new ritual, as the walks had become and the origami had been before that. I figured I'd pull fifty a day and thus clear two hundred acres of grass in a month. I contented myself with the thought that, by the end of the summer, I'd have such great biceps I'd drive the women wild. I spent the rest of summer pulling ragwort. My employees shook their heads as I trotted off each afternoon in my ridiculous gloves.

'You'll never win,' they said.

'Don't be so sure!' I replied.

My employees were right. I was fighting nature and nature was on the high ground. I pulled fifty a day and returned the following to find that, like magic, there were more growing in their place. I felt as though I was fighting nature itself. I doubled down, refusing to be beaten by a yellow flower. The more I pulled, the more they came.

By the end of that summer, I was beaten. The meadows looked as though I'd done nothing at all. My biceps were indeed well buffed but, as nobody was interested in seeing them, despite all that work I'd achieved nothing.

The following year, year three, I choose to simply wait until the council sent me a shitty letter. Year three was a disaster. The ragwort seemed to have doubled. I began wondering whether my original view, that a native plant would never dominate beyond nature's ability to contain it, was simply wrong. By year four, there was almost nothing *but* ragwort.

I comforted myself with the thought that if the council went looking for it with satellite images or drones, they'd see so much yellow they'd assume I was growing rapeseed. Then year five came and something miraculous happened. The ragwort seemed to have declined. Now there were just cases of it in the field, here and there. By year six, the ragwort had vanished completely. All this had happened without intervention. After that first year, I'd given up trying to pull them, and we'd never used any pesticide. So what had dispatched these native 'invasive' plants?

Every day, I was watching the changes occurring in the rewilded areas. I'd noticed a few things whose significance would become clearer later. The ragwort seemed to grow most readily on the harder, more compressed land. I'd observed that huge, thick clumps of it sprouted where there'd been mud, where water sat on the surface of the meadows. When I first started thinking about the ragwort, I'd looked closely at the flowers and buds. Then I'd started looking at what was happening on and below the ground. Back in year one, when I was still trying to pull it out, I'd admired the plant's thick roots. Looking even more closely, I could see that the ragwort was actually loosening the soil. The plant was so exuberant, it seemed to be almost bursting from the ground, as if trying to break free.

Now that the cattle were gone, areas that had once been mud pools were disappearing beneath the ragwort and thistles. Like the ragwort, the thistles seemed to grow mostly where soil had been disturbed and compressed. Their roots also broke up the soil, revealing cracks in the hardened ground into which water could disappear, bringing oxygen with it.

I was fascinated by these changes. They were subtle enough that the casual passerby wouldn't notice them, but I'd discovered a secret garden beneath my feet. Now that I'd begun to really look at the soil and consider what was happening and why, I was full of questions. I turned to books and the internet to learn more about what I was seeing. My mind was blown one night when I encountered a compelling scientific discovery, the concept of mycelium. The very word sent shockwaves through my body as I mouthed it aloud. *What the hell is mycelium?* I wondered. *It sounds like the name of a villain from* Doctor Who.

Mycelium is the complex network of fungi and their root-like structures that connects living plants and trees in the ground. It's often referred to as the 'wood wide web', and is the connective tissue that binds networks together and allows plants to communicate, among other things. The mycelium network is composed of the billions of tiny threads of fungus that stretch everywhere underground; the parts of fungi we see above ground are only a tiny percentage of the fungal organism. I learned that mycelium was a massive piece of the puzzle I'd discovered, and I'd learn a lot more about it as the years passed.

As the wild plants of Dunsany grew and grew, there was a huge increase in the numbers of caterpillars and other creatures living on the flowers and leaves. These insects are extremely attractive to birds, which started to colonise Dunsany in greater numbers and to breed successfully. Many, of course, also ate fruits and seeds from plants on and off the estate, and now they were dropping them, along with their excrement, all over the grasslands. With the newly hospitable environment created by the ragwort and thistles, it was easy for the seeds of other wild plants to gain purchase, and other species started to grow.

The grass, once very uniform, was beginning to develop an assortment of colours and textures, thanks to the flowering micro-plants peppered among it. Over the next few years, the number and variety of wild flowers and grasses increased. The ragwort didn't seem to mind; there was more than enough space for everybody. And as the grasses grew taller and more intense, the ragwort began to recede.

In Irish tradition, ragwort is associated with the fairies and with hidden pots of gold. I'd like to think that this is a way of admitting how important it is to our ecosystem. Another old legend said that gold had been buried somewhere in Dunsany back in Cromwellian times. I told you earlier no one ever found it, but perhaps the *real* gold was something else: the bright yellow of the ragwort, which grew without end and generously opened up the soil to other species.

Particularly in the evenings, the area above the plants filled with flying things and with the many little noises that they make. Now, when I waded through the thick grass, clouds of insects rose around me. It felt like being caught in a tornado of insects as they swirled around me in circles. Mum followed me out one evening and fled, as many of the insects seemed to find her very tasty.

'I haven't seen so many insects since I was a child in Brazil,' she said.

As she speed-walked away, waving her hands to keep them from attacking her, I couldn't help myself: 'City slickers don't belong in nature,' I called back. I continued my stroll, watching as the tiny bug-bodies glinted and shone in the light.

So as not to crush any more grass than necessary, I started to follow the same route day after day, carefully facing today's steps into the path forged by yesterday's walk until I'd made a single-file route that took me all around the land as I watched it transform. One of the most obvious of the major changes was the dramatic difference in the number and variety of bird species on the land. For so long, we mostly saw only the crows, many of which roosted in the old church. There were a few other types of birds, but we hadn't seen or heard them very often. Now the calls of the crows were overwhelmed by the sound of songbirds.

The day of Dad's funeral, as the prayers for the dead were intoned over his grave, the church crows had joined in, as though they missed him too. Now even the church had become home to a more disparate population. Gradually, I started learning how to identify them: barn owls, snipe, warblers, sparrowhawks, red kites, corncrakes and even peregrine falcons.

The bat population started to rebound dramatically too. As if they'd been waiting for this opportunity for years, more and more bats seemed to arrive and to establish themselves in the trees, outhouses and old buildings on the estate. As the sun set every evening, out they came, dancing across the night sky in a silent aerial ballet.

People are taught to hate bats and to regard them as ugly, but I'd defy anyone who's spent an hour or two watching them swooping and diving against an Irish sunset not to warm to them. They're so graceful, and work so hard to feed themselves and their families, it's impossible not to accept them as another wonderful form of life that should be loved and cherished.

People are often nervous at the thought of bats' nests, which are often found in and around houses and other buildings. They rarely pause to consider that one of the reasons why bats choose buildings to live in is because the natural environment has been so altered by industrialisation, intensive farming and the destruction of forests that they don't always have a choice.

I wondered what might happen next. How far could I go? At first, I'd assumed this might be a way to fix the land without chemicals and perhaps make a movie in the process, but what was happening now was something else. I started wondering if my accidental discovery might hold a cure to some of the destruction and ecological collapse of the modern world. Was the magic I was observing a cure for the human destruction of nature? And could I even say that I'd 'discovered' it, when perhaps it was really nature communicating with someone who'd not been able to hear her for years?

Whatever the answer, I was certainly listening now.

Chapter Six

Every Little Life

CHANGE IS SCARY. IT CAN ALIENATE FAMILIES, DESTROY RELATIONSHIPS AND EVEN CAUSE WARS. For the longest time, I boasted I'd *never* change. Why? Because I'm a product of my nature, my upbringing and, of course, our family traditions. But *not* changing is dangerous too. It means you can't adapt, progress, or envision any way other than your own. In turn, this means you can't grow.

In nature, things that cease growing start declining. Look what happens to the human body as we age: we peak when our bodies are no longer developing and begin the transition into decline. It's the same with plants, and with society too. Modern media bombards us with news about the breakdown of the western world. Our society is declining as the pendulum shifts from parts of the world that have dominated for aeons.

I was starting to understand that many of my assumptions were probably untrue. I could see how society was destroying itself by embracing false information, with hubris and by failing to understand nature's resourcefulness. As I questioned everything I'd always believed, I wondered how we'd all remained blind for so long.

It's not clear where the Dunsany deer originated. One theory is that they came with the Ward Union Hunt, which allowed deer to escape from their lands and settle here. Others believe they were simply always here; that's what Dad thought. They're all native red deer, with no apparent hybrids and none of the fallow deer introduced to Ireland in Norman times, or the sika, which came in the nineteenth century. For as long as I could remember, the population had oscillated between about thirty and about sixty. Our deer had always been regarded by the farmers who rented our land as vermin to be exterminated. They ate crops and flattened areas of planted fields where they slept. When my grandfather was in charge, the farmers shot them or allowed local stag hunters to do so. Nobody paid any attention to firearm safety, and many of the hunters weren't skilled marksmen. Often they failed to kill them and wounded deer were left to flee in fear.

Now, every time the deer numbers soared, we heard plenty about it, including threats from our farm tenant to stop paying rent until the problem was under control. In fact, for years we'd employed someone to cull the deer. Peter was a hunting and fishing specialist who worked as a contractor and in tourism. He'd spent his whole life holding a gun and organising events for hunters. He was an excellent marksman. We'd met him in the early 2000s when Killeen Castle – our neighbouring castle, once home to a branch of the family – had been purchased by a hotel group.

As I said before, back in 1981 Killeen had been burned down by nationalist extremists aggravated by what was happening in Northern Ireland. Thankfully, as that side of the family had died out, the castle was empty and nobody was hurt. During the Celtic Tiger years of the late 1990s and early 2000s, Irish appetites for luxury grew. The new owners of Killeen converted it into a high-end golf course with luxury accommodation. They wanted to offer elite sporting experiences, so they hired Peter to manage fishing on the various artificial ponds they created and to locate local hunting opportunities.

One day, when Dad was still alive, Peter arrived at Dunsany to discuss the possibility of a joint hunting experience between Dunsany and Killeen. We were desperate for money, needing to develop revenue streams that would enable us to fix our leaky roof. As we got to know Peter, we were impressed by his knowledge of nature, farming and the world in general. We became friends. But before any of the proposed ventures could bear fruit, the recession hit and Killeen fell into the hands of NAMA (the National Asset Management Agency), a government department that absorbed failing properties and businesses. As the hotel was still unfinished and golfers were cancelling their memberships, Peter was let go. Instead, he'd taken over as the gamekeeper for several large farms and estates.

At this time, Dad's health was failing and we were starting to lose control of the estate. Our farming tenant was becoming increasingly agitated, in particular about the deer. Peter could see we were struggling, and stepped in to help. Refusing pay, he said he'd cover his costs with the deer he shot. Thus, he'd become an intermediary between us and the farmer, who'd have liked every deer in the county to be killed.

Instead, Peter studied the herd carefully. By strategically killing weak or sickly deer he could manage the numbers and keep the deer healthy. As he knew what he was doing, we no longer had to see terrified, wounded deer running across the fields. Although Peter's approach was successful, and I personally respected him immensely, I abhorred the idea of killing such majestic animals, even before going vegan. Then the farmer said he wanted *all* the deer to go, and once more threatened to stop paying rent. How far did he expect us to go?

We were dealing with another threat too: poachers. When Dad got sick and the management started to slide, every local poacher had taken this as a green light to invade again. Peter often encountered would-be poachers and scared them off. He knew many of the local gunmen, and had contacts in the police, so, for a while, his presence scared many of them away. Then the recession had come and, just when lots of people were trying to raise extra cash, the price of venison soared. Now there were so many poachers Peter could no longer manage the situation on his own.

Back before Dad's death, Mum encouraged me to join Peter's patrols, which usually took place before dawn at the weekends and on Friday evenings. We encountered big pick-ups parked at our farm gates, full of camouflage-clad men peering at deer through binoculars. Many fled when our vehicle approached and slowed down, but others were cheekier. We'd roll up to them, wind down our windows and ask what they were doing.

'You're not planning on shooting any deer here, are you?' Peter would ask.

They'd get defensive and say they were just looking. Once in a while someone would claim: 'Sure, we have permission.'

'Permission? Really?' Peter would ask in an innocent tone. 'Who gave you that?'

'The lord.'

'The lord,' Peter would repeat. 'Lord Dunsany?'

'Yeah, him.'

'Right, interesting . . .' Then he'd turn to me and ask. 'Your Dad give them permission?'

I usually responded like someone in a Bruce Willis movie: 'The *fuck* he did!'

At this point, most poachers cursed us to hell before making themselves scarce. These rare moments made driving around in circles at dawn worth it because I discovered something about myself: I enjoy annoying idiots.

But now that the deer were so valuable, Peter was under siege, and even with me helping he couldn't cope. He lived in Kildare and couldn't be here as regularly as he'd have liked. The poachers became more audacious. They'd come at night, shoot a deer, and ram our gates open. One night they shot a stag near the castle, climbed over our bordering stone wall, tied the stag with rope and pulled it across the field from the road, toppling part of the wall in the process. Peter and I intensified our patrols. As we caught more people in the act, they became increasingly aggressive. They sought retribution through vandalism. Gates were destroyed, locks were glued, garbage was dumped at our gate, and sometimes they even hung animal remains on our gates.

The fact that we were also sometimes complicit in killing these beautiful wild animals, just because they were a little inconvenient, troubled me. Why was I fighting so hard against poaching, only to have Peter shoot the weaker deer later on? The deer were a native species, and yet they were out of control.

How could that be? They had no predator, so what would happen if we let them be? Would the entire world be destroyed by deer? Would ecosystems collapse? Would the deer destroy their habitats as locusts do, as we do? Would nature go up in flames? Then I became a vegan, and having the deer killed became unbearable.

'What if we just left the deer alone?' I wondered aloud to Peter. 'If we stopped culling them and waited to see what happened next?'

He smiled, as he always did. Peter was a good sport who never put me down, no matter how outrageous some of my notions. 'Nature needs to be managed,' he said. 'We no longer have a predator to keep nature's wheels turning. There are no wolves left in Ireland.'

I nodded. He was right. Irish wolves, like so many Irish humans, were the victims of Cromwell's brutal rule. While Cromwell sent many of the native Irish 'to hell or to Connacht', he had the wolves dispatched straight to hell. As part of his programme to tame the island, he imported professional wolf-hunters and paid bounties for wolf-kills, leading to the systematic destruction of a species that, while it may have been frightening, was crucial to native biodiversity.

Now, as the estate rewilded, I started to read a little about deer and learned something new, though perhaps it should have been obvious. Grazing animals like deer are essential to rewilding, because when they consume plants and grasses, they also ingest seeds, and they deposit these seeds widely in their dung, as well as carrying pollens, spores and seeds in their fur. I returned to pondering the idea of nature as an intricate web requiring disturbances and reactions to function correctly. Our land at Dunsany was missing certain critical forces to keep the system balanced, so what would happen if we allowed it to be overrun by deer? If we let chaos unfold, would there be no biodiversity? Would nature be unable to survive without our help?

When I first told Rob we weren't going to farm animals any more, he'd responded very dramatically, and all his farming colleagues had agreed with him. They said the land would be destroyed and it would cost a fortune to get it back into a decent state. Lifelong farmers, their way was how it'd always been and they were also sure it was the way it *should* be. Anything else was heresy. When I told Peter, I expected a slightly different reaction, as he spent a lot of his life immersed in nature.

Peter smiled gently. 'Well,' he said, 'the grass will become completely tangled and will render the land useless in the future. Nature isn't what it once was. It needs us to keep it running now. We need to simulate the predators there once were, and the grass needs to be grazed or the ragwort will take over. When you revert to farming, the land will probably require a lot of interventions to make it healthy again.'

While Rob's views had not deterred me, my heart sank at Peter's. I regarded him as a mentor. But still, I was determined to see the rewilding through. Much as I respected Peter, I refused to believe that our arrogance as a species spoke the truth: that nature needed us to function. How could the greater forces of nature depend on our primitive species?

The first four years of rewilding came and went. Everything Peter had warned against had happened, but he never spoke of it. Even as the ragwort and other weeds grew past our shoulders, I'd catch him watching the fields with keen interest. One day I found Peter in front of the castle. He hadn't rung the bell; he was just standing in the shoulder-high grass. I approached him with curiosity and stood next to him. First he just shook his head. I was expecting a flurry of comments about what I should be doing to avoid any further destruction of the land.

'You've created quite a paradise here,' Peter said instead.

'What do you mean by that?' I asked.

He continued eyeing the birds flying over the grass, grabbing insects. 'I'd forgotten what wild land looked like. I haven't seen it since I was a young boy.'

I nodded as we both watched the butterflies fluttering above the grass. 'What are you up to today?'

'Just keeping an eye on the herd.'

I took a deep breath. 'I don't want to cull the deer any more,' I said.

'The farmer's been on to me,' Peter said. 'He wants us to kill more this season.'

I looked at him in surprise. Hadn't he heard me? After a moment I asked: 'How many have you killed this year?'

Peter shrugged. 'None.'

'None! But you've been here loads.'

'Yeah, I've been watching them.'

'He's gonna go bananas if you tell him that.'

'So I *won't* tell him. Don't worry; I'll just show him this.' Peter pulled out his phone and showed me a picture of about eight dead deer, lined up on the ground.

'Did you kill those here?'

'Nah, that's from a previous year.'

I stood and watched Peter. I'd known him for many years. It wasn't like him to be so candid about his job. He put his phone back in his pocket and turned to me.

'Has he paid his rent in full this year?' Peter asked.

I shook my head.

'Well, if he doesn't do what he's supposed to, neither will I. The herd needs a break anyway; the land is doing well with them. Besides who's gonna eat all this grass?'

Peter added that while the deer numbers were increasing dramatically, they were also finding plenty to eat in the reserve, as the grass and other plants had been left to grow wild and therefore had less interest in fields of crops.

Peter and I had never had a conversation like this before. The land wasn't the only thing changing around me.

At that moment Mum interrupted us. She uttered some pleasantries, commenting on how handsome and healthy Peter was looking. He laughed, saying that he was being looked after by a woman who'd been feeding him vegetables.

'She's like you,' he chuckled. 'One of them vegans. She has me eating chickpeas instead of steak; and some other thing, quinoa. It's not that bad.'

Peter never shot another deer at Dunsany. And since then, Dunsany has been a sanctuary for all animals. A place where they can live their lives to their fullest, from birth to death, doing exactly what nature had always intended for them.

Unfortunately, even as nature rebounded, I didn't succeed with my film *Origami*. It became harder and harder to make the pieces fit. The horror genre had taken a downturn since my last short, and financiers were looking for something different. So I folded my last origami and put it into a drawer, at least for now. But I had a new project, a film, one that would be personal to my discovery of nature.

At the end of summer 2017, I began preparing the groundwork for my first feature film, *The Green Sea*. After various mishaps – investors pulling out and the turmoil of trying to make a bid-scoped movie with a fraction of the budget required – I felt like a zombie. My friends and producers – Stephen Lourdes, Helen Serruya and Edwina Forkin – and I were scrambling to get the production together for a winter shooting schedule. We'd managed to secure our lead actress, Katharine Isabelle – a well-known Canadian actress – for a short window for the last two months of the year. We'd have to rush the preparation for the film as after that Katherine would be tied to a TV series in Canada for another year and we'd lose our shooting window.

The story was about a lost writer who is falling down a cycle of self-destruction and finds solace in nature. Well, I had the nature at the reserve, but I needed some urban locations to contrast with the rugged Irish countryside at Dunsany. Nothing local seemed to fit, so I began to search further afield, first in Kildare and then Westmeath, where I'd never been before. The biggest town there was Mullingar, so I set my Google maps and started to drive.

I cruised along a bumpy road through rugged, boggy fields and distant spruce forests, relaxing and enjoying the hour-long drive, listening to my new CD, Shining's *Everyone, Everything, Everywhere, Ends*. The music fit my mood as I travelled along windy roads and finally emerged onto a pristine motorway leading into the town. As I approached, I could see that Mullingar had an interesting aesthetic, with large, ghostly church towers in the distance. I parked and wandered along the main street. After some sightseeing, I decided to stop for a coffee and answer messages and phone calls about film-related issues.

Just off the main street, I found a quaint café. I ordered and sat down. As I typed emails, I saw a slim, attractive young woman sitting at the far side of the coffee shop. She had bright blue eyes, high cheekbones and beautiful long blonde hair. She wore a smart outfit and sat in front of an open laptop, indicating that she was some sort of professional. I glanced over and caught her gaze. She smiled and so did I before awkwardly turning back to my phone. A few minutes later, paying the lady at the till, I turned to the young woman, who seemed to be pondering what she was going to write.

'Writing your memoirs?' I asked.

She turned, caught off-guard by the randomness of the comment. She smiled and laughed gently. 'Hardly,' she said. 'Car insurance.'

'Sounds like you're living the life of Reilly,' I replied.

She laughed gently again. 'Are you busy at work?' she asked, pointing at my phone, which was ringing.

I cancelled the call and turned back to her with a smile. 'Work? I'm trying to skive.'

'What sort of work do you do?'

'Can't you tell from the air of desperation? Filmmaker. How about yourself?'

'I'm an OT.'

I'm sure my face showed I'd no idea what that was.

'Occupational therapist,' she added quickly.

'Right, of course, occupational therapist, love those. . . So you give people . . . career advice or something?' I asked.

She burst into laughter: 'No, I work with people with autism to help them get the support and services they need.'

'Oh.' Embarrassment washed over me like a wave. I could feel my face turning red. She closed her laptop and leant back into her chair.

'So what are you doing in Mullingar?'

I smiled and told her why I was scouting the place and what I was looking for. Her face lit up as she started describing various potential locations. Seeing her enthusiasm, I wondered if I could consult her later on, and asked for her number. I left the coffee shop with the promise of a meeting the following Saturday.

The week dragged by.

Laura and I agreed to meet in town so she could show me all the unique spots. To my surprise, this small town had a lot. As we walked from bar to coffee shop to mini-gallery, I admired her delicate features and her grace. We decided to have dinner together and she suggested a fantastic Asian place, Mekong, where she often went with her friends. I warned her I was vegan, which took her by surprise. She said she'd been a vegetarian since the age of twelve. Some of her family members owned slaughterhouses and her stance on animals was bit of a hot potato with her extended family. I understood only too well, as my family had farmed animals for generations. I told her I'd created a vegan sanctuary in County Meath, where once my family had raised animals for slaughter. Conversation flowed as we ate our tofu.

I didn't want the night to end. I walked Laura home and to her door. We stood at her doorstep, agreeing to meet again soon. From the window, a little face popped out from behind a curtain; a small girl of about five. Laura saw us looking at each other, and waved the child over. The door opened on a charming little angel who approached, peering up at me.

'This is my daughter Catherine,' Laura laughed. Catherine ran towards her mother, hugging her leg. I could see that she was a bubbly, friendly child. I'd never been very good at talking to kids. I don't know why, but they'd always made me feel awkward. But I knelt and introduced myself to the little girl. To my surprise, she politely shook my hand and smiled.

'Time to go to bed,' Laura said. She turned back to me to say goodbye.

'Perhaps the next time we can all go out for a day trip?' I asked.

Laura paused and studied me for a moment.

'You don't have to . . .'

'I'd *love* to,' I said, cutting her off. We agreed to meet again the next week and go for a day trip to a local stately home and gardens. A week later, the three of us explored the gardens together.

I felt a new sensation of tenderness. Laura and her daughter Catherine just seemed to fit, as though we'd always been meant to be together. At the end of the day Catherine gave me one of her own drawings to say thank you for having such a fun time.

As a relationship blossomed between Laura and me, the film-making was drawing closer and I was highly stressed. Whenever I was with Laura and Catherine I could escape the problems of work and of Dunsany, but I also knew that soon I'd have to introduce Laura to my mother.

When Laura came to Dunsany for the first time, she was amazed by the castle, but much more enamoured by the rewilding and by our walled garden, which she thought the most beautiful place she'd seen. To my delight, she and my mother got on. Mum could see how happy I was with her, and was impressed by how caring and sensitive she was. Eventually it was time for Laura to leave, so she said goodbye and drove off.

'She's very beautiful,' Mum said. But before I could react, my phone started ringing.

It was Laura. She was frantic when I answered: 'I've just seen poachers leaving your land with pheasants!'

'Where are you?' I asked.

'I'm following them. They've ducked down a lonely track.'

'Be careful! Don't go after them. They could be dangerous.'

I rushed to help. The poachers made a few excuses when I arrived. As there was no evidence the birds they'd shot were from Dunsany there was nothing I could do. As they flipped us off and drove away, Laura showed me a photo on her phone. 'I got their licence,' she said. 'You should tell the guards for next time.'

Laura left and I went home. Mum was at the door, waiting nervously. When I told her what had happened she nodded, impressed with Laura's fearlessness in pursing men armed with guns.

'Not many modern women would have the courage to stand up to scum like that,' Mum said. 'She's like you.'

All the way through filming, and from then on, Laura was by my side, helping and supporting me in any way she could. We've been together ever since. Mum always used to say, 'Behind every great man, there is a woman behind him pushing him.' Laura has always been there for me, and anything good I do is because of her.

As the Dunsany rewilding progressed, I continued to explore the issues of animal agriculture. As I read, I learned more about how destructive to eco-systems the use of animals really is. I'd always known that places like Brazil were destroying precious rainforest to create grazing land for beef, but I was very surprised to learn that about 80 per cent of the soya grown was for animal feed. I also watched some of the slaughterhouse videos that were emerging on the internet at the time. Predictably, they were absolutely horrifying. When I discussed these matters, people said things like, 'Oh, but that's only in America' or 'Irish animals are happy in the fields'.

The agricultural sector is responsible for far more emissions of greenhouse gas than air travel. In Ireland, agriculture is responsible for 37.9 per cent of emissions, as opposed to 21.4 per cent from transport. Yet while we're all aware of the need to travel less, a lot of people don't want to know about the impact of animal farming on the environment in case they have to give up their burger. Many try to confuse this issue by claiming that many of the fruits and vegetables we buy cause just as much carbon output as animal agriculture, which is far from true. The meat-producing industry creates confusion too, using fancy labels saying things like 'grass-fed beef', 'locally sourced' or 'organic'. But a pound of beef from my area has the same or more carbon usage than three avocados imported from South America.

I pondered the old lessons in religious education I'd received at my various schools. Adam and Eve were created by God and placed in a paradise, where they abused God's kindness and were expelled. Now, that's just a story, but most people believe in a creator, a deity, and that this deity has given us life and this gift of the world. And what do we do? We spit in the face of the creator. We kill, we rape, we trash the world around us and we enslave animals. And after all that, we're arrogant enough to call ourselves God's children. *What would I do if I were God?* I asked myself. The answer came quickly: *I'd send plagues and fires to burn our homes. I'd elevate the sea and watch as humanity drowned. I'd do all this and more ...*

Maybe we were never supposed to take the old religious texts literally, but they were originally intended to direct us towards a higher path. Today, we're supposedly civilised, so we should always attempt to protect those weaker than us, and this world that we've been gifted. We have a duty to live in harmony with nature and animals.

I've never been one to do things by halves. I'd spent years being miserable and, by God, I was *truly* miserable. During my wild years in London, I'd thrown myself into the social whirl and was up for every late night, every experiment, every risk. Now I wanted to take my veganism all the way. With the estate rewilding outside, I wondered if the problem with the human race was even more closely linked to our diet than I thought.

What happens if we eat too much of the wrong thing? It's reasonable to suggest that this would change us mentally as well as physically. If we're meant to be plant-eaters, but have spent countless generations eating things that aren't good for us, won't this affect not just our bodies, but also our mood and temperament? Could diet turn people who'd otherwise be calm and tranquil into beings who are aggressive and negative towards the ecosystem? We seem to be the only species that will consume our ecosystems until they're destroyed, rather than finding harmony within them.

Arguably, human beings stepped out of sync with the natural environment when they mastered fire. No other creature does this. With tamed fires, it became easier for us to survive in otherwise hostile environments. We could use fire to cook meat, making it more palatable and digestible. Now we could spend less time chewing and more time creating. Because of fire, we were free to invent. The many things we've created – aeroplanes, cinemas, cars, electricity – aren't *bad*, but they're also not what was intended for us. I wondered if we'd veered so far from our own original purpose that we'd become a threat to the natural environment, a sort of virus to the world that's forcing its destruction so that it can renew, thousands of years from now. Like a virus, we humans seem not to even try to find equilibrium in our own habitat. These thoughts plagued me to the point of obsession. The only thing that distracted me were the changes I was seeing on the land.

The hares, rabbits, deer, frogs and an apparently infinite variety of bird life that I now saw in Dunsany all cherished their lives just as much as we do ours. I understood now that they all have a right to live their lives fully, to fulfil their destinies. This right doesn't pertain just to species we consider 'cute' or 'beautiful' either, but also those from which we naturally recoil: wasps, horseflies, spiders, fleas, maggots, rats. No one species is 'better' than any other. Just like referring to some plants as 'weeds', referring to some animals as 'vermin' creates a false dichotomy between animals that are 'good' and animals that are 'bad'.

For me, accepting this meant not just abstaining from eating meat and other animal products but ceasing to lay poison for rats and mice and accepting the right of wasps to lives as long and fulfilling as they can be. Much as I didn't want rats to populate my home, I had to respect their right to pursue their own interests, and to recognise their existence as an essential part of local biodiversity. And annoying as wasps can be at a picnic, they're also a vital element of the environment, keeping the populations of certain larvae at a sustainable level, pollinating and no doubt contributing in countless ways that are as yet undiscovered by science.

Being vegan was pulling me closer to nature and I became more open to seeing things I'd previously passed unknowingly. As my walks continued, I began to notice even more patterns forming. I started to see the elements of nature not as singular but as systems with every piece integral to the whole. As I felt my mind changing, I wondered what would happen if entire populations, rather than individuals, adopted veganism. What if the experiences I was having could be extended to others?

People often think that veganism begins and ends with what you eat. In reality, it means trying to avoid harming and exploiting animals; recognising their right to live as nature intended. By embracing the philosophy of veganism I was moving closer to living how nature had intended. Now I considered my family and our beliefs, particularly the words Dad had made me repeat, again and again. Our philosophy at Dunsany is to honour the past, to do something for the people during our time, and to prepare the next generation for their duties. I'd been told the privilege I had was to offer something to those who didn't have anything. I'd never understood how I was supposed to do that. I contemplated how various Dunsany ancestors had tried to uplift their people. Horace Plunkett had worked hard to establish the cooperative system that brought farmers and small business people their economic freedom. My great-grandfather Edward Plunkett had given a platform to artists like the poet Francis Ledwidge and the writer Mary Lavin. Back in the mists of time, St Oliver Plunkett had tried to achieve wonderful things at the time of the English Plantations. I'd always been in awe of and overwhelmed by the stories of these great ancestors, feeling that I wasn't able to do anything. But had I found something now?

Me as a child

On Dad's shoulder

Me in the walled garden at Dunsany

My parents in their office in New York

All the siblings together, Daniel, Joana, me and Oliver

My parents with their dog, Xule

Me with my posters aged about 13

Discovering my love of animals

My dad with his
grandfather, Lord
Dunsany

Dad and Grandad
Randal

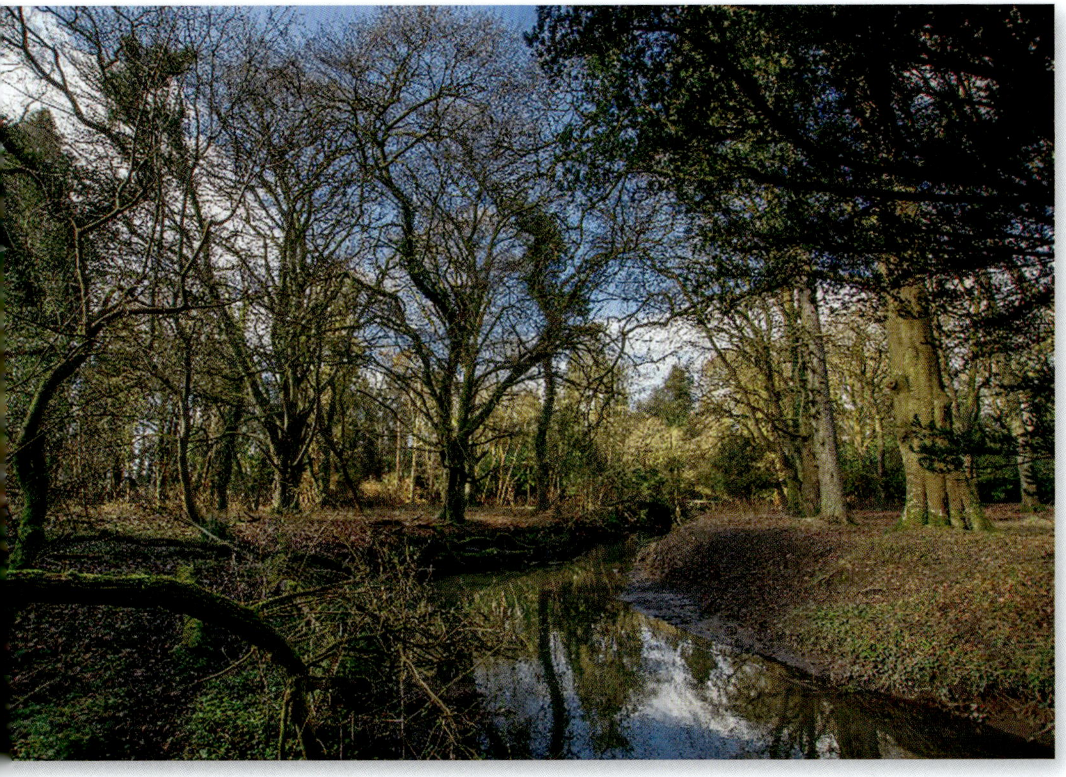

© Daniel Fildes

The River Skane

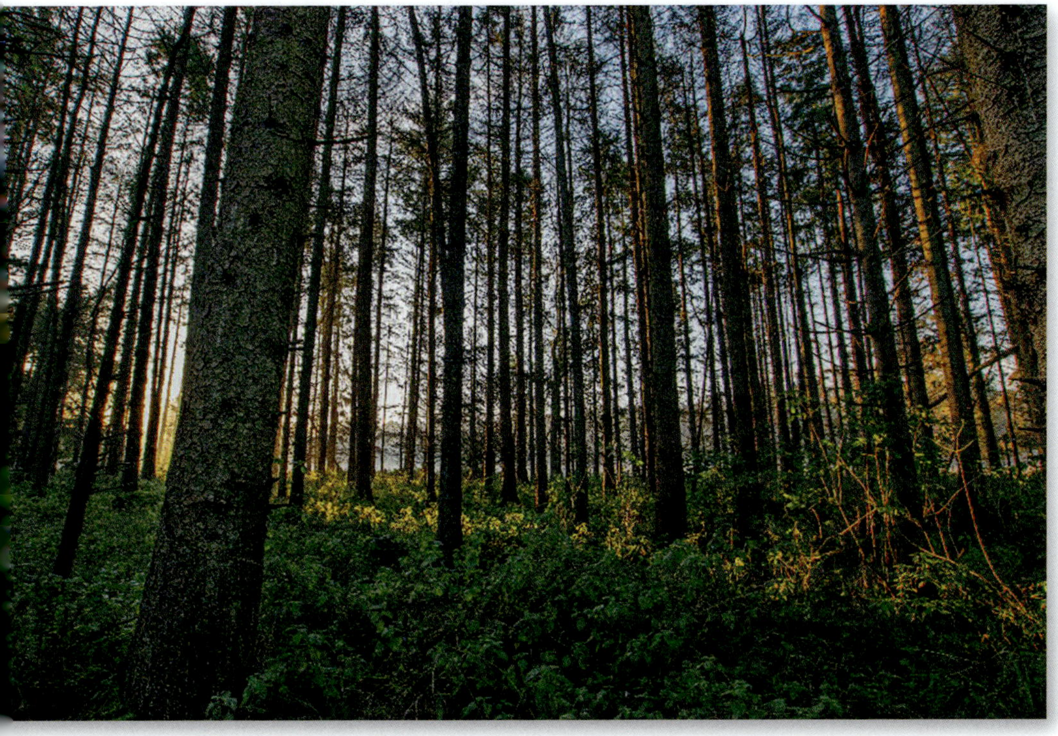

© Daniel Fildes

Woodlands and undergrowth – rewilding plantation forest

Cú Chulainn the stag

Woodpeckers

A buzzard at Dunderry

Dunderry Wood Mushroom

Me at TEDx Innsbruck

Me leading my tours around the Dunsany Estate

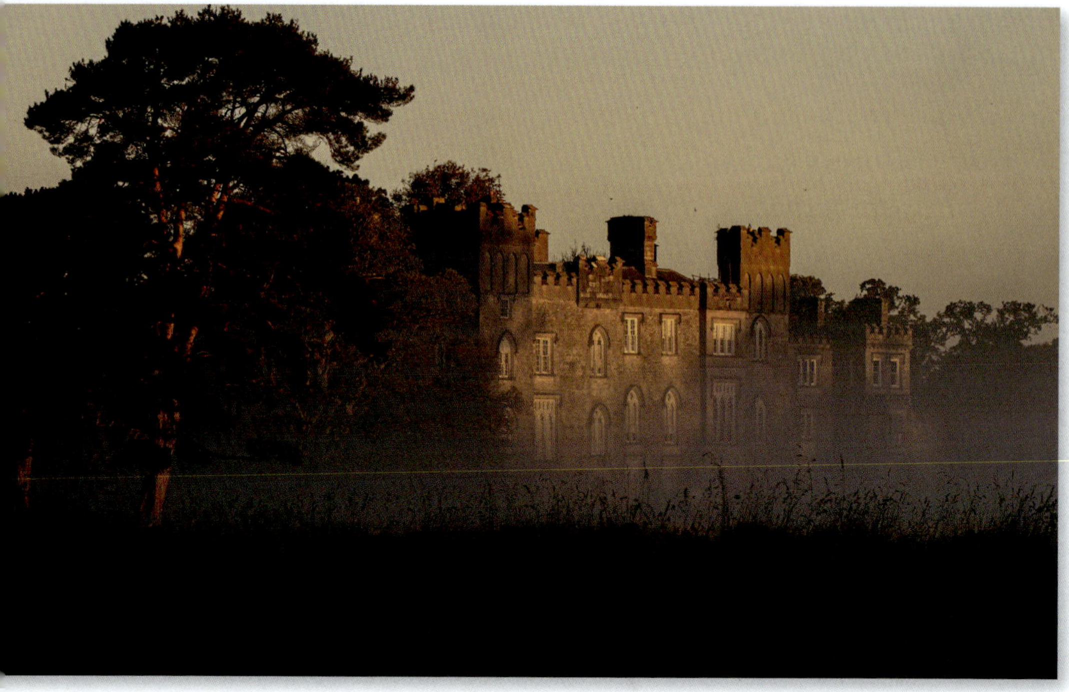

© Finnian Power

Dunsany in the mist

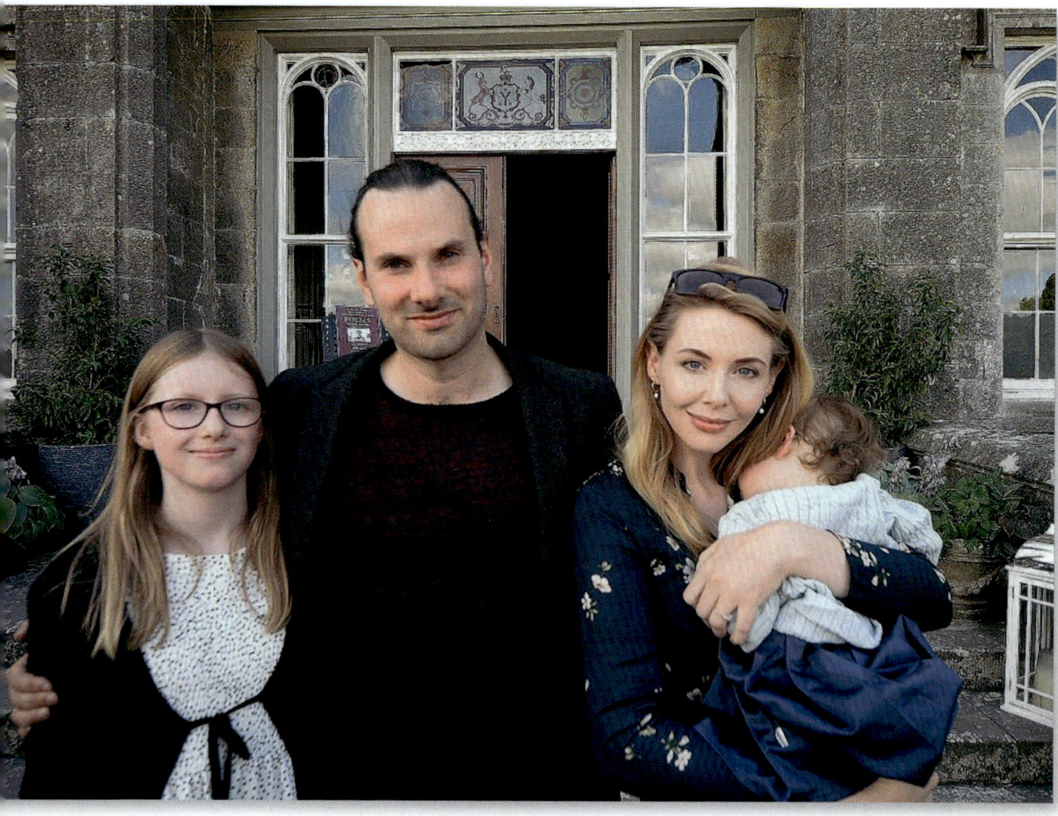

© Seamus Farrelly

Me and my family

Modern society isn't perfect, but it's much less unequal than before. Today, the underclass that needs uplifting is nature, embodied in all the animals and plants I see around me. Not enough people are fighting their cause; too few are standing up against the evil done in the name of our society. Maybe I'd been looking Dunsany in the wrong way for years. I'd started letting nature return to Dunsany, and things had started happening straightaway. I'm descended from a lengthy line of hunters and farmers. My home is decorated with animal heads and pelts. My duty to Dunsany requires me to take care of these old artefacts from past generations, although they challenge my present views.

We can't judge the past for the past, I determined. Every generation has its own ideas and the world has changed a lot. The world I inhabit can grow into something far more worthy of celebration than a hunting trophy. For us to grow, we need to go on a journey of discovery. If we're to learn anything, the road ahead must be riddled with challenges and mistakes that have to be gone through.

Fifteen years before, I'd never have been able to think these thoughts, but my whole past, the many struggles I'd had in trying to inhabit my own skin, had brought me to this point. Now I could see that my road to something better was the endless pursuit of trying to live a life with value, which comes from seeking growth. To have a positive impact on the world, I needed to accept the past – including the parts that brought me discomfort – as part of the journey.

My vegan philosophy was the logical basis of an ideology in which a new type of existence could grow if people embraced and practised it. It would be a struggle to normalise an approach that was currently unpopular, but I was confident that, in time, we could. First we'd need to understand it as a way of life that would gradually allow our mindset to shift, our old ways to be renounced. Like any muscle, it would need to be trained until it became habit.

Integrating a truly vegan philosophy into the rewilding of Dunsany meant no more culling and no more poison. I had to treasure all species equally, to always see the system as a whole. I'd use the lessons Dad had taught me as part of the philosophy of the rewilding projects. My direction, my path and by far the greatest thing I could do with Dunsany in my custodianship was to let the land return to nature, to let it enter a state of *becoming*, and to do so with a vegan philosophy. Even if I achieved nothing, the effort would be worth it.

I was more than just curious and hopeful now. I was *excited*. The more I found out about rewilding, and the longer I spent as a vegan, the more I realised how much I still had to learn. My mind flooded with ideas. I couldn't stop learning, reaching out for more and more knowledge. I scoured the internet for articles about other rewilding projects, and ordered books that described in detail what happens when humans just stop interfering. Although reading long texts has never come naturally to me, I pored over all the material I found, experiencing a genuine sense of wonder with each personal breakthrough. I felt like a detective as I made discoveries every day, finding connections between what I was reading and what I could see happening.

Chernobyl, in Ukraine, was the site of a big nuclear power plant that exploded in 1986. After the initial loss of life, about 100,000 people were evacuated from the area. There were huge fears that a vast zone around the site of the explosion would remain so radioactive it would be a huge danger to human life. The authorities, then part of the government of the Soviet Union, declared an exclusion zone of over four thousand square kilometres, encompassing farmland and the town of Pripyat, which was a planned community built in the 1970s – row after row of Soviet-style apartment buildings – largely to service the huge power station.

In the years immediately following the disaster, many people assumed that the plants and animals in the Chernobyl Exclusion Zone would be very badly affected by the elevated levels of radiation, that many of them would display mutations, and that it would take a very long time, perhaps thousands of years, for the area to return to a sort of normal. In the short term, some plants and animals did display mutations, with leaves changing shape, and some creatures born with deformities. There was also a temporary rise in certain health conditions among human populations affected by the radioactive fallout.

But in the long term, what actually happened in the exclusion zone was very different from the dismal predictions. Levels of radiation dropped much quicker than even the most optimistic predictions had foreseen. With all, or almost all, human activity removed from the area, within just a few years the forests were growing thicker, denser and much more biodiverse, with greater resilience to challenges such as forest fires and climate change, because now the forests were regulating themselves and wetlands were returning to their natural state. At the same time, local wildlife – including bison, deer, elk, lynx, wolves, bears, black grouse, storks and many more species – were present in numbers never seen in living memory. The greater spotted eagle, which had been locally extinct, returned and began to thrive. It was all utterly extraordinary and wonderful. Effectively, the Chernobyl disaster had created an accidental nature reserve and a vast experiment in rewilding. Today, the Chernobyl Exclusion Zone is the third-biggest nature reserve in Europe, and probably the only that can be considered truly wild, because its sheer size means that the animals there enjoy a habitat free from humans.

While many rewilding efforts involve considerable human intervention, from planting trees to introducing species once endemic in the area, the type of rewilding that took place in the Chernobyl Exclusion Zone was passive. In other words, nature was given a lot of space and left alone. Nobody planted trees. No invasive species were removed, and no species were introduced. And, boy, has the reserve got on with things. Acorns became oak trees, all by themselves. Beavers built dams, and fish spawned in the resulting ponds. The percentage of land covered by forest has soared, the amount of wetland has multiplied, animals that were considered endangered in the area didn't just return but have flourished. A place that was once a symbol of misery, of destruction and of innate human arrogance is now a beacon of hope for the future. It's an example of how nature can heal itself or at least transition into a new state – and quite quickly, too.

It was becoming clearer to me that a lot of what I'd been told about nature and about farming isn't really true. Perhaps intervening – even with the intention of making things better – can lead to more harm. We see this in examples of imported tree diseases, which have come as a result of planting trees. Another example is the New Zealand flatworm, which arrived in Northern Ireland and is now devasting the native worm population, on which it predates. This is a big problem for farmers, who rely on worms to aerate the soil through their tunnelling, which also allows water to infiltrate more effectively. The New Zealand flatworm doesn't do this, and as the native worms are destroyed, there are massive risks to the soil.

While Dad, and our ancestors before him, planted trees and maintained wild areas in the estate, most of it had been farmed for centuries, since Norman times. Drains were diligently kept clear, preventing the formation of natural wetlands and inhibiting the ability of species like frogs and herons to flourish. Since the first half of the twentieth century, the farming practice of adding huge quantities of artificial chemicals designed to replenish the depleted soil has become the norm in much of the world.

Until I finally told Rob we weren't going to have cattle and sheep any more, the fields around the castle had been home to domesticated animals, sheep and cattle, which kept the grass cropped close to the ground as they ate and gained weight until they were ready for the butcher's knife. Animals like these have been selectively bred for thousands of years, and no longer very closely resemble their wild ancestors from long ago, physically or mentally. Much like human beings, they've drifted away from nature. Left to their own devices, animals adapt to the landscape. In the hands of human beings, they can acquire monstrous qualities. There are breeds of sheep today, for example, which are so top-heavy when pregnant that if they accidentally roll onto their backs, they can't roll over again and have no choice but to stay there, their four legs pointing accusingly at the sky while ravenous crows pluck out their eyeballs, and then their brains and then peck through their soft bellies to the steaming innards inside. They're living symbols of the awfulness of human greed.

I'd spoken many times to Rob about the impact of animal husbandry on the landscape. He'd assured me that it was benign, pointing out that farm animals contribute manure, and give back nutrients to the soil. Now, the animals gone, I started to read and research and to learn about the many problems associated with farming animals that can linger for years, even after they've gone. The most obvious is the impact of grazing animals as consumers of plant growth. Herbivorous domestic animals have to consume vast quantities of grass and other plants to stay alive. In the process, not only do they remove plants, they also trample the soil. This compacts it and reduces the quality of the habitat for many plant species. It also impacts on the ability of a range of ground-dwelling animals to nest, burrow, or otherwise interact with the environment. It also makes the ground much less permeable, so when it rains, less water is absorbed, and when it rains very heavily, catastrophic flooding can result. They sometimes compete with already challenged wild species for resources. Living in proximity to one another, often in fairly crowded conditions, they're prone to bacterial and fungal infections, for which they needed to be treated. Through their excretions, the land absorbs veterinary drugs and other substances that can be extremely damaging and take years to degrade. Dips and internally administered medications to reduce health problems such as maggots, intestinal worms and other issues remain in the dung and contaminate the soil, where they also kill innocuous, environmentally essential creatures such as dung beetles.

Dung beetles might not sound like the most glamorous members of the rewilding cast, but they're as important as any other. There are more than forty distinct types of dung beetle in Ireland and, for them, access to faeces that are uncontaminated by chemicals is essential. They consume the liquid part of the faeces, so it dries out more quickly, and is more readily integrated into the soil by earthworms, who also play a starring role in the opera of biodiversity. Without both, faecal matter is more likely to drain into water sources, where it can be a health hazard, and is less likely to be effectively integrated into the soil, where it's a vital source of nutrients to the next generation of plants. A healthy ecosystem supports a thriving, diverse population of dung beetles, and these marvellous, diligent and earnest little creatures do incredible work, provided modern agricultural methods and medicines don't stand in their way.

Rewilding is by definition pro-animal. When we rewild, we allow habitats to form. If these are left alone, they'll support a wide range of animals. But not every rewilding project is equal. If a rewilded area is kept free of hunters and never used for animal husbandry, it's compatible with a vegan philosophy. If a rewilded area is sufficiently large – as Dunsany is – those same animals have the space they need to live in a natural way, which will often include creating territories and social boundaries and moving from one area to another as the seasons change. It allows animals that are happier in groups to form communities, and those that are solitary have enough space to stay alone.

Respecting all these creatures has many positive benefits for humans too, because if we embrace the fundamental idea that all living beings have certain rights, we must also extend this simple, essential philosophy to all human populations, and to each human individual, whatever their background, sex or creed. When you take veganism to its logical conclusion, there's no room for inequality, and behaviours such as hating others simply because of who they are, or hurling insults at people on the internet, become anathema.

Veganism made me a better person, because in accepting that every little life is just as important as every other, I also had to remain open to the understanding that every human being, including those who absolutely infuriate me, matters and deserves to be listened to.

Veganism also has the capacity to make the biggest positive difference in the lives of people who have the most challenges. People on lower incomes are the most likely to have to live in areas damaged by agricultural activity. You don't find millionaires building houses near industrial pig farms. Rich people won't tolerate living beside rivers that have been polluted by farming. Countries with high overall levels of poverty are also the most likely to experience the most devastating effects of climate change because it takes money to adapt infrastructures to new realities. By becoming vegan, and by rewilding as much as possible of the land previously used to raise animals, we're making changes that will have dramatic, direct and measurable positive consequences for the most vulnerable human populations.

Rewilding in Ireland has another edge, too; one that resonates with our complex past. Ireland, like many countries, has been subject to various waves of colonisation. Most infamous are the relatively recent seventeenth-century Plantations, when Cromwell's people oversaw the removal of countless native Irish families from the land. The dispossession of so many native Irish during the Cromwellian period had the fortunate side-effect – from the colonisers' point of view – of releasing land for raising farm animals. Several centuries before that, the Normans came – among them, of course, my own ancestors – and before that the Vikings, and before them the Celts, and so on back through recorded time and into the mists of the distant past.

But long before all that, there was another type of colonisation: the colonisation of the land by humans, who first hunted and then farmed and hunted, and who ever since have dedicated themselves to modifying the landscape in innumerable ways – concreting and tarmacking over surfaces, building roads and other modes of transport, lighting our urban environments, and so on – all of which have had many and complex impacts on animal lives, sometimes in unforeseen ways. The same patterns have been witnessed throughout history. All over the world, people have been and continue to be removed from their lands for the purpose of animal agriculture, and the well-being of millions of plant, insect and animal species has been sacrificed to the cause of human convenience.

We can't undo the harms caused by past generations, and while recognising them is important, being angry while doing nothing to change them is not just pointless but also counterproductive, because anger consumes energy that could otherwise be used positively. Living in the modern world can sometimes be stressful and frustrating because we hear all about atrocities taking place here, there and everywhere, and are rarely in a position to do anything about it. Peace can be found in creating transformation where we can.

Reinvigorated by my embrace of veganism, I decided to be as confrontational as possible in dealing with the poachers who'd been a threat to Dunsany for as long as I could remember. To channel Mum's ferocity, her Latin American heat and her determination to stand up for what she thought was right. I started patrolling the estate every evening and at sunrise, spending hours of my weekend doing circles of the field following the poachers' vehicles, rushing out any time I heard the sound of their guns or just instinctively knew they were there. The neighbours began to see me so often I acquired the nickname 'Black Merc' for the old black Mercedes I drive. It would trundle slowly down the road, only the low bass rumble of heavy metal apparent as I approached. As a poacher's car slowed down at a gate, preparing to enter, I'd appear and blast my lights on them.

'We're not doing anything,' they'd say.

'That's good,' I'd answer. 'I'm not doing anything either.'

I'd make a point of staring into their eyes without blinking, so that I looked like a complete madman. My distaste for them very clear, I'd film them with my camera gear and take pictures of their licence plates. They'd get angry and so would I. Often they'd become aggressive and threaten me; I frequently caught their outbursts on film. I'd smile as they incriminated themselves on camera. They'd become uncomfortable and leave. If they tried to return, I'd be there within minutes. I began to build a dossier of vehicles and people. When they attempted to intimidate me, I'd refer to them by name, making them even more nervous.

'You know I'm fucking crazy, right?' I'd say. 'I've got *so* much money and nothing but time, so me hanging out making sure you don't try and kill any animals is my football. I know so much about you already. I know what you had for breakfast.'

They didn't know how to handle this clearly mad behaviour. But if they wanted to see me as an evil, imperialist landlord bad guy, I'd embrace that image, and really make myself a monster in their eyes. I'd become a monster to stop monsters.

It was sometimes frightening, and always disconcerting, talking like this to people bristling with rage and brandishing firearms that could have taken me down as easily as they destroyed a young deer, but I took courage from knowing I was right.

Although I knew the Gardaí were unlikely to help, I contacted them after every single incident and insisted on leaving a report. I wanted to have a paper trail. The Gardaí grew tired of hearing me on the phone and I could hear the weariness in their voices as they recorded yet another incident. To their credit, at least they did it.

As the years passed, I was calling the Gardaí less often. The number of annual calls gradually declined from forty or so to five or six. The message was getting out that illegal hunting in Dunsany was becoming more trouble than it was worth. The economy was doing better, so maybe the poachers had all found honest work, or perhaps they'd simply started killing animals on someone else's land.

Chapter Seven

Wilding the Gilded Cage

AS THE PLANTS GREW AND THE INSECTS, BIRDS AND ANIMALS MULTIPLIED, I STARTED TO READ ABOUT FOLKLORE, PHILOSOPHY AND ECOLOGY TO UNDERSTAND MORE ABOUT WHAT I WAS SEEING, WHAT I WANTED TO SEE NEXT, AND WHAT I COULD DO TO MAKE THINGS BETTER. I was, of course, very interested in Irish folklore, which contains a lot of information about the plant and animal species considered important here, what they were used for, and how people thought about them in the pre-industrial age. I was also attracted by eastern philosophy, and in particular to the concept of yin and yang, which is the idea from Chinese philosophy of a self-perpetuating cycle composed of opposite but complementary forces. We see this simple pattern everywhere in nature: in the passage of light to dark and back again; in the seasons; in the cycles that every living being passes through from birth to death to entropy, and so on.

Walking around Dunsany and seeing a million living things coming into existence, growing, flowering, and then ageing, dying, and in their decaying making way for a new generation, the concept of yin and yang didn't seem abstract at all. I could also see how the concept applies equally to us humans, who experience all those phases in our life cycles too and, if we do things right, set the scene for the next generation to inherit.

I continued to study one tree, plant or animal species at a time, reading everything I could find until I understood how it worked, and how it fitted in with all the other living things in its environment. Steadily, my understanding grew. Before, I hadn't even known the difference between a beech tree and an oak. Now I started to know the minute details of how each tree grows, what it needs to stay healthy and how it strives to survive. Now I understood how absolutely vital extensive rewilding is for our planet's future; how, without it, we're about to lose thousands of species, to continue hurtling headlong into a self-made environmental disaster. I learned how Ireland's green fields, which have so often sparked the poetic imagination, are not the wildlife havens some assume, but largely denuded of life. In fact, they're examples of some of the *worst* ways to manage the landscape. There's more actual nature in many suburban gardens. Huge swathes of the west of Ireland, for example, are essentially a monoculture turned over to grazing sheep. This is one of the most damaging forms of farming and yet for years it's been sustained by state and EU subsidies.

All over Ireland, as in most of the developed world, much of our soil is currently degraded: ravaged by over-grazing, supporting a limited array of plants and other lifeforms, and regularly ploughed. The soil is thus frequently exposed, releasing carbon that the grass had sequestered, making the ground vulnerable to erosion. Year on year, soil quality declines and farmers spread yet more chemicals and artificial fertilisers.

But when the same land rewilds, its quality is restored relatively quickly. Within a few decades, natural plant and animal activity can restore even a very badly damaged environment. In rewilded parts of Dunsany, the areas that once were fields grazed by sheep are still doing less well than other zones, because the land is still processing the massive quantities of chemicals that had accumulated. The soil must be riddled with years' worth of concentrated toxins from the sheep's chemically disinfected feet, and from the medication-laced droppings they left behind. The plastic containers that those medications come in are marked with vivid skull-and-crossbones icons to remind us of how dangerous they are – and yet year after year, we use them in ways that guarantee their transfer into the natural world, and ultimately into human diets, too. The more intensively used the land, the longer it takes to rewild. Our back field, for example, never got a break; our front was periodically left ungrazed so that the grass could grow for silage.

By now, I knew that much of what I'd been told as certainties by people who seemed to know a lot about nature wasn't true at all. The ragwort hadn't destroyed the land. Instead, the grass was growing stronger and taller than ever. The animals that had flocked back to the rewilding landscape, and whose numbers were still growing, weren't despoiling it. They seemed to have found – or to be in the process of finding – their own balance.

I could also see how some of the very basic concepts I'd learned as a bodybuilder obsessed with exercise and diet were applicable to the environment. You build muscle through a combination of stress and rest. If you work hard, stress, or 'overload' a particular muscle using a certain exercise or movement pattern, and then allow it to rest, you'll steadily gain in strength and size, provided you have adequate nutrition. When you return to the same exercise after a period of rest, you should be better at it. I refer to this as the adaption process. Many plant species seemed to naturally apply a similar approach, often exerting huge effort for a year or two, growing and putting down roots, or fruiting, followed by a year of just staying put, or of producing few or no fruits. Effort and rest. Yin and yang.

In the first four years or so of rewilding, changes had seemed to happen in a more or less linear fashion. The ragwort first became ever more abundant, and then ceded to other plants as the more accessible soil it created facilitated their growth. By year four or five, I started to realise that plant, bird and animal life often followed cycles that were longer and more complex than I'd realised. A particular plant species might become more abundant and then die back, only to surge again a few years later. The birds might nest and breed in vast numbers in a particular place for several years, only to move *en masse* for the next season. With birds, this was often because of a surge in predator birds responding to an increase in prey species. The rise in predators would result in a dramatic decrease in prey, which would rapidly become more numerous as the predators adjusted their territories. It was easy to see how this cycle might repeat, essentially, eternally.

I was also seeing interesting things happen with the meadow flowers. In the first years of rewilding, I'd observed a huge rise in ragwort and other flowering plants, including knapweed and meadowsweet. Then, after year five, the ragwort more or less vanished, and meadowsweet had a year of abundance before largely disappearing too. One botanist said the land had become 'too rich' and would require management to make the grass less powerful. I briefly wondered if I'd achieved the opposite of my intention. Had I actually made the land *less* biodiverse rather than more because I wasn't adequately straining its resources? After some thought, I decided to wait rather than panic. Time passed, and the ragwort and meadowsweet started to return. Nothing obvious had changed to make this happen, and I started to realise that nature follows its own schedule, with change coming in waves. Every year since, I've watched with interest to see what will happen next. It's become ever clearer that these ebbs and flows, these complex cycles, overlay and intersect in a vast network of connections that's difficult to see in its entirety, and impossible for us, with our limited understanding of nature, to predict.

I was doing my best to learn from biodiversity experts, but was increasingly concerned that their advice often wasn't based on what happens when you leave nature alone. They, like everybody else, grew up in a world with very little genuinely wild land, and their views were based on observing land for relatively short periods. There was a lot of talk about the importance of encouraging pollinators, with the advice that people should allow wild flowers to flourish. People with big farms or estates, and those with small gardens, were advised to proactively intervene by sowing 'wild flower' seeds. Of course if you plant flowers you'll attract bees and other pollinating insects – but why was this advice so focused on cherishing just *one* element of the natural cycle of growth? What about the next stage? What about entropy, death and

– one of the most important – rot? Where was the advice on letting those same wild flowers fall, lie and decay once the blossoms had faded? Surely *every* aspect of the life cycle matters, not just the pretty part?

It seemed that, despite our good intentions, we're obsessed with preserving certain aspects of nature only; the bits we like. I was reminded of our collective obsession with remaining young. We were forgetting that, for all species, youth is one part of life. Town planners generally aim to create communities with a good mix of ages, because society benefits from having a variety of people at different life stages. The same applies to plants.

Left alone, whatever nature does is part of the same beautiful cycle, the yin and yang. But human beings like simple stories of heroes and villains, rather than complicated fables of catalyst and consequence. In nature, weeds – the plants we dislike – often grow in response to a disturbance. If you clear an area of soil and plant seeds that don't belong there, nature responds by growing an array of greenery. You pull it out, but it returns as soon as you turn your back. I'd already learned this from battling the ragwort. I wasn't fighting just one plant species; I was fighting nature's own cycle.

While cornflowers and poppies look good in photos, is it wise to impose on the plant world an artificial hierarchy of 'good' and 'bad' plants, to encourage a sort of survival of the prettiest? Are cornflowers and poppies intrinsically 'better' than nettles and dandelions? Or is it more likely that they *all* have their place in our natural biodiversity? When we encourage certain wild plants to grow, while eliminating or inhibiting others, it's like going to the gym and only exercising one part of the body. The whole becomes unbalanced, a system compensating for weakness in one area with unnatural levels of growth and activity in the other. That's a health disaster for the human body, and it's just as bad for the natural environment.

Beyond that, I believe that seeing the world as a series of hierarchies is not just simplistic and wrong, but also dangerous. Systemising our world like this has led to many of the problems we struggle with daily. Imposing a hierarchy on nature leads inevitably to social inequalities. If you establish values such as 'an oak is worth more than a hawthorn' or 'a chicken is worth less than a dog', how different is that, really, to 'the wealthy are more important than the poor' or 'men are better than women' or 'white-skinned people are worth more than black-skinned people'? Accepting hierarchies, seeing them as natural and real, leads to racism, war and climate collapse. As I write I realise that, yes, historically my family has benefited from this mindset. But just because you benefit from the status quo doesn't mean the status quo has a future.

I realised that if I wanted to eliminate negative thinking from myself, and if we wanted to see it disappear from the world, we need to take a lesson from nature, to unlearn thought patterns that ascribe value to certain species and beings above others. That if we're going to be serious about equality and diversity, we need to stop thinking in these hierarchical ways. We'll never destroy prejudice until we see all species as equal. It's great that it's not socially acceptable to be overtly racist or sexist, for example, but the problem will never disappear until we've destroyed the very notion of hierarchy. Until we return to a path more in tune with nature, living as we were designed to, consuming what we evolved to eat. By drifting so far from our intrinsic nature, we humans have essentially transformed ourselves from a native into an invasive species.

At Dunsany, I was faced with a grim reality. Although we'd been rewilding for years now, we were lacking key species that once helped to keep our ecosystems in harmony. One was a large herbivore, the auroch, a buffalo-like animal that lived in ancient Ireland. Long extinct, they've been replaced by domesticated cattle, which are limited in their ability to serve nature's needs. The large aurochs created areas of disturbance in grasslands, reducing the grass's nutrient load. Their big mouths ripped chunks from natural meadows. This reduced the height and strength of the grass, allowing more light to filter to the ground, providing opportunities to more fragile plant species. Most of the academic literature maintained that biodiversity was limited without these necessary disturbances. This worried me. What if all the positive things I could see happening took a step backward?

I started reading about what other rewilders and ecology scientists were advocating. 'Regenerative agriculture' was the new buzzword. The idea was that with careful animal agriculture and selective grazing, nature could be improved. Many rewilding projects, I knew, had introduced heritage or legacy breeds of domestic animals. These are often quite similar to their ancestors, the ancient herbivores, and interact similarly with the landscape. That sounded okay in principle, but on closer examination I could see it was just a slightly modified version of ordinary farming, which is a broken system. This was a 'low-fat' version of rewilding, not a serious solution to the natural disaster we're all living through. If I reintroduced cattle, they'd bring the same problems we had before.

One of the big problems with most regenerative agriculture is that sickly animals are treated with antibiotics and other medicines. These enter the ground, changing the soil and, in particular, the fungi. Despite ongoing research, we've no idea how these substances disrupt the soil and what the consequences of using them really are. And what would I do with the animals if I reintroduced them? Would they be pets? As a vegan, I couldn't kill them for meat; that would directly challenge my belief that we can elevate ourselves by adopting a vegan philosophy. Would I have to domesticate them? Give them artificial feeds to keep them healthy, antibiotics when they were sick? Would my good intentions lead to me once again trying to control nature? I'd had a glimpse of what was possible, and now I was worried I'd grown too confident, that perhaps the rewilding of Dunsany had already peaked. I was painfully aware of the limits to my understanding.

As I worried about the possibility that nature might stop flourishing in the absence of large herbivores, I became depressed. But I knew that if I'd listened to the accepted wisdom from the start, I wouldn't have started rewilding in the first place. I also knew I'd never compromise my ethical position. We needed radical change, not a slight tweak to the juggernaut of the animal agriculture industry. Globally, it's one of the main causes of biodiversity loss, deforestation and carbon secretion. It's also the first major obstacle preventing us from shifting our entire way of life. If we wanted to kickstart nature into self-repair, we'd need to view it completely differently. I pondered my original approach to rewilding. I'd started with the assumption that nature is vastly superior to us human beings and can adjust by itself to ensure that its complex needs are served. I decided to refrain from interfering with the grasslands' natural reaction to change, and to wait and see what happened next.

As the grasslands grew stronger, the height of the grass on the top layer rose to above my head. Carefully, I watched what was happening on the ground. I noticed that key species like dandelions would arrive and, shortly thereafter, be consumed by the grass. By the fifth year, I'd noted a small plant starting to creep in, blending into the lower grass. At first I didn't pay it much attention. Then I observed that, where it grew, the larger, heavy grasses receded. Gaps formed in the dense meadow, and where that happened, this apparently humble little green plant started to dominate. Intrigued now, I learned that it was silverweed, also known as *Potentilla anserina* or, in Irish, *briosclán*.

Silverweed, like many native Irish wild plants, grows close to the ground and has a distinctive, subtle beauty. A creeping perennial, it's found all over the island, especially in damp, grassy places. Its leaves are green, silky and divided into toothed leaflets with an attractive silvery tint. In summer, it sprouts long, slender shoots with yellow five-petalled flowers at the top. Before the rewilding, there'd been very little silverweed and almost none in the grasslands. Now it was steadily colonising whole areas. Everyone I asked about it said it was worthless. Even the scientific literature implied that silverweed was a bit pointless: spreading, flowering, dying and rotting without contributing very much to the world. But as it spread, the grasslands became less like a quilt covering the soil, and more like a patchwork blanket, with areas of grass growing tall and proud in the summer, and then falling and rotting over the winter, and large, expanding areas of silverweed, which spread thickly across the ground, putting down roots everywhere it grew, inhibiting the grasses' growth.

As I strode through the fields, I saw what looked like islands of silverweed forming. Then I saw a new pattern. Where silverweed thrived, delicate grasses and flowers could form and live in harmony with it, because where it dominated the lower ground, more sunlight pierced through. The silverweed also broke up the topsoil, facilitating the rooting of other non-grass plants. Here, micro-flowers of all sorts, like purslane and forget-me-not, were flourishing too, and ground-dwelling insects and spiders were making their homes.

Looking even more closely, I noticed that where silverweed flourished, there were many more earthworms. They thrived in the loosened soil, where they could easily reach the surface and feast on the abundance of rotting matter the rewilding was creating. And while it's undoubtedly difficult to interpret an earthworm's psychological state, they seemed . . . happy? They were certainly fulfilled in their little lives.

While the earthworms lived it up in the top levels of the soil, they were joined by astonishing quantities of slugs, joyfully feasting on the surface. I'd never given slugs much thought before. They get a bad rap as they munch through vegetable gardens and ooze across suburban pavements on rainy days. But here, in the grasslands of Dunsany, they were playing a very important part in establishing a self-reliant wilderness, devouring the rotting grass following the flowering of spring and the seeding of late summer, and helping it to return to the soil, from which a new generation of plants would grow. When I knelt on the soft ground to explore, my hands pushed aside the soggy fallen grass to expose thousands of them. And I could see that they were beautiful. Yes, *beautiful*.

Irish slugs come in assorted colours, from black through dark grey to light grey and beige. Their damp skin is often marked by complex striations and whorls. Their miniature faces, with those endearingly inquisitive retractable tentacles, are as individual as ours. Each slug has two sets of tentacles: optical tentacles with which they see and smell – and which they can regrow if necessary – and lower tentacles for feeling, a bit like hands, and for tasting. If you look closely at a slug in motion, you'll see how graceful they are, their damp, mobile bodies rippling forward in a series of orderly muscular contractions. If you get too close, they'll be scared, and – much like a turtle – will retract their little heads in fear until you leave. Next time you see a slug, don't recoil or ignore it. Spend a few minutes having a good look, and you'll see that every one is as much a miracle of nature as you are.

Returning to how nature could cope absent a large herbivore, I pondered the silverweed and how it was forming islands. As I continued to monitor the land, I started to notice some confusing anomalies. Two of the four large fields around the castle, for example, weren't producing trees. The front field, with the most silverweed by far, had less ragwort, fewer thistles and less general diversity, including almost no natural tree growth. The side field had an enormous number of thistles and scrubbier grass but also no natural tree growth. I'd always been told that land left alone would quickly become forest, but years were passing and there was still no tree growth in these two areas. Conversely, the two back fields were quickly turning into scrub and would be forest in a decade or so.

I walked the foresting fields, admiring how they were becoming covered in brambles and rushes, unlike their neighbours. They all had the same type of soil. So why were some fields foresting and others not? Everyone with whom I'd discussed the rewilding of Dunsany had said that if I left the whole estate alone, it'd turn into a forest. They'd also said we wouldn't have any biodiversity without managing nature. Neither was happening.

I'd often been told that when you see a field of rushes you know it's wet, poor-quality land. But the two back fields of Dunsany, now filling with rushes, weren't wet. In fact, they were bone dry, and with their thick, dark, heavy soil, they'd been considered some of the best fields in the area. Rushes are native to Irish ecosystems, but, once again, they're treated as invasive. Before the rewilding, the farmers had killed them with chemical sprays. Now, I began to admire the rushes. Their spiky, stick-like leaves don't cover the ground as the leaves of differently formed plants do. They point up, allowing light to travel down them and reach the ground. Where rushes grew, I saw vast numbers of baby saplings pushing up through the gaps. I started to count them, but gave up after fifteen minutes, as there were multitudes: birch, willow, oak, hawthorn, and even the occasional Scots pine.

I peered over the fence into the next field, where no saplings were growing. Why not? Were the deer destroying them all? That couldn't be it, as there was nothing stopping the deer from entering the foresting field, too. Was it because the two areas had been rewilding for a different amount of time? No, as there was only a year or so in the difference, and the tree saplings had begun to grow straightaway. It was baffling. In search of an answer, I continued to analyse the foresting field. Then I noticed another pattern: the deer tended to avoid trees growing around brambles and hawthorns, both of which grew quickly and abundantly in the foresting area, often close together. As they did, oak and hazel saplings grew between them, like a second wave of foresting. I learned that this process is referred to as succession.

As the foresting fields gradually became woodland, it was going through certain cycles. I liked to think of it as 'the advance system'. A typical cycle starts as grass, which is often followed by brambles, hawthorns or hazel. This is known as the infant system. These plants grow in patches, creating a food source for birds, which feast on their berries. Within a few hours, the birds dispose of their seed-laden faeces, and where they fall, a new tree might grow. As the birds have also been consuming berries in already forested areas, their faeces often give rise to the growth of trees such as birch, hazel, alder or even willow. This is known as the adolescent system. These trees grow more quickly, creating in the process a second tier of growth, permitting the development of slower-growing trees like oak, hornbeam and maybe yew. Fast forward a few more years, and these slower-growing trees will be starting to outgrow the smaller ones, which would become the understorey. The trees in the understorey don't dominate the forest in terms of height, but grow happily beneath colossal trees like the oak. In a rewilding ecosystem, they're the first line of restoration, allowing an immature forest to become a mature one.

By year seven, I'd begun to notice a plant I'd never seen in Dunsany before. It was horsetail, *Equisetum arvense*. I first observed it growing on the edges of the woodland, and then it gradually started cutting into the grasslands. To me, it has a rather alien appearance: a stem covered in furry leaves, like a hairy asparagus. Horsetail has remained essentially unchanged since dinosaurs walked the earth. Today, it grows all across temperate and Arctic parts of the northern hemisphere, putting down roots in the grassy areas it likes. Its rhizomes can reach up to nearly two metres beneath the ground, so – to the chagrin of gardeners and farmers – it can be very difficult to eliminate. Next I saw the horsetail expanding in a very straight line across a row of ancient beech trees growing along a ditch in our front field. It cut through the dominant grass with little effort, creating bush-like sections. Intrigued, I read more about this strange little plant. I encountered many websites calling it 'the worst thing since Japanese knotweed' and 'the invasive destroyer of gardens and graveyards'. I found these descriptions entertaining until I learned that horsetail is actually native to Ireland. Another native species described as invasive! I decided that if this little plant found itself in Dunsany it must be here for a reason. I started observing it closely.

For the first year or so, little happened. The horsetail seemed to just spread along the route it had chosen. Then, suddenly, I noticed something growing underneath. I pulled back the stalks, revealing underneath them an array of little oak saplings. It seemed that wherever horsetail grew, it was followed by slow-growing oaks, and no other tree species. I also noted that the deer never grazed these little oaks. Wherever horsetail grew, a new generation of oaks seemed to be spared. I don't know if this is also the case elsewhere, but it's a clear pattern at Dunsany. For now, let's just say that to a rewilder like me, horsetail is almost magical. Its high silica content moderates the effects of copious amounts of water around root systems, so wherever horsetail grows, other plants follow, among them the next generation of trees.

Parts of Dunsany had always been prone to flooding and waterlogging. For countless generations, we'd fought this by digging drains and clearing them regularly. Everyone said that if I didn't maintain this practice, swathes of land would revert to bog and flooding would become a big problem. I decided to wait and see. None of the predicted terrible flooding actually occurred. The drains, which had been necessary to create arable farmland that was easy to manage with machinery, were redundant in a landscape quickly reverting to nature, with wetlands that didn't encroach upon or threaten other areas. The formerly drained areas became waterlogged as the artificial channels filled with vegetation. Within a couple of years, they were natural wet areas, growing entirely distinct species of plant to the drier areas around them. There was little flooding, just our usual seasonal lakes. The soil was far more able to deal with surface water than before, absorbing it within a day. There were also substantial areas of wet soil supporting reeds, rushes and an abundance of other wetland species.

Meadowsweet is a plant native to Europe and parts of Asia that grows in waterlogged soil. In spring, it sprouts clusters of creamy-white flowers in a lace-like formation with a sweet, distinctive, almost intoxicating scent. Each plant supports a large population of insects, which in turn support birds, frogs and – in areas with watercourses – fish. Moth caterpillars feast on its green leaves. It's a true life-bringer, and it was filling our wetlands. Watercress started to grow too. I'd only ever seen it before in bagged salad. Now, confident that it was uncontaminated by chemicals, I could pick and eat my own. The rushes were creating space for a new generation of black poplars, a native Irish species that grows in very wet soil. Currently quite endangered because so much of our farmland is drained, it's safe in Dunsany. Suddenly, everywhere the water pooled, there were mountains of frogspawn in the spring, followed by a large, noisy and growing population of adult frogs, and an army of long-legged herons greedily eating them at every stage of their life cycle. Where once there'd been drained fields, now there was a thriving wetlands community.

Only about 11 per cent of Ireland is forested. Much of that is commercial forest of variable, but mostly quite low, ecological value: largely densely planted monocultures of coniferous forest supporting relatively few wild species. Parts of Dunsany were already forest – a blend of self-seeded native and non-native species introduced at various stages. Until now, we'd managed the forests quite aggressively, removing dying or dead trees vigorously and clearing the undergrowth to give the trees 'more room to grow'. I decided to apply the same rewilding principles to the forests as the fields; we'd just leave them alone and observe. I soon realised that the trees are not a discrete community. Instead, they interact with grasses and other types of plants in all sorts of amazing ways.

In a natural forest, there's growth at multiple levels, each supporting a unique array of insect, plant and animal species in delicate balance. When a tree dies and falls, part of the natural canopy disappears, allowing a gap for the light to pierce deeper to the forest floor, giving the younger trees beneath more scope to grow upwards and gradually replace it. While the trees in the ancient woodlands of Dunsany grow in a somewhat natural manner, large, mature trees comprise most of the external canopy. Various levels of understorey try to reach the gaps between the mature and dense rising understorey beneath. Although all the woodland had been managed, the younger forested areas that Dad had planted as a commercial enterprise were different. Here, the trees were densely packed together, with little or no undergrowth. The idea had been to periodically thin them out and allow the strong ones to grow larger. Thus, the estate would earn money from the thinnings, with the prospect of a big payout when the more robust trees reached their full height and the area was clear-cut. Then the cycle would start again. Although not harvesting those trees would be costly, I couldn't bear to destroy them. I've always been uncomfortable with cutting down forests, even planted ones, leaving exposed, damaged land. I decided to also leave the newer plantations alone.

Most spruce plantations are dark and silent. Because of the compact way they're planted, and because they're all planted the same size, at the same time, all the trees grow more or less at the same level, creating a closed canopy and a bare understorey. Dunsany has several areas of coniferous plantations, but they're not really like that. The grounds underneath the trees were busy with abundant green growth. In many areas, they'd even begun growing an understorey of young trees, often beeches, sycamore and alder, different species from the planted ones. I'd trip on brambles that were doing very well despite growing in an artificial planation. Why were the spruce plantations at Dunsany so different to those I'd visited elsewhere? There were a few subtle differences. They were always planted adjacent to natural mixed forest. The trees were larger, with less space between them. Although some of the plantations had been planted over seventy years before, they'd never been thinned.

A forester once explained to me that trees can't grow wide and dominate unless they're managed. This contradicted much of what I saw. In the forests, different tree species battled for access to light. Generally, the most durable would win. Isn't this the principle of natural selection? But why were the conifer plantations at the reserve doing so well? Left alone, many of the trees in these plantations had grown tall and thin. Many had died, been out-competed, or had grown to the point whereby the sun could now shine through, creating spots of light where once there'd been darkness. It's very unusual for plantations to reach this age without intervention or management. My grandfather, who'd mismanaged the estate so badly, had been an accidental rewilder.

I decided not to do anything with Dad's much younger plantations. They were still less than fifteen years old, and had been actively managed until now. I anticipated that if we left them alone, the trees would grow thin as they competed for light and resources. Gradually, some would die and fall, leaving gaps and allowing space for pools of light that would create oases of growth beneath. Well, that's what I hoped.

Year on year, through a combination of natural selection and the activities of the Dunsany deer, the stronger, more robust trees began to gain traction and the smaller, weaker ones started dying off, as I'd anticipated. Vibrant signs of a new forest began to emerge underneath the trees that Dad had planted as saplings. Bramble, sycamore, ash, hawthorn and beech started growing. We were allowing an understorey to develop naturally. Gradually, an artificially planted forest was becoming as diverse as a natural one. In the wetter areas, Dad had planted almost a monoculture of alder. These now exploded with immense, diverse quantities of regrowth, while their companion plantations – mostly oak and Scots pine, lagged behind. Eventually there'd be no way to tell the difference between the planted and the natural forests. I began to feel a sense of achievement as I daydreamed about these plantations slowly becoming towering forest and my descendants walking underneath them, surrounded by birdsong.

Meanwhile, in the native forest, we gave the forest's natural mycelium (fungal) network time and space to heal. We'd stopped removing most of our dead trees from all the forested areas, from the hedgerows, and from what had once been fields or parkland. I was considering our relationship with nature and how we humans have benefited endlessly. We use farmland to produce food. We till the land, plant monocultures of crops, spray chemicals to stop insects and other pests from taking any benefit from our creation, spray fertiliser to make crops grow faster, and spray again to keep weeds down. Then we harvest, leaving nothing behind. We're in a relationship with nature, but we're doing all the taking and none of the giving. Any relationship without harmony, without give and take, without yin and yang, is unbalanced. In a human relationship, a lack of balance generally ends in divorce and you'll be left sitting on half a couch. So what about our relationship with nature? Over time, if we keep taking and never giving anything back, nature will express its discontent through weather and climate. We can develop a more nurturing, sharing and caring relationship with nature. We can do this by letting it experience a full circle of life.

Everyone knows the concept of the circle of life. We're born, we grow and mature; we're beautiful, we fruit and flower; we get old and decline and then we die. And then we have to rot. It's the same for every living thing. But we generally mess it up at the rotting stage. Farming, for example, fulfils certain stages of the cycle but it never allows any natural breakdown, so the soil never gets what it needs to refuel itself. We think we're helping nature by removing all the dead matter, but we're not. We're not closing the circle of life. A broken circle generally ends up looking like a C. C stands for crap, and that's what we have. So I decided to introduce a new rewilding protocol: give and take. From now on, we'd allow 50 per cent of the wood and debris that fell to remain there, slowly rotting. This was already happening in the grasslands, and they were thriving. While I couldn't enforce this rule in the farmed parts of the estate, I could easily do it in the rewilding areas, where it would act as a necessary counterweight to the pressures on the ecosystem.

Trees support abundant life during their lifetime and even more when they're dead. A native Irish oak can provide a habitat and/or nourishment to up to a hundred species when it's alive, but up to *twice as many* after death. Trees continue to be a vital part of the ecosystem until the last molecule has been repurposed, which can take years. How cool is that? From now on, unless a dead tree was actually overhanging a road or house, we'd leave it standing. If it fell, it would remain where it landed, returning slowly to nature. All we had to do was avoid standing underneath dead trees in a storm. Easy to accomplish.

I did decide to intervene a little when it came to planting trees. As we already had several forested areas, by creating corridors of trees we'd make it easier for forest-dwelling species – squirrels, pine martens, shrews, stoats and hedgehogs – to move between them. This would create a much more viable habitat and give each group a bigger gene pool to breed within. I started planting native saplings, mostly oak, hawthorn, willow and birch, to connect the forested areas and along the perimeters of the estate, where the land meets the road. These swathes of baby forest would steadily become a buffer zone between the rewilding and the threats to nature represented by artificial light, motor traffic and suburban crawl. Thus began my tree-planting journey.

Most tree plantations use plastic tubing and fences to protect young trees from grazing deer. Despite claims that they're biodegradable, they're ugly and terrible for the environment. Thousands of young trees had started growing by themselves since we'd begun rewilding, so in my planting I decided to imitate nature. I'd accept that some saplings wouldn't take, that some would be eaten, but that the rest would grow into forests. It was going to be perfect. I started assembling trees. I grew some in pots, took donations and bought some from a well-regarded local nursery. I began to plant. Recalling how funny I'd looked when I'd tried facing down the ragwort in pink gloves, now I was at it again with a wonky shovel, the same trusty pink washing-up gloves and sacks of trees. I attacked the ground like a man on a mission, opening up gaps and slowly sinking the little trees into the soil, patting their bases tight. In the first year, I planted a thousand native trees. In the second, I planted nearly two thousand.

By the end of the second summer, all the saplings I'd planted had been eaten by the rapidly growing deer population. All that remained of my baby trees were stubs. From a castle window I watched the deer resentfully. They looked very happy in their large herd, standing in the tall grass. I gave the deer my best evil stares. They didn't care.

It was bad enough I'd lost all the trees; now I had hands like a carpenter and had endured several episodes of lower backache from all the labouring. Deer are notorious for destroying and ravaging forests all over Ireland, and a lot of conservationists want to cull them for this very reason.

I certainly looked silly now to everyone who'd watched me plant thousands of saplings.

But in the nearby forest, there was an *explosion* of young trees. There they grew – oak, beech, alder, willow, ash and massive amounts of hawthorn – completely undisturbed by the deer just a hundred metres away. Looking more closely, I noticed hawthorn growing everywhere a tree had died and opened the canopy. Among and between the hawthorns, the slower-growing trees seemed completely undisturbed. I'd observed a similar pattern before with the brambles, among which willow or birch grew tall. Bramble and hawthorn are both very spiky. It didn't take a genius to understand: they were nature's plastic tube. The deer clearly avoided the spiky bushes, allowing the saplings to grow there.

Then I noticed something even more interesting. In the forest, the tree saplings seemed to grow unimpeded by the deer even when they *weren't* growing among spiky bushes, and although the deer tracks showed they'd been walking right past. Considering this, I reflected that there'd been very little natural undergrowth in the forest before we started rewilding. In the woodlands, there was less damage to the trees from the deer, not more, although the herd was much bigger. A rarely visited woodland area in particularly good condition had very little damage at all. Passing an oak seedling much like the doomed ones I'd planted, I decided to do an experiment: I'd dig up a bunch of oak seedlings, let them grow, plant them the following year, and see what happened.

I took nine oak seedlings and grew them in pots for a year. To make the experiment seamless I used only the soil from the forest they came from. After a year, I carefully distributed them around three of my forests: three in each. For the sake of comparison, I planted them near naturally seeded oaks and went away for a month. When I returned, every single one of my nine oaks had been destroyed, while the neighbouring oaks – often growing less than a metre away – remained untouched! I'd used the same soil, and planted the same trees beneath a mature oak, so what was going on? Why did the deer destroy these? I had no answer . . . not yet.

Rivers and their management are a matter of ongoing debate in Ireland, as elsewhere. For a long time, the conventional wisdom was that human intervention could help rivers to function normally while serving agriculture and industry. Natural streams and rivers rarely flow straight; usually they bend and twist. This slows the flow, allowing nooks and crannies to form at the sides, where fish and amphibians can spawn. Rivers also steadily fill with debris. After heavy rain, their banks break, depositing much of it in the flood plains. Like volcanic ash, this nutrient-rich matter gives a serious boost to biodiversity. When farmers created drainage systems in waterlogged fields they dug ditches into which excess water flowed. Responding to gravity, these often ran towards larger water systems, along with all the dirt and debris that washed off the fields. But when we started straightening rivers and lowering the water table by digging into the riverbed, rivers could no longer break their banks, which meant that none of this valuable debris could form or redeposit on the river banks or forest floor. The water flowed more quickly too, so pools of more slow-flowing water no longer formed, and it became more difficult for the various species that once nested there to do so. We also cleared many of our waterways of falling debris such as rocks, timber and other disrupters of flow.

All across Europe, local authorities and other managers of waterways have for years removed fallen timber and other obstructions to keep rivers clear and flowing speedily through the landscape. While this reduced biodiversity, it also reduced the frequency with which rivers broke their banks. More recently, climate change has introduced new weather conditions. Very intense rainfall has become much more common in northern Europe, leading to more frequent and extremely dangerous flash floods.

The Skane flows along our fields and through several of our forests. Many years ago, it had been full of life. As I said before, back in the nineties when Oliver and I played *Rambo* – our favourite movie – in the woods and in the river, we'd imagined our cherry-laurel-clogged forest to be very similar to Vietnam. With our trusty sticks, we'd waded through the Skane's murky waters looking for enemy combatants: always on the lookout for Charlie, ready for an ambush! Every so often, as we splashed through the dark, cloudy waters, we'd see bubbles floating to the surface and bursting there. We'd never actually found any Vietcong, but we'd always returned in need of a shower and clean clothes. Then we got older, discovered girls and other entertainment, and stopped playing in the river. I hadn't given it much thought for years, and only now did I learn that the fizzing and bubbling in the water had been caused by sewage pumped into it by the local council, and that Oliver and I'd spent many childhood days wading through shit. Horrified, I arranged for every medical test available to ensure I hadn't contracted any lurking disease. Having left leaving the doctor's office looking like a pincushion,

I can safely say I'm clean and can confirm I've no hepatitis. Thank you for asking.

The revelation of the sewage dump had caused considerable local embarrassment, and although the county council had stopped discharging sewage into the Skane, there'd been no life in it for years. Then one day I was walking along the river when I noticed movement in the water. I looked carefully and saw a little fish I'd later identify as a brown trout. After all these years, the fish were back!

About a year later, a member of the Board of Works arrived at my door. He explained that he was representing the state, and that Irish waterways are the remit of the state, not individual landowners. He said he needed to clean the Skane to protect it and keep it clear and, without understanding the implications, we gave him access. Sometime later, he arrived with several diggers and used them to dredge the river, digging out lumps of mud and dumping them on the banks. To my horror, my employees noticed living fish squiggling in the mud. We quickly helped them as best we could, picking them up and throwing them into the water as the men and their diggers worked.

By the end of the day the river was 'clean'. There were no branches left to slow the waterflow and the riverbank bore several large piles of forest debris and a large number of plastic containers that been washed downstream. I glanced into the water, thinking that it looked ravaged. Instinctively, I knew that this was all wrong. I decided that, no matter what, I wouldn't let anyone do this again. Gradually, the river returned to its normal state. As winter storms came and went, boughs and even whole trees fell into the river and started to form natural dams, and some of the river banks collapsed, creating small twists in the water.

People are used to seeing tidied, manicured waterways. At first, when you see fallen trees and submerged branches in a river, it can be a little disconcerting. But when you think about it, obviously this is the natural condition of rivers, because they've been flowing through the landscape since long before humans existed. These fallen trees and branches create environments ideal for fostering life in and near the water. For example, salmon require rocky river beds in which to lay their eggs, and young salmon require pools where the current is relatively slow in which to feed and grow. Because the Skane passes through farmland before reaching Dunsany, it unfortunately carries mud deposits from drainage channels. This mud settles on the river bed. Because the river can't break its banks, the riverbed is not a good nursery for young salmon.

But the river was still in much better condition than it had been for very many years. Diverse fish, including trout, gradually became a frequent sight, the sunlight that filtered through the tree cover overhead dappling on their skin. Otters returned to hunt and to raise their young on the muddy river banks.

When the world refers to rewilding, predator species are widely discussed. There are lots of examples of natural environments from which predator species have been removed because their presence was inconvenient or a threat to humans. In Ireland, as we've seen, the last of the native wolves was killed in the seventeenth century. As carnivores like wolves represent a threat to valuable livestock – and, to a much lesser extent, sometimes to humans – it's easy to understand why people wanted to get rid of them. But removing predators from a landscape also causes new problems, because now the prey species will become more numerous, sometimes outstripping the natural environment's capacity to support them, at which stage they'll become a threat to crops.

Famously, grey wolves were reintroduced to Yellowstone National Park in the United States in 1995, having been locally extinct for about a century. Relatively quickly, their presence moderated the elk population, which reduced the degradation of the areas around water sources, allowing other plant and animal species to thrive there. Beyond Yellowstone, some other places that have reintroduced predators have seen quite dramatic environmental changes, which are often for the better, as the numbers of prey animals have become more sustainable, with positive repercussions for plant diversity. But there are significant challenges to reintroducing predators, particularly when lands available for rewilding are small and often adjacent to agricultural land, and to towns and suburbs.

Should we in Ireland reintroduce predators such as wolves? There's understandable pushback against such an idea from the farming community, which has reasonable concerns about the impact on domestic animals, and from the general population, worried about the potential for attacks on people and pets. In principle, I'd love to introduce a pack of wolves to Dunsany, at least partly to irritate my critics. They are – or once were – a native Irish species, and their return would naturally ensure a balance between predator and prey species. But, in practical terms, it's probably too late to introduce wolves to an area like Dunsany. Ireland's forests and wild landscapes are very fragmented now. Ireland has too few areas where wildlife is free to roam. Some animals have adapted to this status quo, such as the fox, which has learned how to live in urban environments, but wolves are pack animals that are far bigger, more aggressive and more dangerous to people. They'd cause havoc in an urban setting. They cause almost as much in agricultural settings. In recent years there's been a lot of pushback against rewilding in continental Europe, especially when wolves have been reintroduced to parks and reserves, as many of them have ventured into local farmland and killed cattle. Some people have even started illegally killing wolves. One of the big problems with wolf packs is that they need a large territory and these are disappearing quickly from most of Europe. Without large territories, projects involving the reintroduction of predators like wolves are unlikely to succeed, while also making rewilding unpopular.

Killing animals like deer seems like an obvious way to imitate the role of predators in the natural environment, but in practice it's not that simple. The Irish government persistently loses control of deer numbers. I've often heard government ministers calling for a mass cull because the deer population has grown out of control. More deer-hunting licences are granted every year, but the number of deer continues to increase. For example, according to the National Parks and Wildlife Service of Ireland, 78,175 wild deer were culled in the twelve months up to February 2023. At the time of writing in 2024, the government is calling for another major cull, as despite the enormous numbers of slaughtered animals, the population of wild deer continues to soar.

Exploring the real impact of the culling programme, it might be that the number of people shooting deer is actually making things worse. Deer breed in the rutting season, which normally starts in late September/early October and lasts for a few weeks. The testosterone levels of stags soar at this time, reaching up to 300 per cent more than normal. The calls of the males attract the females, and ultimately the males fight each other for access to does. Generally, the largest, strongest stags dominate, and many of the smaller, weaker ones are left with few opportunities to mate. Now, enter the hunters. They typically want to kill the most spectacular-looking males. With alpha males removed, the younger, weaker males have access to the females and more females get pregnant than if a small number of stags were dominating. This may be one reason deer numbers continue to grow despite efforts to reduce them through hunting.

I wondered if the natural order would be able to adjust itself if we didn't assume the role of the predator. The growing numbers of deer did pose a challenge to my desire to increase forest cover at Dunsany, so it was a real conundrum. Early in the rewilding, I'd declared my intention to both cease culling the deer and to engage in substantial reforestation. Many people said these two goals were mutually exclusive, because the deer would eat all the baby saplings as soon as they were planted. It *was* true that the deer quickly gobbled up the saplings I planted, but it was also true that in the already forested areas, where the saplings planted and rooted themselves, they gradually ate fewer and fewer.

As the years passed and the size of the deer herd increased, the saplings showed less damage from deer, and a new generation of understorey trees was growing fast and thick. This had never happened before, when we'd still been managing the deer population, and it also doesn't happen in national parks around the country. By the time the deer population of Dunsany had tripled, the deer had also largely stopped eating the saplings in the forested areas. How could that be? I believe that in the absence of predators, prey species will often find their own balance if they're left alone. We held tight, and eventually, the deer population seemed to have settled, to have reached a natural equilibrium.

Since we stopped interfering with the forests, the new growth in the understorey increased dramatically. It included many species that weren't here before, evidently introduced by the many birds finding a home here, and by deer, foxes, badgers and other creatures that consume fruits and berries and transport seeds and pollen in their droppings and on their fur. We've observed how shrubs and smaller trees that are often considered irrelevant or even harmful, and are removed, actually foster and encourage the growth of other species. I've already spoken of how the bramble and hawthorn seem to repel deer and shelter baby trees from the grazing. Brambles, often regarded as a waste of space, are also among the greatest absorbers of carbon, while the fruits produced by both the bramble and the hawthorn are nutritious to birds, animals and humans. A healthy forest is home to many bird and animal species.

Now that disturbances to our forests were minimal, they could produce a lot of food. Birds were coming to eat blackberries and to nest in ever-greater numbers. The fibre-rich blackberries encouraged healthy digestion, and as they deposited faeces on the forest floor, they dropped seeds they'd eaten here and elsewhere, organically introducing new plant species, increasing our biodiversity and refreshing the gene pool of our naturally occurring trees and plants.

One of our biggest assets at Dunsany is the size of the reserve. There's enough space to create something absolutely meaningful.

The animals here are not confined; they also roam beyond our borders into all the land around us. As the rewilding progressed, Dunsany became a sort of oasis for local wildlife; a place they could enter that was free from hunting and provided lots of food. As time passed, I have interfered with the rewilding less and less. If rewilding required our constant attention it would actually be new age gardening. The emphasis of rewilding must be on the 'wild'. But I couldn't help wanting to make my own discernible impact on Dunsany. Don't all humans feel a need to influence their surroundings? I'd sought to do something that would 'put a bow' on what was already happening rather than interfere with it. I considered how the human body requires circulation, and how we're products of nature. Where there's flow, there's health. In the human body, blood carries oxygen and nutrients and, where there's good blood flow, there's generally better health. Similarly, a nature reserve is healthier when there's more movement of birds and animals. Gradually, the tree corridors we'd planted, using biodegradable cardboard tubes containing no plastic to keep the saplings safe from deer and rabbits while they were still young and tender, were creating connections between the forests, making it easier for keystone species to establish or re-establish themselves at Dunsany.

Life sometimes brings people together at just the right moment. In summer 2019 the phone rang, and when I answered it a woman from a local wildlife refuge introduced herself as Nicola. She'd heard about Dunsany and wondered if I'd be interested in returning a trio of orphaned foxes she'd been caring for to the wild. She was running out of options, as most country people see foxes as vermin, and many of them are involved in, or at least sympathetic to, fox hunting.

(I learned later that country foxes and urban require very different things to flourish and when urban foxes are repatriated to the country, or country foxes to urban areas, they often fail to adjust.) I'd no problem with foxes. In fact, I quite liked them. I'd often put my neck out fighting with local fox hunting clubs, and we'd exchanged many hearty insults. As with the trees I planted, this was a moment when I interfered with nature. For me, Dunsany had become a symbol for the voiceless, the ones in need of protection. For the unwanted. It's an oasis for all nature in which all creatures would be treated equally. Of course, I accepted immediately.

The foxes – three lovely creatures – arrived one Saturday. Mum, who also liked cute, fluffy little things, immediately wondered if we could keep them as pets. Nicola wasn't sure whether or not to take her seriously. Laura and Catherine helped with the cages as we all walked to a small woodland, Bluebell Wood, near the castle. As we walked, Nicola looked up and around in surprise. 'I can't believe there's such a big wilderness in the area and that so few people know about it,' she said. As we walked, I explained how and why the land looked as it did, and our ethos for rewilding.

We arrived where the woods met our giant meadow. The grass was easily five and a half feet tall, and the trees blew gently in the air. We placed the cages down and prepared to release the young foxes. I nodded at Catherine and she sprung open the door of the first cage. The single fox shot out and disappeared into the large meadow. The second cage opened and Nicola nudged it. The second fox leapt out, ran a short distance and slowed down to a trot through the long grass. Unsure about the whole thing, the third remained pressed against the back of the cage. Nicola tapped the cage and lifted it, trying to usher him out. Eventually he took off and ran away before stopping to peer back for a moment. Then he jumped into the deep grass and disappeared. Nicola picked up her cage.

'Well,' she said, 'another one down. I'd better be getting back now. I've loads of patients still waiting for their dinner.'

I helped Nicola carry the cages. As I placed them in her car, I said that she if ever needed a place to release animals, they'd be safe here.

'I was just about to ask,' she smiled. 'What's your view on wood pigeons?'

Soon I was receiving orphaned animals from rescue organisations all over the area. Considering my conflict-filled relationship of long standing with the local hunt, I made a particular point of taking foxes. I made sure everyone knew about it, too. It was two fingers to the hunt, and we all knew it. The releasing of orphaned and injured animals was a success and social media was electric. Big surprise: people love to see fluffy animals being released in nature reserves. Now we were getting diverse types of animals: foxes, birds, hedgehogs and more. But much as I was thrilled to see all the animals released here, I wanted to do more. It wasn't enough.

In the summer of 2019, Laura and Catherine moved to Dunsany. We stayed in a house in the coachyard to have privacy. That allowed me to spend time with them and also to look after my mother in the castle next door. It was a glorious summer and they settled in easily. Catherine enjoyed the woods with my troupe of dogs; I had six now. Laura talked happily about foraging and learning how to identify the different types of mushrooms and edible plants on the estate. She was eager and anxious to learn more and more about the plants, trees and animals surrounding us. New life had been breathed into Dunsany again. My world was changing in so many wonderful ways. Was it just me hitting life goals as I got older, or was it the magic of the place?

Gradually, I found that local people who shared my interest in wildlife started thinking about me differently. I stopped being that awkward guy above in the castle who liked to make things difficult for the hunt, and became the fella who was interested in animals and seemed to be doing his best to help them. Until now, I'd been called 'English cunt' once or twice a week by people who didn't like how I parked, or took exception to seeing me picking up groceries at the supermarket. That was happening a lot less often now. In fact, people occasionally approached me in the local café to say they'd seen a red kite in their garden and assumed it was 'one of mine'. Some said I was doing excellent work, and were happy it was happening in the area. Next, the local schools heard about Dunsany Reserve and invited me to talk to the kids about nature and inspire the children's projects on local wildlife. Now I wasn't just the chap who likes foxes, I was the local man who took time to show the primary school the reserve and tell stories about animals to the kids.

Finally, I'd started to belong.

Chapter Eight

Networking

ALMOST EVERY HUMAN SOCIETY HAS BEEN BASED ON THE PRINCIPLE OF HIERARCHY. We generally extend this idea to our understanding of the natural world, too. Here in Ireland, for example, we seem to observe a hierarchy of trees, with some considered important and noble, and others barely considered at all. The Irish oak, a beautiful, slow-growing species whose acorns were once part of the Irish diet, is regarded as an aristocrat among trees, whereas the scrubby hawthorn – although important in folklore and tradition – is often seen as little more than filler, a nuisance-tree that can easily be removed from the landscape with no ill effects.

In reality, the fates and fortunes of all tree species are deeply intertwined and interdependent, on each other and on all the other natural species in the wild environment. Gradually, I realised it didn't make sense to see plants, trees and other species as individuals. Instead, they're networks in which every single element is intimately intertwined with every other. We've seen how baby trees that take root in areas thick with brambles, thistles and other thorny plants have more protection in their early years and can grow until they're less vulnerable to the deer. Meanwhile, another tree would have reached the end of its natural life and fallen, and in the clearing caused by this departure from life, young brambles and hawthorns would already be starting to grow.

I began to learn more about species that are often overlooked, and that have a role in the natural environment so important that 'essential' sounds like an insult: fungi. Up to half of the living biomass of the ground is composed of networks of fungi. Without fungi, there's no life at all. Living in an old, damp building as I do, I had already spent a lot of time pondering fungi, mostly in terms of the black mould that forms on our walls every time a roof tile comes off and water seeps into the castle. Now I learned that there are literally millions of types of fungi, and they're at the heart of everything. The part of the fungi we typically see – sticking out of the ground or poking from a pile of rotting wood – is just a tiny part of the whole. Most of the fungal organism consists of an extensive network of mycelium, the millions of tiny threads that twine through the soil and wrap themselves around tree and plant roots. If you pick up even just a handful of soil from the forest floor, it could easily contain hundreds, if not thousands, of metres of mycelium. The mycelium is essential to a healthy environment because it breaks down rotting matter and returns it to the soil, and it delivers essential nutrients and minerals to trees and other species, as well as forming a means of communication – of threats, of times of plenty – between them.

When a plant or a tree has a symbiotic relationship with a fungus, it's known as a mycorrhiza. The fungus establishes itself among the plant's roots, where the plant supplies it with the sugars or lipids it makes through photosynthesis. In turn, the fungus supplies the plant with nutrients from the soil and with water. Most plants have had close relationships with fungi since the earliest of them evolved from the water-based algae from which all plant life is descended. Thanks to this relationship, plants of all sorts gradually colonised the land, and in their growing, living and dying made the very soil come to life, enabling the eventual appearance of birds and animals, including humans.

Not only do individual plants have these relationships of mutual benefit with fungi, but nutrients can move between different plants throughout the mycorrhizal network. Every healthy, functioning forest has a mycorrhizal network that allows trees to communicate and even cooperate. In a forest, every plant is connected through this system, and they can all be actively involved in transferring nutrients, such as phosphorus and carbon via the mycorrhiza, which are microfilaments, fifty times thinner and up to a hundred times longer than even the narrowest, longest plant root. If one species has more of a particular element than it needs, it can transfer it via this network to another species, in exchange for something else. The mycorrhiza also fosters a strong immune response in plants, making them less vulnerable to disease.

Plants can also use the network to communicate threats to other network members. We've all been taught about how evolution and adaptation are driven by competition, and that's part of the story, but they're driven by cooperation and networking too. The implications for how human beings can and should interact with forests are huge. Active management of forested areas typically involves removing dying and dead trees, and often includes the thinning of the understorey, with the idea of giving young saplings more space to grow. But dying and dead trees are a vital part of the forest. As it nears the end of its life, a tree can redistribute carbon and other elements, via the mycorrhizal network, to younger trees. After death, fungi break it down, returning all its nutrients to the soil and feeding the fungal networks.

Active forestry management also often means removing species that might seem less important, so there'll be more space for favoured trees. But these 'less important' species are connected through the same fungal network with the others in a complex relationship of mutual benefit. Removing them can be catastrophic. Interfere with even just one element of the forest, and you can disrupt the entire system. There are many parallels with human societies. A community entirely composed of very young people is likely to be extremely unstable, because youths benefit from the steadying hand of their elders. A community entirely composed of the elderly doesn't really work either, because they need the support, excitement and stimulation that only youngsters can offer. A healthy community – whether a forest or a human town or city – is a complex network of individuals from all walks and stages of life, interacting with one another in various ways.

I could see all this working at Dunsany, every single day. Surprising things had started to happen. Most of the Dunsany elms died at the height of the outbreak of Dutch elm disease. But now the elms started to grow again. Despite predictions they'd soon wither and die, most seemed to be flourishing. Our forests contain what may be the largest elm trees left in

Ireland. How did they survive? These few ancient trees shared one thing: they were all deep in our oldest woodlands. None of the elms that grew alone in the middle of a field survived. Could the forest itself be the cause of their survival? Could the new trees returning to our woodlands represent the first wave of immunity or was it something else? Perhaps our policy of non-interference allowed a healthy mycelium network to flourish, affording the elm a degree of protection in the face of a significant threat?

Research into exactly how the mycorrhizal network functions is still ongoing, but it seems likely that symbiosis and even cooperation between plant species are more crucial to evolution than competition, as is often assumed. Many studies show that mycorrhizal networks can transfer elements crucial to life, such as carbon, nitrogen and phosphorus, between plants, helping them all to thrive. As the fungus network depends on the forest for its wellbeing, and vice versa, this exchange loop is fundamental to keeping the complete system healthy and active. And that's not all: plants may be able to use the mycorrhizal network to communicate threats and hazards. If a particular tree species, for example, is under attack from a parasite or other hazard, it seems to use the mycorrhizal networks to communicate this information to other trees of the same species, and they respond by increasing their defences against the specific threat. In a system that's working really well, a virtuous circle is established, as the health of each individual organism – plant or fungus – is enhanced by the others' good health, with the complete system in turn becoming a more advantageous environment for life.

I've mentioned that when I started planting trees to create corridors between our forested areas, all the saplings I placed so carefully in the soil were quickly eaten by the deer. Initially, I thought that maybe this was because they'd been planted in open grassland, so I started planting saplings in the forest. They were eaten too, while nearby saplings that were self-seeded seemed to have had no damage at all. Why? I believe the naturally seeded saplings are part of the system, plugged into the mycorrhizal network from the moment they start to grow, and this gives them a certain amount of protection; whereas when I introduce saplings by digging a hole and planting one, I'm disturbing the connectivity of the mycelium network, which has to restore itself around the new arrival, a complex process that can take a lot of time.

Obviously, when we humans intervene in the landscape by farming, deforesting or adding artificial chemicals, we interfere with the mycorrhizal network. We typically don't destroy it, because it's complex and multi-faceted, but we stress it, making it less effective. It's still able to function to a degree but, like when increased distortion is added to a phone line, the interference becomes more intense and it's increasingly difficult for plants to communicate. Their resourcefulness as a community falters. They become more vulnerable to disease and other threats. Left alone, though, landscapes can heal themselves relatively quickly. The threads of fungus begin to weave their delicate structures with a little help from their first wave of restoration: the common weeds we so often fight.

Our natural self-planted forests have changed over the centuries. Today, most include a wide array of invasive species that grow wild among native plants. Some rewilders believe that *all* non-native species – like beech, introduced to Ireland in the 1600s – should be uprooted and removed. Others feel we can't erase the past and should work with what we've got now. I fall into the latter camp, as I've faith that, left to its own devices, nature will either find a way to coexist with non-native species, or will discover its own way to eliminate them. I feel the role of rewilding is not to restore the past, but to create a new future by letting the ecosystem learn how to manage itself. The beech and the brown rat were originally foreign to Ireland, yet they've found a way to work well within our common shared land.

The cherry laurel, a common sight in Ireland with its shiny green leaves and springy branches, growing tight and near to the ground, is an evergreen from the cherry family. It's native to south-west Asia and south-east Europe, and was introduced in centuries past as a decorative shrub. At Dunsany, they were often planted in the forest to give cover for pheasant shooting. Unfortunately, the cherry laurel absolutely loves our mild, damp climate and seems to thrive in almost any type of soil, particularly the acidic soil that is common in Ireland. With the help of birds, which find its fruit delicious, eat them, and then spread their seeds abundantly, it quickly jumped over garden walls and colonised vast swathes of the whole country. Many introduced species can coexist with native flora and fauna. That's not the case with the cherry laurel. As no Irish animals consume its leaves or saplings, it spreads rapidly through forests, filling the understorey with abundant stalky and leafy growth. The thick, leathery, waxy leaves, with the high levels of cyanide that give them that almondy smell when the sun shines on them, prevent the sunlight penetrating to the lower levels and severely inhibit the growth of other species. When the leaves fall, they cover the ground like a carpet, further inhibiting the light's ability to penetrate, and taking longer to decay than most forest debris. Together with rhododendron ('the gruesome twosome' as I like to call them) these plants are in the government's sights, with vast sums spent every year on chemicals to kill them. As with the war on deer, Ireland hasn't managed to restore a balance and in some places, like Killarney National Park in Kerry, it appears to have gone backwards.

A few years after the rewilding started, the cherry laurel at Dunsany was doing less well than before. Some trees had died, and others were looking weak and scruffy, with fewer leaves and some completely bare branches. Then I started seeing areas wholly cleared of cherry laurel, where the branches were rotting and, in some cases, had fallen to the ground. Most of the leaves had fallen off. I'd no idea why.

One day, doing my usual walk through the rewilding part of the estate, I was enjoying the moist evening and listening to *Wrong One to Fuck With,* the new Dying Fetus album (side note: this is a *great* record), I'd turned down a track by the river when I heard something heavy knocking on wood. *Is someone cutting down a tree?* I thought. In the past, we've had people breaking into the forest and stealing the wood. I turned off the death metal and listened carefully. There was silence for a moment and then I heard wood breaking. I reached for my phone and glanced down: no signal, I was too deep in the forest.

Although we'd had plenty of timber thieves, it had never happened so close to the castle before, or in the part of the forest that required crossing the river. Whoever these people were, they had big balls. I was alone and wouldn't be able to call the police until I got out of the trees, so I prepped for conflict, puffing up my chest and advancing, armed with little more than bad language. I sped down the path towards the sound. Bursting around the corner towards it, I was greeted by . . . no one. I was in an empty clearing. I looked around stupidly. The sound had vanished. Had I gone mad? Or perhaps I myself had been rewilded?

Then I glimpsed a flash of movement. I heard the crack of wood. I turned to see a stag with large antlers colliding with a small tree, forcing it to crack. He paused a moment, shook his head, banged his horns against the tree and moved away. I noticed another large male stag with equally big antlers. The first stepped back and the second took a running start and rushed at the tree. His antlers crashed and the tree twisted and heaved, one of its lower branches snapping with a screech. We've all seen those wildlife documentaries by David Attenborough, with footage of deer rubbing their horns on young trees to scratch off the surface or whatever. This wasn't like that. It was more like a Warner Brothers cartoon when a bull chases somebody wearing red.

The first deer began to move towards the tree again and I slipped my hands towards my pocket to retrieve my phone and take a photo. The deer turned their heads at the movement and noticed me. As the three of us stared at each other, my hand continued slowly towards my pocket. It was like a Mexican stand-off in a Clint Eastwood film. My hand would draw closer, and a stag's head would bob up. Not wanting to spook them, I'd stop moving. It was close to mating season, and I'd heard that stags can be dangerous at that time. Finally, I pulled out my phone. I needed a picture so people would believe me when I described what I'd seen. My phone screen went on. Code required. Damn. I began to type my code, failing first time because the screen was damp. I failed a second time. The third time, I'd begun to punch in the code when the deer snapped out of their reverie and began to run. My phone unlocked and I hit the camera button. The result? A deer's blurry backside. *Damn*, I thought. *I've never seen anything like that before and all I have to show for it's a splodgy image of a deer leaving through the undergrowth.* Nothing suitable for Instagram. I cursed at my phone, slipped on my headphones, pressed play and listened to Dying Fetus as I walked on.

I've seen some pretty strange things over the years, and if that had been the end of it, I'd have just dismissed it as animals being odd. But I started to observe the laurel thinning out more than could be explained by deer just smashing through and leaving gaps. Whole branches seemed to be dying on the trees. In December that year, as I was taking my evening walk through the meadow, my foot hit something so hard I gasped in pain and released an avalanche of bad language. I peered down and found a thin laurel tree lying in the field. What was going on?

My first port of call was to Gerry, the man in charge of our timber business. Gerry's a strong bulldozer of a man, with hands like clusters of bananas. He'd been working with us for about ten years and I regard him as a friend. But if he'd been cutting down trees, we were going to have a word, because I'd told everyone we weren't going to, not even the invasive ones. I found Gerry in the woodyard splitting timber. He spun around, startled, when I called his name.

'Jaysus, you scared me,' he said. He put down the chainsaw and lit a cigarette. 'What can I do for you?'

I smiled and sat down on a log. 'I was walking through the woods the other day,' I said. 'There's a lot more space than I remember.'

He nodded. 'It's winter, I guess. Fewer leaves on the trees.'

'This was in the upper part of the woods near the river. You know, where the laurel is.'

Gerry nodded.

'Have you been doing some extra work?' I asked.

'What do you mean?'

'Have you been cutting any cherry laurel?'

'Why the hell would I do that? It's useless. You can't even burn it. It's poisonous.'

'Conservation, then?'

He paused and took another drag of his cigarette. 'Lord Dunsany –'

I'm in trouble, I thought. *I've offended him. He only calls me 'Lord Dunsany' when he's annoyed with me.*

'Lord Dunsany, what would make me want to cut down cherry laurel? It's good for nothing and I'm sure not gonna do it for my health. Besides, you're the meanest boss I've ever had – and I worked in the prison service.'

'So you haven't been cutting the laurel in the woods? I asked again.

He chuckled. Good. I hadn't offended him.

'God, no.'

'Well, keep up the good work, we'll have to visit your pub for a drink again sometime.'

Last time we'd gone, he and his friends had me downing shots and I'd ended up on the side of the road puking whiskey and poitín. A great night. But if it wasn't because of Gerry, *why* was the cherry laurel dying?

I spent the night googling to see if a disease or parasite could be destroying the trees. Nothing. Then one night, as I turned into the drive on my way back from a rock concert, the headlights illuminated a stupefying sight. Four does at one of the laurel bushes were ripping the leaves off and eating them! I stopped to watch but the deer moved on quickly when they saw the headlights. I rolled up to the bush and looked at the damage. The branches were ripped apart – not enough to kill the tree, but sufficient enough to severely reduce its ability to flourish.

I returned to the woods the next day and looked very carefully at the cherry laurels. All the branches had been removed or picked dry. I continued to monitor them, noticing that new shoots were removed almost as quickly as they formed. New forests often fail to thrive when deer eat bark off trees, causing them to weaken and, often, die. Cherry laurel is hardy, but it will also die if the bark is removed. Like many trees, cherry laurel feeds itself through the membrane. The cherry laurels were being pruned so aggressively that light was beginning to hit the ground as it never could when they were flourishing. I also saw that many of the dead cherry laurel branches had a variety of fungi growing from them. The wood was already breaking down. The deer had been dragging trees from the wood and depositing them on the grass. I'd heard that elephants do something similar to stop the savannah grasslands becoming jungle. Could the deer be doing the same thing?

Because cherry laurel is poisonous, deer don't generally eat it. If they did, it would never have become such a problem in our national parks. Most efforts to eliminate it rely on the heavy use of chemical poison, injecting it straight into the tree, or spraying harmful chemicals on the ground. I asked all my employees if they'd ever heard of deer destroying cherry laurel before. They all confirmed that deer don't eat it because it's poisonous and said it had never happened in Dunsany. And yet, I'd seen it happening several times, and the deer looked healthier and stronger than ever. I started asking every learned person I knew, and researching every evening. It seemed that the behaviour of Dunsany's deer was anomalous. Could it be hormonal, relating to the time of year? It couldn't be a lack of food because we'd hundreds of acres of long grass.

Months passed and the deer continued to systematically destroy the cherry laurel, especially in the forests. They'd focus on one area until the trees started dying and then pick another. They'd attack one section and ignore another. The areas being cleared began to have undergrowth again, as young trees and plants grew beneath the cherry laurel where the ground had been bare before. Despite their aggressive grazing of the cherry laurel, the deer often spared new saplings, of species they usually ate, beside the laurel. I was fascinated, feeling as though I'd discovered a secret.

There are nine forested areas in Dunsany, and the same thing was happening in each of the seven that had cherry laurel. They also grow on my closest neighbour's farm, and although he has plenty of deer on his land, his cherry laurel remained untouched. In the more agricultural areas of Dunsany, the cherry laurels were similarly unharmed. They were only being destroyed in the rewilding parts of the estate.

Pondering this, I asked myself: *What is a mature forest, really?* Sure, there are trees and plants, but it's more than that. A healthy, mature forest is an advanced, complex system. It includes animals and birds and, of course, the mycelium. Clearly, the mycelium is strongest in areas of ancient or mature forest. It's a complex web connecting vast areas of the planet, but by building and farming we've weakened and partitioned it. It hasn't been destroyed, but its ability to function and regulate is massively diminished. Consider Ireland: how many mature woodlands or bogs remain free of human management? We use chemicals to fight invasive plants, and much of our land is heavily grazed and constantly disturbed by human activities. We've very little wild forestry in which dead trees are allowed to fall and rot. We limit the mobility of animals, wild and domesticated, with control fences. Very little of our land is truly healthy.

But in Dunsany, we'd stopped interfering with the fields. We'd let the grasses grow, die and rot. We'd limited human access. We'd removed fences and stopped trying to prevent the animals occupying their natural habitat. Could it be that, beneath our noses, the mycelium was growing, reestablishing itself, and connecting itself more securely to the habitat? Our rewilded lands were full of large trees, some hundreds of years old, and now the land was no longer intensely grazed, and large swathes of it were experiencing natural decay and the return of many native plant species. Could it be that the fungal networks were stitching themselves back together, slowly filtering out the toxins that animal agriculture had left in the soil, and enriching themselves for the first time in generations with the abundant decaying matter? Was the system was coming back online as the impacts of human interventions on the land declined? As the fields rewilded and the forests bloomed with fallen timber, was the mycelium starting to connect one patch of forest with another? To link *all* the species of the forest – plants *and* animals – to one another in a complex web we don't yet understand?

Suzanne Simard, a Canadian forestry scientist, developed and ultimately proved her theory that trees communicate by passing nutrients through the soil. She examined the concept of the mother tree and its ability to recognise its young by signals passed via the mycelium, and to protect them by emitting tastes and smells to ward off grazing animals. That would explain why the saplings I'd planted had been destroyed, while the naturally seeded ones nearby survived. Could a similar process be impacting on the deer? In order for the mycelium to function properly, allowing trees to protect their young, the system needs to be healthy. But what if the threat to the forest was not the deer, but an alien plant, like the cherry laurel, whose presence threatened the entire system? In that case, how would a forest self-regulate itself? How would it control such a threat? One way might be fostering the presence of a plant disease that could eliminate the threat. After all, disease is often nature's way of rebalancing. But what if there was no plant disease that could do it? Would nature just let cherry laurel and other invasive species take over the world? Was it possible that trees, which can release smells and tastes to ward away grazers from their young, could also attract a grazing animal like deer to eat something new, or even to see the plant as hostile, and in this way use animal behaviour to bring sustainability to a mature system? Maybe. In our arrogance, we seem to believe that nature can't function without our interference. But in Dunsany, our forests were flourishing as never before in my lifetime. We were seeing astonishing regeneration and declining numbers of cherry laurel, all without chemicals or other invasive procedures. Although I don't understand how, I believe the healing forest itself was prompting the deer to eliminate an imposter threatening the viability of the complete system. Now, this is just a theory, I've found little to no literature to support it, and there's no money to be made in sitting back and trusting nature. But try a thought experiment. Suspend your disbelief. What if I'm right? What if we really *have* discovered a secret? What if the forest has spoken? If nature can fix itself, there's hope for the future – for us all.

Dad told me I've a duty to do something for my people and my time, as so many of my ancestors did. I'd never felt able for this momentous responsibly. After all, I'd barely made it through school. Could *this* – the rewilding of Dunsany and the insights it offers the world – be my contribution? By leaving nature alone, and simply observing it, by rewilding with a vegan philosophy, could I do something worthwhile for animals, for plants, for the future of our planet? Could I create a template that would help others to do something similar? Before, I'd always been focused on the castle and on myself. I'd been able to see the bars of my gilded cage, but I'd never been able to see the handle on the door that would allow me to open it from the inside, and let me out to fly. Finally, I was beginning to understand my mission in life. Nature needed someone to champion it. I was determined to fight until I could fight no more.

Chapter Nine

She was Proud and so was I

STEPHEN AND I JUST COULDN'T MAKE *ORIGAMI* WORK. Time had passed and the landscape of independent film had changed. We decided to make a new film, hoping to revisit *Origami* once we had proven ourselves. After a few months, we'd created a new film, *The Green Sea*. Making *The Green Sea* was the first time I'd I truly embraced everything my mentor Karim Traïdia taught me. I'd put all my fears and emotions into it. Much of it was made on the estate, and watching it now I saw not just the movie, but also the significant, tangible changes that had occurred in the landscape since my earlier films. The film was shot in the end of 2017 and after numerous production issues we finally finished it at the end of 2019. And now our sales agent would be bringing it to market in the hope we could show it to the world in 2021.

Mum, who'd been watching me work on *The Green Sea* for several years, was eager to watch it. She didn't go to cinemas and had never come to a screening so I prepared a private screening for her in the living room. She cried when the film finished. She'd recognised much of the subject matter and the personalities: the film was deeply inspired by our lives and by her difficult childhood. She was proud and so was I. I'd made something honest, something completely me, my own wacky interpretation of the world I live in. Mum was buzzing, sure that people would flock to see *The Green Sea*. For a while, I thought so too. I had to. The stakes were high: I'd spent all my savings finishing it. Finally, I was going in the right direction.

In March 2020, together with much of the world, Ireland went into lockdown. Suddenly nobody could do anything other than work from home and go for walks outdoors. The film was shelved for a while and we were all stuck at home, watching what looked like the beginning of a post-apocalyptic film unfurl. We didn't know what to do, so we locked ourselves into the castle. Laura was a frontline worker and couldn't risk infecting my mother, so for now we lived apart. All the employees stayed either at home or outside. We felt under siege.

Mum had always had a 'weak chest' that tended to play up in spring and autumn. She was prone to infections and we'd lost count of how often she'd had pneumonia. The idea of a virus like Covid terrified us. We decided to take a conservative approach, went nowhere, kept everyone out of the house and cleaned our shopping with disinfectant. We both panicked when we heard her first cough. We'd been locked down for at least a month. When she developed symptoms, her doctor assured us it was her seasonal chest infection. He prescribed a course of antibiotics, which usually worked.

But instead of getting better, she grew steadily worse. The doctor prescribed more antibiotics, and then more again. I could see her growing slowly weaker. All the while, she kept working, using her architect's pencil to design the post-production studio I was then planning to build in the farmyard. I felt awful seeing her trying to pencil designs in bed, but the work seemed to keep her mind off how miserable she felt. For a day or two, she seemed to be improving, but then she deteriorated suddenly. I wanted to bring her to the hospital, but Daniel convinced me not to, worrying she'd catch Covid in hospital and die because she was already so weak.

Within a few days Mum was nearly unconscious, and I rang the ambulance. When it arrived, it was full of paramedics suited and booted against the virus. They loaded her into the back and took her away, leaving her sketchpads and pencils on the bed. I wanted to go, but the pandemic laws forbade it. When Mum got to the hospital, the doctors ran a Covid test. She'd had the virus the whole time.

I never saw my mother again. The hospitals weren't admitting visitors. She died on the isolation ward and was returned to Dunsany bagged in plastic in a closed coffin. My siblings couldn't come to the funeral and I wasn't allowed to open the coffin to say goodbye. It was just me, two estate employees, the dogs and the local priest – Father Toner, a long-time family friend – burying Mum beside Dad in the shadow of the old estate church. We all stood two metres apart and Laura and Catherine waited in the distance, under a tree, as Father Toner delivered his blessing. It was a beautiful day. The spring sun was cutting through the trees and the birds seemed to be singing louder than ever. The dogs, of course, couldn't say anything. After the burial I found one of them,

Chow, lying on the freshly-dug soil. His eyes told me that he understood. I was no one's child now.

Laura and Catherine were still living in the courtyard next door to the castle. They wouldn't move in with me for several weeks, and I had barely seen them for several weeks before that, as I'd been caring for Mum in her illness. With Mum gone, the castle and estate still needed my attention. We were facing bankruptcy as our farm tenant had not paid his rent. There wasn't time to mourn. I'd have to respect Mum's memory by keeping the show on the road.

I walked around the empty, quiet rooms of Dunsany Castle with dry eyes. I hadn't cried before or during the funeral either. I'd sworn not to cry when Dad died and now, no matter how bad I felt, stoicism just seemed to come naturally. I was glad about the Covid restrictions, because they meant nobody could visit and tell me how sorry they were for my loss. That might have tipped me over the edge, and I had a lot of work to do.

I considered how things were about to change. Since Dad's death, Mum had often taken the reins at Dunsany. It was all on me now. I set about cutting back on expenses as much as I could and started exploring ways to increase our income.

My old friend Peter – our hunter turned conservationist who had been working at Dunsany for years – died during Covid too. When I went to his funeral, his girlfriend and brothers told me how much our friendship had meant to him. Discreetly, his brother and father told me that they felt Dunsany had had a lasting effect on him. While he'd spent his whole life shooting animals, in the last few years he'd tired of hunting and had adopted a different kind of conservation. Nobody knew exactly why, but the rewilding of the estate made him change his position on many things.

Peter was probably the only other person who walked under those great tall trees and waded through the green sea of meadows as often as me. Like me, that changed him.

I like to believe that the magic of Dunsany didn't just whisper in my ear, it whispered in Peter's too. And if that was true, there was no reason it couldn't also speak to many others. My mother, Peter, my father, the animals: we'd all tried to protect this wonderful place. It was time for me to bring light back to Dunsany and, hopefully, let it shine beyond these walls. The wild was calling me, and I couldn't ignore it.

I reminded myself I'd just begun to fight and that I couldn't do it on my own. I needed to build something that went beyond just me. I needed scientists to explore and explain what I was seeing, and lobbyists who'd help me communicate its importance. I was a bottom-of-the-class loser, but I could make things easier for far more learned people than me, I could bring the noise and perhaps inspire others to listen. I needed to use the self-promotional skills I'd learned from the film industry. Dunsany had shown me something and I didn't want to be the only one to see it. I needed to share it with my people, to show that there was hope we could change our trajectory. The sense of purpose I felt was going to be the most important thing in my life.

For years, I'd tried to live in an entirely unnatural way. I'd tried to be self-sufficient and had felt frustrated when I failed to thrive. Just like any tree, I needed a network to be the best possible version of myself. When I found Laura and Catherine, I'd taken a huge step forward, but I also needed other people in my life: colleagues, friends and a like-minded community. For me to succeed – as a person, as a film-maker, as a rewilder – just like the trees and animals of Dunsany, I needed a network. I needed a community.

The next day, I got to work. The world needed to know what rewilding with a vegan philosophy was doing for Dunsany, and what a similar approach could offer others. While everyone else was making banana bread, I'd be working to get the story of Dunsany out.

After weeks of emailing people I still hadn't heard anything. Then – at last – I received an email from Stephen Waldren, an associate professor of botany in Trinity College Dublin. When we spoke, I explained that I'd created a sort of Jurassic Park and asked if he and his students would like to study it. Like most scholars, at first he was polite and non-committal, but he arranged to come and see what Dunsany might offer his PhD students. Shortly afterwards, I took Stephen and several of his colleagues for a nature walk. I was so excited to be with people who knew all the plants and species by name. I must have seemed like an eager student as I tried to soak in every tidbit of knowledge. As we walked, I told them about the marvellous things I'd seen as the land changed. They asked why there was no glamping or horses or rock concerts. When I said the land was reserved solely for nature and the pursuit of understanding I expected them to giggle or scoff, as so many had before, but they were enthralled and accepted my offer to introduce their students to Dunsany in case any were interested in doing research here. I was thrilled as they drove away. It felt like the first step in a crucial process. First, we'd use Dunsany to get knowledge, *real* knowledge, about what was happening here. Then we'd franchise. Surely then vegan rewilding would spread like fire.

For the first time I started to record what I was seeing happen all around me. I wrote down what I observed about the animals and plants, exploring what had changed and how. Although I'd never particularly enjoyed writing, I enjoyed this. Putting it down in plain text made it clearer than ever how big, how important the rewilding project was. Then I found myself writing in a different way. For the first time, I started to write poetry, capturing not just the changes but also my emotional responses to them. I used my camera to take shots: candid photos that documented what was I seeing, and atmospheric images that also reflected the mystery and wonder of the changes, and something of my emotional relationship with the landscape.

Meanwhile, working on my computer one day, I found an article about Ireland's first wild animal hospital. In lockdown, people in rural Ireland had little to do but spend time in nature, and many more than before were caring for injured wildlife. A group of nature enthusiasts had converted the back of a pub into a fully kitted wildlife hospital. I looked up the address and was excited to see that it was five minutes from my home. If this wasn't fate, what is? I called them immediately, trying not to sound too mad. They'd no idea Dunsany Reserve existed, and so close to their hospital.

'How soon can you come?' I asked.

Thus began my relationship with Wildlife Rehabilitation Ireland (WRI). They had a mission to help Irish wildlife and relied on their volunteers, who worked tirelessly. They had almost no financial support from the government and depended on donations. They were running on a shoestring. I wasn't surprised, as although Dunsany was getting ever more media attention we'd never had any financial support for the rewilding, and any government interest was strictly local.

I wasn't satisfied with the impact the rewilding of Dunsany was having on wild birds and animals. Providing an oasis wasn't enough to bring change. We needed to level up. A relationship with WRI provided an excellent opportunity. I looked at the old farm buildings that, in my grandfather's time, had been full of farm animals – pigs, sheep, horses and chickens – to be sold or exploited for the needs of the house. Most of them had been built by Horace Plunkett, my great-grand uncle, who founded the agricultural co-ops and established the Department of Agriculture and Technical Instruction for Ireland in 1899. His farmyard had been state of the art then.

Despite Horace's forward thinking and wonderful intentions, I couldn't help but contemplate how those animals didn't see their sheds as agricultural progress. For them they were more like prisons. How can we sometimes forget that these creatures also have souls, wants and desires, just like ourselves and our children?

As soon as the idea popped into my head, I blurted it out: 'What about using some of my buildings here to look after your patients?'

Aoife, one of the people running WRI, agreed almost as quickly. Together, we determined that as WRI didn't have money to enhance their facilities, I'd convert some of our farm buildings to help them. As I went to bed that night, I pondered the irony of turning what had once been prisons and symbols of oppression into hospitals, which are symbols of hope. I thought about how, when I was younger, I'd often gone to bed dreading the stranglehold Dunsany would have on me one day. Now I went to bed thinking about the trees I'd plant and the animals I'd save. How far I'd come.

Before long, Dunsany was where animals would come to get ready to be returned to the wild. Animals that have spent time in care can struggle to adjust to freedom if they're released too quickly. 'Soft releasing' has been proven to work. Animals are transported from the hospital, where they had been kept in small pens, with lights and noise and humans constantly in sight. They can become too familiar with people and with being provided for. With soft releasing, they go from a hospital to a pen.

Our former pig pen – a quarter of an acre in size – contains many self-planted trees and shrubs. The foxes it now housed couldn't escape it, but once released into it, human contact was reduced to when food was brought in by people who didn't engage with them directly. Gradually, the animals learned how to fear people again, and in the enclosure they became accustomed once more to digging, playing and even hunting worms or rodents. We used video monitoring to watch their development. As we prepared them for release, we reduced the food they were given. Finally, they were lured into a cage trap and transported to their new homes, or the door was left open and they disappeared into the wild.

At one point, we had almost thirty foxes. Even after their release, other species continued to multiply. As foxes are very territorial, it's likely that the interlopers left Dunsany to found their own territories elsewhere. But I do meet a particular one on my regular walks around the estate. She pauses when she sees me and watches me pass, with no evidence of fear in her thoughtful dark eyes. Maybe she remembers me as the one who brought treats when she was young. I liked to think that the foxes' animal instincts told them I posed no threat.

Then WRI had a new problem: otters. Otters can be aggressive, and they need different things from foxes, including water. WRI had no area big enough to keep a group of four growing otter orphans in their care. They explained that otters are hard to rehab. They spend much longer with their parents than foxes do, and these orphans were too young to be released, although soon they were also going to be too dangerous to keep in small pens. They'd need to be kept somewhere that met their requirements for over a year. Aoife and I looked at the farmyard. It wasn't suitable for otters. Aoife looked downhearted, but I was smiling.

'What are you so smug about?' she asked.

I said nothing, but indicated that she should follow me. Together, we walked behind the castle, through the now almost six-foot grass and around a giant bush, where there was an old disused tennis court. Dad had taught Oliver and me how to play tennis as kids, but neither of us had liked it much. The tennis court had become overgrown, and now a layer of moss and wild plants was growing from the tarmac. We stopped in front of it. Almost speechless, Aoife stared at the tall fence around the tennis court. 'Is there *anything* you don't have?' she asked. Over the next few weeks, WRI volunteers fixed the holes in the fence, carried in a large bath and other water features, and prepared a pen for the young otters. The new pen was a tremendous success. WRI and I looked after the four orphans for a year, and then they were released. Another win for nature.

We've continued to use the soft-release method at Dunsany, and have rehabbed hedgehogs and rabbits as well as foxes and otters. It's been a wonderful experience. We also partnered with another organisation, Kildare Wildlife Rescue, doing the same thing.

I'd started posting pictures of the rewilding on Instagram and was growing an online following. I'm not a trained photographer, so my pictures were cute but hardly professional. I wasn't able to get good pictures of the wild animals. One evening, a young photographer called Daniel Fildes sent me a message. He was interested in photographing nature and wondered if he could walk around and take a few photos. My naturally suspicious nature stopped me from agreeing straightaway, but I agreed to meet and discuss it. Daniel was a gentle, athletic young man. We walked together as I showed him Dunsany. I could see his eyes light up as we crossed the open meadows and spotted rare birds overhead. I explained what I was trying to achieve and why I was hesitant to allow too many people into the rewilded area in case they disturbed the animals. He agreed with everything. By the end of our walk, I'd said that he could come and take photos, so long as I could post some on Dunsany Nature Reserve's social media.

The next day, Daniel arrived and disappeared into the wild. That evening after work, I went to let the dogs out. As I did, Daniel emerged from the reserve, covered in grass and leaves. He'd been here all day. He pulled out his camera and excitedly started to show me his photos. Daniel became a great wildlife photographer and also stepped into the shoes of my dear friend Peter, observing the wildlife, becoming the reserve's eyes and ears and letting me know what was happening.

Meanwhile, Stephen Waldren from Trinity College had found three PhD students who wanted to study the rewilded areas. We made an appointment for them to visit. By the end of the day, each of them had a project. One would focus on grasses (the poor woman nearly melted when she saw how big the fields are). The second would look at insects, especially butterflies and beetles, and the third wanted to explore the forest and identify the natural regeneration of the trees. They'd spend the rest of summer here, each compiling data for their dissertations. All I asked for in return was for a copy of their reports. I wanted to start building a database of unfiltered information, an essential future resource.

Stephen Waldren, his students, and Daniel all learned a lot from Dunsany and I learned even more from them. If I was going to lobby for Dunsany and for vegan rewilding generally, I needed to know as much as possible. As if I was about to sit an exam, I focused on growing my knowledge. I'd been learning more about nature and the environment every day since the rewilding started, but I still wanted to hear the experts. Would they agree with my view that I'd tapped into a real opportunity to make a difference?

As news of the rewilding gradually spread though environmental activist circles, I started to engage with schemes intended to improve the numbers of species under threat, partly to help them and also to raise awareness of what we were doing. It was still lockdown so visits were limited and most organisations were still unable to bring people together, because of Covid restrictions. For now, I'd have to be patient.

One day I received an email from a lady whose father, Pat, was a member of BirdWatch Ireland. She'd been cycling in the area when she heard a woodpecker. The last time a Great spotted woodpecker was officially spotted in County Meath had been more than a hundred years ago. Pat had spent the weekend on the roadside outside my forest watching and waiting to catch sight of this little bird. Not only did he manage to identify the nest, he even got a photo. Pat would become a great friend of the reserve, regularly supplying us with information about other new arrivals. The news about the woodpecker excited a lot of bird-watching groups, which organised a big excursion to see this oasis. The bird population had been soaring for years, but it had been very difficult to specifically catalogue what we were seeing. The experts would know better than me.

Then BirdWatch Ireland suggested a possible collaboration. They could see plenty of scope for even more birds, and for an ever-greater variety. Having just identified our first kestrel return – something to celebrate, as kestrels hadn't been seen at Dunsany for many years – they suggested that I allow them to install kestrel boxes, ready-made habitats where kestrels can raise their young. We timed this just as the Green Party – seeing an opportunity for some positive publicity – released some kestrels that had been in the care of WRI. This moment was captured by newspaper and TV channels and was even featured on Sky News. Dunsany's rewilding was making waves.

Wanting to help more than just kestrels, with the help of neighbours, I soon had some donations of owl boxes. I'd seen barn owls at Dunsany once or twice, but the Irish population of these birds has massively declined. Some of our social media followers, still stuck at home because of Covid, began to build custom-made owl boxes and donate them. We quickly set them up. The houses were soon aflutter with owl action. There were more little rodents everywhere, as the abundant grasslands provide them with a wonderful environment, so there was plenty for these native birds of prey to eat.

As we were still in lockdown, all the journalists were looking for a good news story that would pique interest at a challenging time. A story about rewilding was perfect, and there was a bout of media interest. Inevitably, they were intrigued by the fact that the guy who was doing it was a heavy metal fan who looked the part. I was a little embarrassed by all the fuss, but also pleased. I knew the project needed positive attention, and I was increasingly confident that what I was doing really could make a difference.

I also needed to keep learning. The scientists and wildlife experts I'd met had far more training than me. I was grateful for their insights, and proud that many of them could see that I was doing something truly valuable. At the same time, I realised that in many ways I was seeing more than them, because while I didn't know the Latin names for the creatures and plants I witnessed every day, and didn't necessarily understand the finer details of natural processes like photosynthesis, I was walking the rewilded land day after day after day and had the immense privilege of observing changes not just on a macroscale, but in the minutest detail. I also had no preconceived ideas about what could or should be happening. It was all new to me, and I was open to every learning opportunity.

Beyond Irish academia and environmental activism, I searched for and connected with global experts. One was Nicholas Carter, a Canadian researcher who'd spent years exploring how the mass adoption of plant-based agriculture, and a plant-based diet, could solve many of today's problems. I also joined the Rewilding Europe organisation; its first Irish member. This group, which has been operational since 2011, has members across Europe who work both together and separately to rewild European landscapes. Most of them see as a vital element of their work the reintroduction of species still present in isolated parts of Europe but locally extinct in many areas. All are dedicated to the regeneration of natural plant and animal life. Now I was part of a team, a network, with a shared vision of a better future. I was excited because I knew that many of the other rewilders had been doing it for longer than me, and that they had knowledge, expertise and experience. I was also excited at the thought of being able to share what I was seeing at Dunsany with others, knowing that my own growing expertise would help them, too. Rewilding projects in places with a similar climate to Ireland, such as the Netherlands and Belgium, have a comparable array of flora and fauna. It'd be fascinating to see if the plants and animals in those places were responding in the same way as in Dunsany, or if they weren't.

I quickly learned that even within the rewilding community there are quite significant differences. Many see a place for quite significant levels of human intervention. Many integrate 'regenerative grazing', the introduction of domestic animals that graze the land. Some of these are doing very interesting work, but I don't consider it rewilding at all, as there's nothing 'wild' about animals that have been artificially bred for generations, and whose interactions with the landscape developed under human management. There are others who see a place for activities such as hunting in rewilded areas, which I disagree with very strongly. They argue that it raises revenue and helps to manage populations of animals such as deer in areas now lacking wild predators. But I have faith that, left alone, nature will find a way to stabilise animal populations, and I believe it's simply wrong for humans to hunt for food in the first place, when they no longer need to. I'm also not in favour of some projects' plans to monetise rewilded areas by turning them into Disneyfied theme parks where tourists can go glamping and play Robinson Crusoe. It's not really rewilding if there are tents, barbecues and toilet facilities all over the place. But having said all that, I *am* delighted there's significant and growing interest in rewilding. Even if some projects are doing it in ways I don't entirely approve of, I'm still glad they're doing it: we need all the help we can get.

A phrase suggested to me by a friend and long-time supporter Nia Timms of Heartstone Sanctuary, which I helped coin, is V-wilding – distinguishing my work at Dunsany from projects using regenerative grazing. It's a better description of what I was trying to promote; a vegan rewilding movement in which all animals are considered precious, but not a commodity.

My view of the many hunting trophies in Dunsany has shifted since I became a vegan. Previous generations of Plunketts shot wild animals on safari in Africa and elsewhere, and had them taxidermied and mounted or posed for display on the walls of our home. A tiger skin, head intact, embellishes our library floor. Now I'd eschewed the idea of killing animals or consuming meat, I often felt uncomfortable beneath their glassy stares. Some friends suggested taking them down and warehousing them. I thought about it, and decided not to. We cannot learn from history by hiding it. Lest we forget, we need to always be aware of it. We can move on from it, but we can't – and shouldn't try – to erase it. We're all the sum of the parts formed by our ancestors. I decided the hunting trophies could stay, no longer as decorative items intended to say something about how strong, how manly, how great the Plunketts are, but as a sombre reminder of how careless past generations were with our natural biodiversity, which was so much richer then than it is today. 'You killed us,' the slaughtered animals seemed to be saying, when I first decided to be vegan. Now they seemed to be saying something different: 'Never again,' and 'It's not too late to stop.'

For years, Dunsany was locked away from the public. We'd always been deeply concerned about the constant incursions of hunters and poachers, and worried about theft. At first, the rewilding had felt deeply personal, a battle I was fighting all alone. The many years of invasions, of threats, of destroyed perimeter walls, of slashed tyres, and even of bullets being fired at the castle, had given me a fortress mentality. Me against the world. Now I could see that while the work I was doing with social media, with scientists and with wildlife groups was important, the general public is too. After all, they're the largest group. For people to really understand vegan rewilding, V-wilding, they needed to hear the story and witness the reserve.

I just wasn't sure how to reach out. I couldn't just open. If loads of people were walking around, it'd cause enormous damage and maybe even reverse many of the benefits of rewilding. Then I had an idea: I'd create an event, a nature walk, at which they would hear all the stories, walk the landscape, and listen to me talking about rewilding, and how vegan rewilding differs from traditional approaches. I'd built it, and now I needed to let them come.

I invited people to register for a visit. When the social media post went out, my email inbox exploded. The first day, I received about three hundred emails. The second, it was almost five hundred. Everyone was fascinated by the idea of buying a ticket to this wonderland. Caught a little off-guard, I realised this wasn't going to be a one-off. I decided to keep groups small and infrequent to minimise damage. Lockdown restrictions were still in place, but we could practise social distancing. I began seeing two groups a week, of about twenty each time. It was exciting and touching to see how many really were interested, that they cared about the land and could understand why the rewilding was such a big step. Gradually, I started to sense pride in other local people that such a big rewilding project was happening on their doorstep, and that they could be part of it.

My friend and mentor, Karim Traïdia, often told me that no film project can work unless it contains the authentic self, and the real emotions, of the director. I realised now that this doesn't apply only to film. It applies to the rewilding of Dunsany too. Unless the rewilding of the estate felt personal to me, unless I was truly involved on an emotional level, it would never work.

Rewilding a substantial portion of the estate has been the most rewarding thing I've ever done. The strangest part was that changing my relationship with the land seemed to change how people saw me. I started seeing more friendly nods and smiles. I started returning them. I started rethinking my position in the community, and increasingly seeing myself as part of it, as a stakeholder in the area who wants to work with others to make it a nicer place to live. For us all.

Chapter Ten

Taking the Helm

AS DUNSANY GREW EVER WILDER, LAURA AND I WERE GROWING OUR FAMILY. In 2021, with Ireland still under lockdown, our daughter Constance was born. Now we were parents of two wonderful girls. I remember holding this tiny, squirming little person in my arms and realising that it was time for me to start actively planning for my own death and the handover of the estate. For as long as I could remember, Dad had talked to me about The Future, when he'd be dead and I'd have to take over. For most of my life, I'd dreaded it. Even when Dad did die, and I inherited Dunsany, I'd continued to think of The Future as a vague point in time, when somehow I'd mysteriously know what I was doing.

The next generation had arrived, kicking and screaming, and I suddenly started to think about The Future in a different, new way. All at once, life had become both much more complicated and much simpler. Like me, one day Constance will have to make her own peace with Dunsany because, whether she likes it or not, she's going to inherit it, and she'll have to find her own way to put her stamp on it. She's already been a gamechanger, because from the start Dunsany has always been inherited by eldest sons, and Constance will be the first female custodian of the estate, and – thank God – perhaps the first who won't be handed the absurdity of an aristocratic title.

We've always followed the old ways, but some ways are better left in the past. Today women must stand as equals in all things, and at Dunsany that starts with Constance. As she grows up, I'll teach her all I know about our shared heritage: the history of this place and its people; the deep sense of obligation we all have to keep it safe. I feel an overwhelming sense of responsibility to keep Dunsany secure for her so that when she grows up and takes over she'll be at the helm of a viable enterprise that respects nature and helps to make the world a better place. I'll do my best to show her how special Dunsany is, to help her understand the natural environment, and to accept her responsibility in cherishing it. Ironically, although I often hated it, I'll follow my parents' example of telling the stories of the past that I heard from childhood. As she grows, I'll make her repeat the very same words I was made to utter. No doubt she'll have reservations about this, as I did, and she may feel much the same way I did. Perhaps I'll spend the last years of my life as Dad did, unsure if she'll follow the path we've all taken for hundreds of years. It's part of the process.

Dad resented Dunsany and might have given it all up at one point. He never really succeeded with it as he'd hoped but, like me, he was part of something bigger than us all.

Like him, today I say what Dad said about me: I'll sacrifice everything so that Constance can stay here and do something great, something for her generation. I made a promise to Dad – on his deathbed, no less – and I'll be expecting Constance to do the same for me.

Beyond Constance, I feel responsible for all the little ones starting their journey through life. Many weren't born with the advantages I was given, but we all have a shared future. None of us will be spared the hardships of the looming ecological collapse. Our species needs people to stand up and fight, and I'm determined to do that. We still have time to make changes that will create a better world for future generations. The time to make those changes is definitely now.

I've always been fascinated by stories of self-sabotage, perhaps because for years I was very prone to it myself. One of the remarkable stories of Greek mythology is that of Orpheus, whose wife Eurydice died. Orpheus discovered her body and such was his heartbreak that he played mournful songs so moving that even the gods wept. Following their advice, he travelled to the underworld, where he managed to persuade Hades and Persephone – in charge down there – to let Eurydice return with him to the land of the living. As is always the case in these stories, there was a condition: Orpheus had to remember not to look back until both he and his wife had returned to the upper world. The two left, with Orpheus walking in front and Eurydice following him. No sooner had Orpheus returned to the upper world, he couldn't resist turning to look triumphantly at his wife. In an instant, Eurydice disappeared, returning to the land of the dead, and leaving her devastated husband to a lonely life without her. They'd only been a few feet from salvation.

For me, this story of self-sabotage begs the question as to whether it was ever really about getting the wife back at all. Were Orpheus's laments genuine, or were they self-serving? The situation of humanity today reminds me very much of this old story. We're very good at wringing our hands and bewailing the terrible things happening to the environment and to the plant and animal species that live in it, but even though we know what we have to do, we don't seem to be able to resist *not* doing it, just to satisfy our own desires. Are we, like Orpheus, doomed to suffer the most awful loss imaginable, and then further doomed to know that it was all our own fault and we could have saved ourselves?

Because so much of Dunsany is being rewilded, while most of Ireland is subject to farming, which is heavily skewed towards the production of meat and dairy, researchers have a perfect research environment here. I've converted enough landmass from agricultural use to nature reserve for the various species that live here to behave almost as they would have long ago, before agriculture was invented. The deer have space to roam, the mycelium space to expand and grow, and all the tree and plant species and the abundant insects and mammals they host have entered into an expansive phase that's entirely natural, but had been denied to them on these lands for centuries.

Living in the castle in the twenty-first century as a family man is very different from past times. Up to my grandfather's generation, the family was fortunate enough to have a large staff dancing attendance on them. That staff, many from families whose lives had been connected to mine for generations, had taken care not only of the people of the castle, but of the building itself. Their tireless work kept the rooms warm and dry, and aired and fresh. They polished the furniture and dusted the innumerable paintings and *objets d'art*. Now I live in the castle with just my small family and we take care of ourselves. We spend most of our time in just a few rooms and inevitably the fact that most of the castle is not really lived in has taken a toll.

I can understand why so many people from backgrounds like mine eventually sell their homes to hoteliers or golf clubs or hand them over to the state. And yet I remain stubbornly in place, scraping money together to mend every hole in the roof, treat every damp spot. I've gained ever more respect for the army of servants who cared for Dunsany Castle.

I've often wondered what Dad would have made of all the changes in Dunsany since I started rewilding. I like to think he'd have been proud and excited to see buzzards and peregrine falcons return to our skies, to hear the first woodpecker here since the mass deforestation of Ireland in the seventeenth and eighteenth centuries. If I could ask him why we see so many more animals now, perhaps he'd pause and say 'they are the beneficiaries of our success in V-wilding'.

Rewilding Dunsany meant questioning a lot of received wisdom, and many of the decisions my ancestors took over the years. I had to learn to think of the forest as something intrinsically valuable in and of itself, not just as something getting in the way of farming, or as a commercial crop to be managed. Obviously, we do need timber for all sorts of things, so we need commercially grown forests as well as wild forests. But look at how we grow commercial timber: we plant trees in rows so tight that few species can live in the understorey, and then when they are ready to cut – because we typically grow patches of forest of one species only – we slay them all at once. One result may be a generous payout for the harvested wood, but another is exposed topsoil, now vulnerable to being carried away by heavy rain or wind, and less likely to rejuvenate in a natural manner. Another issue is that the baby forests thus planted are not attractive habitats for birds, as they have nowhere to build nests, and many fewer opportunities to forage – and birds are very necessary for the healthy development of a forest, as the seeds they excrete from the fruits they eat lead to the spontaneous growth of a healthy understorey, including young saplings that will gradually take their place among the trees.

There are other ways of growing wood commercially and harvesting it that are less damaging, but of course they require more work. Ideally commercial forests, like wild forests, would include diverse species at various stages of growth and development, so that when mature trees are removed there are growing ones ready to take their place with minimal disruption to the understorey. With judicious planting alongside benign management of naturally occurring species, we could have forests that are commercial while also providing a habitat for an abundance of plant and animal species.

Much more important, of course, is to preserve extant wild forests, while also fostering the growth of new ones. Thankfully, we've been able to do both in Dunsany. The estate had always had a certain amount of forested land, but the patches of trees were separated by fields, most of which hosted a large number of cattle being raised for meat. By planting native species – while leaving the existing trees, native and invasive alike, alone – I've created corridors of forest that connect these patches of forest. Fifteen thousand trees have been planted so far in collaboration with the Irish Trees organisation, which is headed by Bob Hamilton. Bob retired from a career in business to follow his passion doing environmental restoration in a business-like manner. Together with Bob and his partner John, we've been able to create corridors of forest that block light and noise pollution, while also connecting old and new forests. It's a work in progress, with many more trees to come. This endeavour has even helped bring a little money into the estate to finance our ongoing science-testing and data collection, which are proving to be so important for the argument in favour of rewilding with a vegan philosophy.

Planting young trees in this way is one of the only active interventions we've made in our rewilding project, because native Irish tree species grow very slowly, and with careful planting in areas adjacent to extant forests, we can make an enormous difference. You'll have seen young trees in managed plantations growing inside plastic tubes, intended to protect them from deer or other creatures that might want to eat them while they're still soft and tender. As I've explained before, ours are made of stiff cardboard that gradually breaks down over two or three years, and then rots with the rest of the organic matter. Year on year, the young trees are growing tall and strong, and as they do, they naturally bring with them the plants that grow in their shade, and the animal species that depend on them. These corridors of trees permit the free flow of tree-dependent species from one area of the estate to another, and facilitate the development of a rich biodiversity not just among and under the trees, but across the entire nature reserve.

I started to engage with the public even more. I was touched and excited by the interest that persisted even when the

Covid-era restrictions lifted and everyone returned to their normal lives. Although obviously the numbers I could bring around the estate were quite limited, I was hopeful that the people who came would fall in love with the rewilding, as I had. I learned how to bring groups around the estate without disturbing the rewilding land, following the perfect example of how to manage groups in this environment that is right in front of me. There are hundreds of deer in Dunsany, but until you get close to them, you'd never know it. They have a negligible impact on the landscape because they walk in single file, and can all make their way through a field of tall grass without flattening it. Human populations in places like the Amazon Rainforest do exactly the same. Taking them as my example, I accompany small groups on single-file walks through the rewilded estate, avoiding areas where birds are nesting. Everyone's excited and fascinated by what they see. They're all supportive. Our rewilding perspective may be unfamiliar to them, but deep down they sense that this is a natural, homeopathic approach to the environment. They often leave saying that they feel inspired to explore what they can do with their own gardens, farms or balconies. Interacting with all these interested people, answering their eager questions, and seeing the friendly smiles on their faces, I realised again how lonely I was, for years. It's wonderful to share what I am seeing in Dunsany with them. To make people fall in love with nature, the way I have. All the research we do here at Dunsany is available to the public. We're working on building an online resource where all the information can be downloaded, but at the time of writing it's available to anyone who asks to see it.

The funds raised from these visits have given us the possibility to measure and survey, giving us insight into the bat population, insect numbers, the amount of carbon sequestered by the rewilding. I've realised that if I'm going to talk to the experts about what I see happening here every day, I need to know their language. I need the data, I need to be bullet-proof in my methodology and, most importantly, must never lose sight of why I'm doing this. It's not about making money. It's not about interfering.

It's funny that I'm currently spending so much money on bats because they're flying rodents, and I've always been afraid of rodents. Even before the rewilding started, there'd always been plenty of bats in Dunsany. I'd never enjoyed it when they swooped around my head on my many forays onto the roof to examine missing or damaged tiles. Now there were more than ever, and when I read about them I realised how integral they are to Irish biodiversity, and how interesting it is that Dunsany has so many, and such a range of species too.

In the past, farming has often represented as being a 'natural' activity, the harnessing of nature for benign ends. Of course we need agriculture because we need to feed a massive world population, but there's something seriously wrong with how we are doing it. If it's so 'natural', why do farmers consistently have to augment and 'improve' the soil with chemical additives? Do we really need to eat all that meat? Are we sure the way we're doing things now is the right one? Isn't there room for nature in farming? Can we really have farming without it? What if we started to change our eating habits for the sake of the animals, for our own health, and for the future of the planet?

Agriculture has always been a very important part of the Irish economy, and although Ireland is increasingly urban, it still is. Many people are interested in the greening of agriculture, but while the government does take modest steps towards reducing the damage agriculture wreaks on the landscape, it's never enough. I'm not anti-farming; the rewilding of the reserve and much of our research is funded by the farming of other parts of the estate. I know very well how hard farmers work. We need farmers to grow the food crops that keep us all alive, and we also need farmers to engage in conversation about how they can work in a way that supports biodiversity, and can be compatible with rewilding of adjacent lands. Ideally these conversations will be held with individual farmers, not the powerful agro-industrial lobbies that have dominated the conversation for too long.

While respecting that we all need to eat, and that farmers need to make a good living, it'd be foolish to pretend there aren't points of potential conflict between farming and rewilding. The threats to our world represented by climate change and shrinking biodiversity have no easy solutions, and we can only work together to solve these problems by engaging in dialogue and reaching compromise. Compromise, of course, with one another, not with the overarching aim of feeding the world while also respecting nature.

As my vision for Dunsany grew ever clearer, I realised that at its heart lay the fundamental concept of equality and equity. That's the cornerstone of veganism, really. I could also see how I had a huge opportunity to promote equality – not just of humans, but of all living beings. For years, my parents drilled into me the fundamental knowledge that it's unacceptable to squander privilege. I won't let that happen. I'll allow my little corner of this small green island to become an oasis in which plants, insects, birds and mammals can all thrive and have the sort of life for which they've evolved. Because once we've decided that every living being has the right to life, we can't pick and choose. We've got to extend the same right to them all, even the ones that are personally inconvenient to us, or that – for whatever reason – we dislike.

In my case, for example, I've always detested bees. They just freak me out, and in the past I've been known to swat them. As a vegan, though, I've got to respect them. As if they somehow know that, the bees of Dunsany have taken to infiltrating my office, which now requires me to laboriously capture them in a glass and release them outdoors. It sometimes seems that they're treating the whole exercise as some sort of adventure-park thrill, and coming straight back in again.

Did you know that bees are currently doing better in cities and towns than in the countryside, largely because of the astonishing amount of chemicals used in agriculture today? These urban environments certainly can't support all the pollinating insects the planet needs, so what can we do about it? While we need to start incorporating more nature into urban areas (a lot of data shows how this is good for communities and for people's mental health), and cities and towns can play their part, it is not nearly enough. We need to make it easier for farmers and other people who live and work in rural places to do so in a way that's compatible with bees. We also need to increase awareness of the diverse types of bees. Did you know that the poor, beleaguered honey bee is just one of many distinct species? People often believe that by buying and eating Irish honey, they're supporting vital pollinators, but honey bees compete for resources with a variety of other bee species. Captive honey bees are also quite prone to disease, because beekeepers take most of their honey away and replace it with processed sugar, which keeps the bees alive during the winter but doesn't contain the honey's vital enzymes and other properties, leaving them weakened and very vulnerable to the wide range of parasites and viruses that can attack them. Here in Ireland, the native black bee almost went extinct in the twentieth century, although it's had a resurgence since. It's still under threat today, however, largely because of cross-breeding with non-native bees imported by the honey industry – legally, because bees are considered livestock, and therefore can be moved freely throughout the European Union.

Here at Dunsany, we're doing our bit to encourage the Irish black bee population by installing bee lodges made of insulated Douglas fir that provide habitats in which they can live and from which – hopefully – they can spread. By using lemongrass to lure them in – it mimics bees' natural pheromones – we've established numerous thriving colonies that are left to make their honey undisturbed, and from which they can establish other colonies. In the process, we've ensured a healthy system of pollination that benefits not just Dunsany, but also the neighbouring farms; neighbours say they've observed higher yields from crops grown in fields adjacent to our rewilded land, and have even asked me to establish more bee colonies on the boundaries between our land.

There are many tensions and divergences of opinion in the rewilding community around exactly how to approach the task of returning an area to nature. Some people feel that rewilding can encompass a certain amount of animal husbandry, with domestic species like sheep and cattle playing a role. My feeling is that raising grazing animals for food, which has already been categorically proven to damage the land, and which is known to reduce the amount of carbon in the soil and thus contribute to climate change – while also raising a host of ethical issues relating to animal rights – can't play a part in any serious rewilding effort. There are lots of little things we can all do to help the environment. However, the only way to sustainably feed the world in the long term – while also combating climate change and fostering biodiversity – is taking veganism beyond our diets. We need to make it a way of life, a philosophy, informing every single thing we do. Just imagine what we humans could achieve if we adopted a more civilised approach to our world. Imagine how our society would change. Consider how ethical approaches to life would gradually penetrate our minds and influence our collective behaviour. What kind of society would we have then?

One of the big challenges of many, if not most, rewilding projects is funding. Land that's been set aside to rewild is, by definition, not producing an income for the landowner in more traditional ways, such as using it to grow crops or graze domestic animals. We all have expenses, and some rewilding projects have tried to marry the competing goals of rewilding and bringing in an income by introducing grazing or foraging animals that can roam free before they're slaughtered and eaten, or by allowing hunters onto their land during designated hunting seasons. I don't believe that either of these approaches is actually compatible with rewilding. Nor are they realistic approaches to feeding the world because meat from animals raised in this way will never be sufficient to feed everybody, so if people want to eat meat, factory farming will persist, while land cannot truly be said to be 'wild' if it's supporting a population of farmed animals. No matter how 'organic', no matter how 'natural' the process, domesticated grazing animals were never supposed to exist in the numbers required by animal husbandry, and they're always going to impact on the land in a plethora of ways.

Some argue that in the modern world, where many natural predators have already been destroyed, a certain amount of management of wild animals by culling or hunting them is actually necessary, but as I've seen – and as I've shown you – if you leave the animals and plants alone, nature will find a way to manage itself. Rather than attempting to meld rewilding with sustainable forms of agriculture, my own view is that the two enterprises simply cannot occupy the same space, so while I've watched and observed what other so-called rewilders are doing with animal agriculture, my general policy has been to do the opposite. At Dunsany, we believe in letting nature take the lead.

However, sustainable agriculture can certainly operate in parallel with rewilding. In fact, it has to. By removing animal-based foods from our diets, we'd quickly reduce our need for vast swathes of grazing land and huge quantities of crops destined for animal feed. By some estimates, about 70 per cent of all agricultural activity on the planet is devoted to animal agriculture, which in turn only produces less than 20 per cent of our calorie intake. Currently, the types of food that most of us have grown up eating – particularly meat and dairy – are very hard on the landscape, requiring much greater swathes of land than growing the vegetables, cereals and fruits that are actually all we need to be healthy and well. Approximately half of all the habitable land on the planet is used for agriculture, and of that more than 70 per cent is used for raising animals, with just 20 per cent used for growing plant crops. Moreover, a huge percentage of the vegetable matter grown in agriculture goes into animal feed. One of the most grotesque aspects of the global food economy is that farmers in very poor countries often work hard to grow crops for export that are used to raise farm animals, when the same land could have grown nutritious plant crops in much less damaging ways. Big fiscal interests are behind decisions about land use that have huge environmental consequences that impact on every living being, including us. We've also developed very unsustainable types of farming that take far more from the soil than it can give. Even with crop rotation and the use of manure and other forms of fertiliser considered 'natural', much of the land being used for farming becomes depleted of vital minerals, or suffers from soil erosion because we've taken out all the wild plants whose roots used to keep the soil in place.

But what if we reduced the number of animals being raised for consumption and dairy? What if – whisper it – we worked towards eliminating animal products from our diets completely? Even if human population levels remained steady or grew, we wouldn't need to devote *nearly* as many hectares to agriculture, because growing edible crops is much more efficient than using it to raise animals for meat. More land would become available for rewilding, and as it returned to nature, insect, plant and wild animal species would all start to recover, with uncountable benefits for the fight against climate change, biodiversity generally, and the health and wellbeing of humans.

Because food is so closely linked to issues such as cultural identity, family pride and history, the thought of completely changing the way we eat can seem utterly overwhelming.

There's a role here for transitional foods, which resemble meat and dairy products in terms of taste, texture and nutritional profile, which will enable people to eat their favourite shepherd's pies and sausage rolls without actually eating meat at all. Gradually, as consumers become accustomed to these alternatives – which will also increase in quality and variety as demand grows – it'll become much easier for them to countenance a future in which they eat no animal products at all.

Modern technologies, when partnered with our rich food heritage, will also play a key role in shifting eating habits. Precision fermentation, for example, is a form of technology that has been used for years in creating vaccines and medications. It involves engineering a protein's gene sequence into a bacterium or yeast strain, and can be used to create dairy and meat alternatives that are remarkably similar to the original, but much less damaging to the environment. Gastronomy doesn't have to be sacrificed in the process of veganising our lives.

If everybody ate a plant-based diet, much more of our landscape could be used for both rewilding and sustainable agriculture, with different areas designed for each activity. My experience at Dunsany has shown that a rewilded area will quite quickly become a habitat for large numbers of wild bees and other pollinators, and that this in turn will have a positive knock-on effect for crop agriculture, which will benefit from their work. Far from being incompatible with feeding the world, in this way rewilding can help make it happen.

Anyone who wants to make a difference can start by changing a few simple things in their own lives. The most obvious first step is to become a vegan. I know that the idea can seem daunting at first, but I also know that if I can do it, anyone can. Quite apart from the massive benefits for the environment, the data is already in about the personal benefits of a vegan diet. We already know that a diet high in meat is bad for us, even carcinogenic. We already know that our oceans are so full of microplastics that every time we eat a fish we're also ingesting plastic. If the question is 'What can we do about it?', the answer is staring us in the face: 'Just don't eat those things. There's no need.' It's really that simple.

Cultural change often takes a long time, even generations, to become embedded, but it can happen quickly too. If we're serious about addressing the many challenges facing the planet, we need to start working hard to ensure that the next generation grows up with a different attitude, a separate set of values. Children are naturally drawn to animals and nature, and yet because of increasing urbanisation and our technology-focused way of being, many of them have limited opportunities to experience them at first hand. Rewilding projects like Dunsany, as well as much more modest rewilding and sustainable agriculture projects, can work hand in hand with schools to instruct kids about the environment, and also about diet, fitness, crop production and many of the skills they'll need to live healthily in the modern world.

At the time of writing, Dunsany Nature Reserve is subject to many threats. First, it is facing the same threats that are challenging all of the natural environment: climate change, pollution and the suburbanisation of the landscape. More specifically, as the suburbs of Dublin continue to sprawl across the green fields of its hinterland, it's also threatened by development. Irish property developers appear to be obsessed with constructing low-rise suburban homes that swallow up vast swathes of countryside, bringing with them noise, traffic and light pollution. And once the suburbs are constructed, the demand for public transport links increases. I am obviously in favour of public transport, but to minimise the disruption to the environment I'd like to see it stretch alongside motorways and other extant major arteries rather than ploughed through previously undisturbed land, where it disrupts the movement of animals, interferes with fragile ecosystems, and creates noise and light pollution that interferes with animals' general wellbeing and their ability to successfully procreate.

The sometimes competing needs of modern urban societies and nature have to be balanced and carefully managed. At the time of writing, the Irish transport authority is planning to extend the train line from Dublin all the way to Navan. This will allow commuters to settle further outside the city, and to travel to work in a relatively environmentally friendly way. One of the issues with this plan is that the current proposed route will bisect the nature reserve I've spent years creating at Dunsany. The most likely route will restore an old single train line that cuts through Dunsany and would devastate our largest woodlands. The line was built at a time when woodlands in Ireland were more plentiful, but Dunsany's forests are the last left in the area.

The road to hell is paved with good intentions. While we do need trains, we cannot create infrastructure at the cost of the few natural forests left. When I asked a government official why this route was necessary, particularly considering that most of the population growth is on the other side of the county, he said: 'Planners like straight lines and there's a lot of money in rezoning new areas of farmland as developers buy the land cheap. It's a rotten system and like so many other projects in this nation of ours, it's not fit for purpose, just wallets.'

If these plans are realised, the new train line will be a large dual line that will sever the reserve and all the lands around it in half. The noise and vibrations will drive animals away and what remains of the forest will be shaken. It will become impossible for many species to travel from one part of the reserve to the other. All the work we've done here will become practically useless as the animals will no longer be free to roam, their breeding and feeding will be interrupted by light and noise pollution, and the maintenance of the train line and the land around will disturb plant growth and the all-important mycorrhizal network.

Some people will say I'm being selfish and just don't want a train to spoil the view from the castle, but that's not the case at all. I could cope with the sight of a train moving through the estate. But that's not the point. I feel, honestly and urgently, that with Dunsany Nature Reserve I've been given both the opportunity and the duty to use my land to improve biodiversity and – crucially during this time of rampant climate change – to both sequester carbon and provide researchers with the perfect experiment in how lands can be returned to nature.

I know my experience of life is atypical in a lot of ways. I'm deeply aware that I come from immense privilege of the sort that looks increasingly anachronistic in today's world. That gives me a huge responsibility to make the world a better place, and I'm doing my best. One of my motivations for rewilding comes from my sense that I have a responsibility to give something back. I'm lucky to be able to give back in a particular way: to have the luxury of being able to rewild seven hundred acres and still manage to get by. I know not everyone can do that. But beyond me, and beyond Dunsany, I've also concluded that we're *all* responsible for doing what we can. The world is in a new era, threatened by global warming and massive species die-off, all of which will have consequences as yet incompletely understood. I've been gifted the opportunity to be a guardian of nature, and I feel honoured to do what I can.

I see a direct parallel between the various waves of destruction that have crashed over Ireland in the course of history, and the situation that we are living through now. Back in the 1600s, when Cromwell banished my family from their home, they left for Holland and stayed safe there until they could return and claim what was rightfully theirs. Today, not just Dunsany, but all of green Ireland, and indeed all of the natural world, is under attack from over-development, intensive agriculture, and our species' apparently insatiable appetite for consumption.

Every generation has its own battles to fight. Ours is climate change, along with all the associated issues and challenges. By and large, we already know what we need to do: reduce and then cease releasing unnatural amounts of carbon into the atmosphere, while also allowing nature to become a carbon sink by allowing to grow carbon-rich plant species. Scientists estimate that about 20 per cent of greenhouse gas emissions result from the degradation of the natural landscape. We can make an enormous difference by both not allowing any pristine landscapes to degrade while also allowing as much land as possible to return to a natural state. Of course, trains and other less environmentally damaging modes of transport are part of this picture, but we need to develop infrastructure intelligently, locating new lines near already existing infrastructure, such as extant motorways and major roads. This will provide the modern transport systems that we need as twenty-first-century people, while keeping disruption of the natural environment to a minimum.

We can all create habitats too. Wherever we live, and however much space we have, we can plant flowering shrubs to support insect life, and then leave them insecticide-free so that they can support species that will, in turn, support others. You might live in a small inner-city apartment, and assume there's very little you can do, but you'd be wrong. If you have a terrace, a balcony, or even just an outdoor windowsill, you can grow plants that support insect life that will in turn support birds. If you have a large garden, a small farm or a field or two that you can relinquish to rewilding, you can be part of a green revolution.

Whether your own rewilding is taking place in a window-box or across several acres, you'll be surprised by how quickly you'll see new life appearing. Those plants that you once considered weeds will attract butterflies, bees and other insects, which will in turn attract birds and other wildlife. The leaves you used to brush or blow off your flowerbeds when they fell will rot and feed earthworms and slugs. Wherever you live, you can engage in judicious planting of native wild flowers that attract insect life – although a word of caution here, because the packs of 'wild flower seeds' on sale don't necessarily reflect the natural variety of any given location. For example, in Ireland most wild plants produce flowers with rather muted colours – think of the soft cream or purple of native clover, or the light purple of a flowering thistle. Insects are generally attracted to the brightest flowers in any given environment, so sometimes well-intentioned planting of seeds marketed as 'wild' can inadvertently result in many native species being overlooked.

You can also start growing some of your own food. If you have a garden, you might be surprised by just how much you can grow there, and even if you only have a window ledge, you can invest in a few plant pots and fill them with herbs. There are few pleasures as great as eating food that you grew with your own hands, and even if you only have space for a couple of pots of parsley, growing it at home will help you to appreciate how generous nature is in providing us with all we need in the form of the edible plants and seeds that keep us alive.

If you're a town or city planner, you can look at making systemic changes that will make it easier for wildlife to flourish in urban and suburban environments, including looking carefully at street lighting and maintaining or creating wildlife corridors in urban and suburban environments that make it easier for plant species to spread, and for animals to move around.

You can petition your local politicians to fill any available spaces in your area with plants that will enhance the environment – and hold them to account. And again, if we all do it, we'll see positive results, probably more quickly than you'd ever have imagined. While rural and suburban biodiversity will never be enough on its own, it'll contribute to making the planet a healthier place, and will play an even more significant role in helping people to develop a new mindset, a new way of understanding the natural environment and their place in it.

Perhaps most important, you can also demand that the government both creates and supports nature reserves and rewilding projects, one of the most vital tools we can implement against climate change and the decline in biodiversity; and that it promotes a sustainable approach to agriculture. In much of the developed world, the farming community depends quite heavily on subsidies. It's in everyone's interest to have a thriving agricultural sector, rural areas and small market towns and villages that are populated and well serviced, so clearly subsidies can be important. But agricultural policies intended to make rural areas thrive, to support farming families and communities, often seem to have been designed to bribe farmers to wreak havoc on the natural environment. In recent decades, as part of the European Union (previously the EC and EEC), Ireland has been part of a pan-European system of agricultural policies that have often rewarded farmers for seriously damaging the natural environment. At times, subsidies and other forms of direct income support have required farmers to uproot wild plants and trees considered to be 'encroaching' on agricultural land; in other words, to actively reduce species variety in areas adjacent to agriculture. Surely subsidies would be better spent on helping rural people to support, rather than despoil, the natural world?

The problem is that many subsidies are given to people who are farming and living in ways that we already know are extremely destructive to biodiversity, and often producing foods that we don't need or that harm us or the planet. There've been various efforts on the part of entities like the European Union to reward farmers for supporting biodiversity, but they've never gone far enough. Typically, they encourage people to set aside small, unconnected parcels of land where wild plants can grow alongside the usual destructive forms of agriculture. There are almost no schemes to support more ambitious approaches, such as the Dunsany rewilding project. I've only been able to create a reserve here because I have other quite extensive lands that I can use to personally subsidise the rewilding. What hope does someone with a more modest smallholding have? Even if they want to rewild, and are prepared to make sacrifices to do so, where is their financial incentive, given that we all benefit from these efforts?

Most of the rural landscape of Ireland, as elsewhere, is owned by the farming community. Farmers, like everyone else, are rational people. Their job is to use their land to make money to support themselves and their families. If they can make extra money in the form of subsidies, many will choose to farm in a way that maximises their income, even if the environment continues to be seriously damaged in the process. If they were offered subsidies to engage in sustainable farming using methods that support the presence of wildlife, that's what they would do instead.

Some countries are already taking steps towards supporting making the consumption of plant-based products the norm. In 2023, for example, the Danish government, with the support of political parties across the spectrum, produced an action plan that includes using subsidies and other incentives to encourage farmers to invest more in plant production and developing a food culture dominated by the consumption of plants. If we all start to work together in this way, we'll see a difference much more quickly than seems possible now. I know because I see that difference happening around me every day.

I've also personally started to explore some of the ways in which a rewilding project like Dunsany can monetise its efforts. The more ambitious I become for the rewilding project, the clearer it is that I need to find a way to raise funds. Not just for me, but also to create a sustainable model that can be replicated all over the world, to franchise the idea and allow vegan rewilding to be a tangible method for farmers and landowners to replace animal agriculture with nature solutions. In 2024, the European Union passed a new, very important law that will require all large business to declare their carbon emissions. Hopefully, a new business culture of accountability will raise the profile of projects such as Dunsany and make it easier for us all to do what it takes to nurture biodiversity, capture carbon, and start to heal the world.

When a local businessman, William Butterly, contacted me with his idea of selling biodiversity credits to environmentally aware businesses, I could see that this was a real opportunity. The idea is to work with businesses seeking to offset their carbon uses. Dunsany is a huge carbon sink, and we can offer environmentally aware businesses the opportunity to invest in the rewilding project. Dunsany signed an agreement with the Irish business Coffeeangel, which committed 5 per cent of their annual profits to us, helping us to continue our work here. We hope to be able to see many more developments in this area, not just for us but for any rewilded landscape that is capturing carbon in a meaningful way and finds in this a means to raise some funds to support the project.

We also need to study and learn more about the different ways in which a natural landscape absorbs carbon. A rewilding landscape has a sort of mind of its own. Long, long ago, before any humans settled on the island of Ireland, it was much more heavily forested than it is now. Interference with the natural landscape dates back millennia, so we've collectively forgotten what a truly natural landscape should look like here. People often assume that if everyone in Ireland disappeared, the entire island would gradually become an enormous forest. But our experience at Dunsany has been that while trees are growing, reproducing, and extending their range, big swathes of land are remaining grassland, where trees show absolutely no interest in sprouting and laying down roots. Ten years on, while parts of the reserve have started to reforest, others remain completely free of trees, even though they are adjacent to forested areas.

Moreover, while the forests are important carbon sinks – which is why environmental activists around the world place a heavy emphasis on reforesting – mature grasslands are also very significant carbon sinks. According to Ireland's food and agriculture development authority, Teagasc, Irish grasslands typically absorb between four and six tonnes of carbon every year. In 2022, a study backed by Oxford University showed that our grasslands at Dunsany were absorbing almost twenty tonnes of carbon. That's more than semi-mature forests, which typically absorb about twelve tonnes, and a similar amount to peatlands, which can absorb from eighteen to thirty tonnes. How is that possible? Because unlike grasslands that are rotated with crops, or that are regularly grazed down to the ground, our grasslands have been allowed to experience their full life cycle, from germination to full growth, to flowering and then seeding, and in the process they have developed complex root systems beneath the ground. I believe my Norman ancestors chose this place precisely because of these natural grasslands, which today are reclaiming their own space, filling with wild flowers, and supporting a vast insect population, and consequently a wide array of bird life.

Just before the reserve celebrated its ten-year anniversary salmon started spawning here for the first time in about seventy years. I'd received a call from Inland Fisheries Ireland, a government body in charge of the waterways and fish population. They requested a visit, as they had a matter to discuss with me. My guard was already up, expecting trouble. To my surprise they explained that, because of the EU, Ireland is under pressure to return the health of its waterways to a minimum standard set by the EU. Apparently, Ireland's waterways are among the least healthy in Europe, and the country could be penalised if it doesn't make improvements. The fisheries visit quickly revealed that salmon had been spotted laying eggs at the south side of the river. They couldn't explain why salmon, which are very sensitive to the health of watercourses, had suddenly returned to a river considered to have very little viable habitat for them. They said the Irish government didn't know how to improve Irish waterways, and they'd told their organisation and the Office of Public Works (OPW) to figure out a strategy. One idea that had emerged was to repeat a strategy that had been tried in the UK – the rewilding of the waterways. They were seeking a landowner who wouldn't mind the river slowing down, and wouldn't be perturbed to see areas of their land becoming waterlogged. Someone silly enough to have reversed generations of agricultural progress, planning and labour.

'You're in luck,' I told them. 'I'm that idiot.'

'Now, now,' they said. 'We're not looking for an idiot; we're looking for a *progressive*.'

'Potayto, potahto,' I replied. And that was it. We'd begun.

As the officials walked along the river, they were surprised to see so much debris in it, along with bows and dams starting to form. They chuckled, commenting that they understood why the salmon had returned. They may have been happy, but I was even happier, because from that day on I was in a joint project with the Fisheries and the OPW, to create the first waterways rewilding project. Over the next few months, we'd help the river by pushing in even more forest debris and supplementing this with a large quantity of stones that would turn the riverbed back into an ecosystem suitable for salmon. I'm confident we'll succeed.

As the first female custodian of the estate and the castle, Constance will feel under pressure to make her mark, perhaps even more than I have. Fortunately, she's inherited her mother's integrity and courage, which are qualities that will serve her well when she receives Dunsany, which by then will – hopefully – be several decades into being rewilded.

At the time of writing, Constance isn't even in school yet, and already I've started preparing her to succeed me. Laura and I are raising her with a strong sense of her Irish identity: she'll be educated in Ireland, in a local school, and her friends will be kids who live in our area. Here at Dunsany we no longer empty our chamber pots out the window, as they did in Norman times, and we no longer send our children away for an English education that will isolate them from their own people. The world has changed, Ireland has changed and is changing, and we're changing too. *I'm* changing. I've learned not to hate Christmas as I used to. I even finally managed to cry and to wear my tears with pride.

When I die – and I sincerely hope that I won't for a long time, because I want to spend the rest of my life watching Dunsany return to nature and because, finally, I truly love this place, and I truly love Ireland – I want to be buried here. I'm proud of our history, of the country we are living in and of the country we'll be in the future. I want to do my best until it's time for me to take my place among my people in the family graveyard outside our private church, deroofed by Cromwell in the 1600s, but very much still standing.

I have to laugh sometimes at the huge pride I feel when I relate the stories about my ancestors that I learned from Dad. I used to hate those stories, but now I love them, because they inspire me and confirm to me that I'm where I am supposed to be, doing what I was always meant to do.

All my young life, I desperately wanted Dad to be proud of me. I knew he loved me, but I worried that I wasn't clever or accomplished enough to make him proud. I thought that I needed to be more academic and more talented. Now, years after his death, I think he *would* be proud of me, and of what I'm doing with Dunsany. I think he'd enjoy seeing the changes I'm witnessing, and would appreciate the changes that have taken place in me.

For the longest time, I was a ghost floating through the halls of once-great men, feeling that I was the one who'd deal the crippling blow that would see the place collapse. The one who'd see the end of hundreds of years of history in this mysterious place. Gradually, through rewilding, I started to see Dunsany not as a cage but as a defence. I realised that the bars of this cage were not a cage at all but a gateway to being able to do something worthwhile, the way my ancestors did. The way I'm doing now.

Through the process of rewilding – or, to be exact, V-wilding – I learned how to accept myself, flaws and all. Above all, I became able to recognise that I'm part of the magic of this wonderous place, not the owner but the protector. That I've a role to defend those weaker than me, those without a voice. I started this book describing my Damascus moment, when I met a small group of Dunsany deer, and realised in a flash what my purpose in this world is. From that instant, there was no going back. In the final stages of writing this book, one of the researchers studying Dunsany brought me wonderful news: among the many birds living in Dunsany she had identified curlews, which are critically endangered in Ireland, and the nuthatch, which has only been spotted in Ireland a handful of times.

I've learned a lot about how death is as much part of life as birth. Dunsany is home to countless animals now, and obviously they die all the time. Often, on my daily walks, I come across the remains of deer that have died and fallen where once they nibbled trees or mushrooms or the tender stalks of young grasses. It's fascinating to see how quickly nature deals with the remains. Badgers and foxes, which are omnivores, will happily scavenge, and birds such as buzzards, kites and ravens all join the feast. Flies will lay eggs on the remains too, and the maggots that hatch from those eggs will gorge, fatten, and enter the next stage of their development. Within a very few days, there's nothing left but a few scattered bones. Within weeks, even the bones are no longer in evidence, and after a year has passed, you won't see anything, although the grass that grows there will be a little greener than before.

If you stay somewhere long enough, you become that place. Generations of my ancestors lived here, in their numerous ways leaving their mark on the land, on the castle, on Ireland. They're all dead, of course, but in many other ways they're all still here. I've already started to embody Dunsany and one day, my earthly remains, like theirs – like those of every dead creature here – will rot and return to the soil in their resting place mere steps from the castle that's been our home for nine hundred years. Like those of any dead thing, they'll fertilise the place where they lie. They'll return to nature here, in this hated, beloved, special, wonderful place of mine.

I'm happy about that.

I really, *really* am.

Further Reading

WHEN IT COMES TO LEARNING ABOUT REWILDING, THE INTERNET IS YOUR FRIEND. Rewilding projects often have websites with lots of information, links to articles and helpful bibliographies, and plenty of people working in this area have created presentations and lectures that are now available on YouTube and other channels.

There are also some terrific books out there, of which the following is a sample that you might find interesting as you continue to explore the concept of rewilding and what it might look like for you.

- Bekoff, Marc. *Rewilding our Hearts: Building Pathways of Compassion and Coexistence.* New World Library, 2014.

- Hakansson, Emma. *How Veganism Can Save Us (Survive the Modern World)*. Hardie Grant Books, 2022.
- Monbiot, George. *Feral: Rewilding the Land, Sea and Human Life*. Penguin Books, 2014.
- Sheldrake, Merlin. *Entangled Life: How Fungi Make our Worlds, Change our Minds, and Shape Our Futures*. Bodley Head, 2020.
- Simard, Suzanne. *Finding the Mother Tree; Uncovering the Wisdom and Intelligence of the Forest*. Allen Lane, 2021.
- Wohlleben, Peter. *Walks in the Wild: A Guide through the Forest*. Penguin Random House, 2017.

Acknowledgements

As I reflect on this journey and the immense support I've received in writing this book on the path to V-wilding, I'm filled with deep gratitude for the many individuals and communities who have walked beside me. This endeavour is not merely a personal narrative – it is a collective effort, shaped by the passion, dedication and kindness of countless colleagues and supporters.

First and foremost, I extend my heartfelt thanks to my colleagues in the scientific community. Your unwavering commitment to understanding and preserving the natural world has inspired me daily. Special thanks go to Dr. Stephen Waldren and his Trinity College students – Rudraksh Gupta, Cara Shields, Clare Lynn, Colin Lewis, Elena Hernandez Perez and Thomas Buckley. I also acknowledge the valuable ongoing work of Dr. Jimmy O'Keeffe and Dr. Darren Clarke of DCU, as well as Dr. Pat Moran and his colleagues at FERS.

Your expertise and contributions to our foundational data collection have been pivotal. You have been a cornerstone in developing the evidence shared in this book and in shaping many of the insights and theories explored in its pages.

Beyond our academics, a must-mention is my friend Nicholas Carter, Ecologist and Director of Future Food Systems (IFFS.earth). Your depth of knowledge in ecology and your continuous stream of new data – particularly regarding rewilding and vegan-influenced conservation – have guided and shaped this project profoundly. Your work never ceases to inspire me and has fuelled my relentless pursuit of deeper understanding.

I am also deeply grateful to those who have dedicated themselves to animal care and protection. To Aoife McPartlin, Emma Higgs and Leyton Jones of the WRI; Dan, Viv, Sean, Zanna and Marie of the Kildare Animal Foundation; and the volunteers of the Irish Bee Conservation Project – thank you. None of these vital connections would have been made without Nicola, whose involvement with animal charities served as the catalyst for so much of our work.

There are those who, though often not present in person, have offered unwavering support from afar. One of the most significant influences in recent years has been my dear friend and tireless supporter, Nia Timms of Heartstone Sanctuary. You pioneered the term V-wilding and were the spark that led to this book being written at all. Your network and influence helped me discover the people and relationships that laid the groundwork for what this book has become. Though you have yet to visit Dunsany Nature Reserve in person, your spirit and friendship have shaped it in countless ways.

Dunsany Nature Reserve is more than just a place – it is a village, built by a community of collaborators. Daniel Fildes, your photography has opened the doors to many, telling the story of Dunsany through imagery. Your dedication and protection of this idea have been essential to its continued growth. Finian Power, like Daniel, has lent his talent to our cause, helping build public support through stunning visuals. My thanks also go to Tony McKeown, Monica McManus and Natasha Efole, who now carry forward the legacy you all helped create.

To the wonderful team who has worked at Dunsany over the years, including the late Peter Lynch – you would be proud of what this place has become. To my trusted confidants – Derry Farrelly, Philip McMaster and Gerry Leddy – your ongoing support of this generation and the last has been invaluable.

I must also acknowledge my collaborators in sustainable rewilding efforts, such as Bob Hamilton and John Doran, whose work with Irish Trees has significantly increased awareness and helped connect our forests for future generations. I also thank BioNua – William Butterly and his team, Vanessa Von Appen, Tatiana Gorgacova and WeiWei Xi – for their quiet but crucial behind-the-scenes efforts. Their connections with forward-thinking partners like Coffee Angel have brought vital financial support to our work, laying the groundwork for a future where rewilding might be sustained through innovations like biodiversity credits.

This book – and the story it tells – would not exist without those working diligently behind the scenes. I offer deep thanks to my literary agent Max Edwards and his team – including Alex Osmond, Checkie Hamilton and Tom Lloyd-Williams – for securing the right publishing partner in Eriu. My gratitude extends to the team at Eriu, especially Deirdre Nolan, who discovered this project and fought to bring it to life. Alongside her, Lisa Gilmour, assistant editor with Eriu. To the team at Gill Hess, Declan Heeney, Helen McKean, Simon Hess and the marketing and publicity team at Bonnier Books UK – thank you. I also acknowledge my appearance agent, Grainne MacAnthony of Carol & Associates.

A special mention must be made for my dear friend and writing partner, Deirdre Nuttall, who first approached me with the idea of this book and worked tirelessly to help shape and structure its content. Your efforts, patience and unwavering belief in this story are impossible to measure. It was an honour to share my journey with you.

To my closest friends and work colleagues – Karol Daly, John Phillipson, Kat Green, Colin McCracken, Helen Serruya, Luciana Gomes, Walter Moura, Justin Hoey, Cat LaBelle, Stephen Lourdes, Hasan Tezer and Mike Judd – thank you for standing by me through thick and thin. A special tribute goes to my dear friend Eric Branden, who sadly did not live to see this book come to fruition.

To Joe Doyle – my closest non-blood family member – and his wife Lu and their children Marfa and Agnia: you are family in every way that matters. Joe, I truly believe that without your unwavering presence, we would not be here to celebrate this book and all that we've achieved. My gratitude to you and your family is deeper than words can express.

To my actual family – Daniel, Oliver and Joana – thank you. I also remember with love my father Edward and my mother Maria-Alice, who would have been proud to witness this milestone. I offer my thanks to Terry Dillon, who assisted with proofreading and notes; a big thank you to the entire Dillon family.

Finally, to my beloved wife Laura, whose steadfast support has carried me through and to my daughters Catherine and Constance – your love and encouragement have been my anchor and my inspiration.

And to you – the readers – thank you. Your willingness to engage with these ideas makes this journey meaningful. I hope this book not only informs but inspires you to join the movement toward rewilding and to rediscover your relationship with the natural world in powerful, lasting ways.

Together, we can foster a deeper understanding of our environment and create a future where nature thrives. The future is ours to write, we all have the power to change the world we live, I pray that vegan rewilding may be a step to realising a new paradigm.